FEMALE FRIENDSHIPS

FEMALE FRIENDSHIPS AND COMMUNITIES

Charlotte Brontë, George Eliot,
Elizabeth Gaskell

PAULINE NESTOR

WITHDRAWN

CLARENDON PRESS · OXFORD

1985

Oxford University Press, Walton Street, Oxford OX2 6DP

Oxford New York Toronto
Delhi Bombay Calcutta Madras Karachi
Kuala Lumpar Singapore Hong Kong Tokyo
Nairobi Das es Salaam Cape Town
Melbourne Auckland

and associated companies in
Beirut Berlin Ibadan Mexico City Nicosia

Oxford is a trade mark of Oxford University Press

Published in the United States
by Oxford University Press, New York

© *Pauline Nestor 1985*

British Library Cataloguing in Publication Data

Nestor, Pauline
Female friendships and communities: Charlotte
Brontë, George Eliot, Elizabeth Gaskell.
1. Women in literature 2. English fiction—
Women authors—History and criticism 3. English
fiction—19th century—History and criticism
I. Title
823'.7' 09352042 PR868.W6
ISBN 0-19-812838-X

Library of Congress Cataloging in Publication Data

Nestor, Pauline.
Female friendships and communities.
Bibliography: p.
Includes index.
1. English fiction—19th century—History and
criticism. 2. Women in literature. 3. Friendship in
literature. 4. Community life in literature.
5. Brontë, Charlotte, 1816–1855. 6. Eliot, George, 1819–
1880. 7. Gaskell, Elizabeth Cleghorn, 1810–1865.
8. English fiction—Women authors—History and criticism.
9. Women novelists, English—19th century—Biography.
I. Title
PR878.W6N47 823'.8' 09352042 85-10529
ISBN 0-19-812838-X

Set by DMB Typesetting, Oxford
Printed in Great Britain at
the University Press, Oxford
by David Stanford
Printer to the University

For my sisters

Acknowledgements

I am indebted to Wolfson College, Oxford, and the Rhodes Trust for awards which made the undertaking of this study possible. I am also grateful to Nicholas Shrimpton for his supervision of my doctoral work in this area and to Jeri Johnson for her help and support in the final stages of composition. My particular thanks go to Marilyn Butler for her generous encouragement and advice.

Contents

Introduction

In 1818 Jane Austen's heroine, Anne Elliot, disallowed Captain Har-
ville's appeal to literature as proof of women's inconstancy, protesting
' "Men have had every advantage of us in telling their own story. . .
the pen has been in their hands." '[1] However, by 1852 things had so
changed that George Lewes could confidently refer to the 'advent of
female literature', while seven years later the female editors of the
English Woman's Journal claimed for women novelists 'a prominent
position in the field of literature, the value and importance of which it
is not easy to over-rate'.[2]

Of course, when Jane Austen complained of the male monopoly of
the pen in *Persuasion*, she was not unaware of her sister authors. She
delighted, for example, in the works of Maria Edgeworth and Fanny
Burney, and regularly read other women writers of her day such as
Mme. de Stael, Mary Brunton, and Anne Grant. Indeed, women were
writing in the eighteenth and early nineteenth centuries in considerable numbers and individuals among them achieved notable success.
Beyond the celebrated authors such as Maria Edgeworth, Fanny
Burney, Hannah More, Anne Radcliffe, and Jane Austen herself, lay
a gallery of women who earned distinction, or, more humbly, earned
a living for themselves and their dependants by wielding a pen,
women such as Lady Mary Wortley Montagu, Charlotte Lennox,
Elizabeth Carter, Eliza Haywood, and Charlotte Smith.

Thus, the rise to prominence of women writers lauded by George
Lewes in the middle of the nineteenth century was not so much a break
from earlier periods as an important development. It was not until the
middle of the century that the emerging consciousness of a female
literary tradition coincided with an unprecedented concentration of
talented women writers, and earlier moments of individual insight
and professional self-consciousness gave way to a sustained and articu-
late assessment on the part of women writers of their relations to each
other and to the literary endeavour. The opportunities provided by a
literary community, which male writers had long enjoyed at court

---

[1] Jane Austen, *Persuasion* (1818; rpt. Oxford: Oxford University Press, 1980), p. 221.
[2] George Lewes, 'The Lady Novelists', *Westminster Review*, July 1852, p. 131; Review
of *A Life for a Life* by Dinah Mulock, *English Women's Journal*, Sept. 1859, p. 60.

and in the coffee-house, club, and university, were becoming newly accessible to women.

With the pen firmly in their own hands, then, and a consciousness of their sister authors writing beside them, what image of women and women's relationships did female writers project? This study seeks to answer that question in relation to the three major women novelists, Elizabeth Gaskell, Charlotte Brontë, and George Eliot, who wrote within this new context. It is not simply a study of women novelists' female characters or a comparison of the heroines of male and female writers. It is rather an examination of relationships between women, both in the life and the fiction of three important female writers, the three luminaries 'shining in the firmament', during a period which lent particular interest to the subject of female friendships and communities.[3]

The mid-nineteenth century saw this literary phenomenon of an emergent community of women writers coincide with the social phenomenon of an excess of females in the population, which stimulated a widespread reassessment of women's role and drew many minor women writers into the discussion of women's relationships. Between 1840 and 1880 women novelists not only reflected, but deepened, the more general debate, and this book endeavours to examine those insights against this background of a broader controversy.

Literature is commonly seen as offering its own unique insights into a period. More than simply another source of opinion, literature in any age provides access to deeper levels of consciousness, liberating its own truth in fiction. Thus, Rebecca West argued succinctly: 'nonfiction always tends to become fiction; only the dream compels reality.'[4] Nor was the idea foreign to a pre-Freudian age. Eliza Lynn Linton, for example, suggested that songs were the expression of the political temper of an age and 'novels show the current of its social morality, and what the learned would call the psychological condition.'[5]

This inclination to privilege the insights offered by literature is particularly marked in regard to the nineteenth century when the popularity of fiction made it perhaps the most potent form of social

[3] Mrs Parr, 'Dinah Mulock (Mrs. Craik)', in *Women Novelists of Queen Victoria's Reign, Mrs. Oliphant, et. al.* (London: Hurst & Blackett Ltd., 1897), p. 219.

[4] Rebecca West, 'And they all lived unhappily ever after', *Times Literary Supplement*, 26 July 1974, p. 779.

[5] Eliza Lynn Linton, *The Girl of the Period* (London: Richard Bentley & Son, 1883), II. 243.

commentary. The spread of literacy, the repeated connections in literary reviews between novels and public morality, the merging of fact
and fiction in the 1840s with novels drawing on blue-books for source
material and the blue-books incorporating the popular literary feature
of woodcut illustrations, the reliance on didactic fiction even in Evangelical pamphlets, all attest to the profound relevance of fiction at this
time and suggest its capacity not merely to reflect, but to amplify and
deepen contemporary debate. Thus Dinah Mulock described the contemporary novel as 'one of the most important moral agents of the
community. The essayist may write for his hundreds, the preacher
preach for his thousands; but the novelist counts his audience by
millions. His power is three-fold—over heart, reason, and fancy.'[6]

It is perhaps not surprising, then, that students of literature offer
blithely ahistorical readings of texts, thinking nothing of making a
study of industrialism by reading Dickens and Gaskell, with the more
adventurous straying to Kingsley and Disraeli, and yet ignoring the
writings that Engels was producing in Manchester in the same period.
At the same time the obverse of such ahistoricism is even less satisfactory. To view literature as historical source material, a simple reflection of a recoverable 'reality', is naïvely to ignore both the nature of
the creative process and the limitations on our access to the past.

The relation between life and literature is not, of course, one of rigid
causality. In this book the social and biographical contexts are considered as a means of illuminating rather than explaining the literature itself, which remains my primary interest, for, as suggested, the
period in which Gaskell, Brontë, and Eliot wrote was one of particular
interest for the whole question of women's relationships with women.

The perennial question of woman's nature acquired a new urgency
in the middle of the century because, as the 1851 census revealed,
there was an 'excess' of half a million females in the population, and
with the number of women who were likely to remain unmarried increasing, the fate of the 'Superabundant Woman' became a matter of
'awful importance'.[7] If it was no longer inevitable that women would

6 Dinah Mulock, 'To Novelists—and a novelist', *Macmillan's Magazine*, Apr. 1861,
p. 442.
7 Anna Jameson, *Sisters of Charity* (London: Longman, Brown, Green & Longmans,
1855), p. 61; *The Census of Great Britain in 1851* (London: Longman *et al.*, 1854)
reported that the total population consisted of 10,223,558 males and 10,735,919
females on 31 Mar. 1851 (p. 88). It also noted that of all persons above the legal ages of
marriage (14 years for males and 12 years for females) 3,110,243 were bachelors and
3,469,571 were spinsters (p. 40).

be supported by husbands, how were they to support themselves? Periodical articles earnestly debated the merits of various possible professions, and societies such as the Governesses' Benevolent Institution, the Society for the Promotion of the Employment of Women, and the Middle-Class Emigration Society were founded to tackle the problem. Sisterhoods, long the 'refuge' of Catholic maidens in Europe, began to spring up and so too did schools for the training of nurses.

Women, then, were banding together and 'taking the initiative' in facing the problems of single life.[8] Ironically, the prospect of women caring for themselves was far from reassuring. This 'modern principle of association', rather than offering a simple solution to the dilemma of an excess of females, raised more fundamental problems.[9] How far could women be trusted without male supervision? How healthy were relationships between women? Indeed, were women even capable of friendships with their own sex? Negative answers were predictably forthcoming, with periodicals such as the *Saturday Review* leading the hue and cry against women's collective action. Autonomous communities of women were seen as dangerous, as a thriving anti-conventual fiction in the period makes clear. And if concerned observers were not taken in by *Sister Agnes; or the Captive Nun: a Picture of Conventual Life* or *Geralda the Demon Nun*, they could turn to the pages of *The Times* to discover that the Solicitor-General in opening a case for defamation brought by a Sister of Mercy against her religious superiors declared that

the facts about to be presented to the jury were a strange and painful revelation of conventual female nature, showing as they did what women were capable of when they shut themselves up from their kind, and did violence to the instincts of their nature, and the great, though mean and petty, cruelty they could wreak upon a sister in the name of a religion of love.[10]

The period provided a gallery of easy targets—spinsters, nuns, nurses, political and philanthropic activists—for misogynistic satirists

[8] Louisa Hubbard, 'Englishwomen and Their Work in Queen Victoria's Reign', *The Englishwoman's Year-book*, VIII (London: Hatchards, 1888), 25.

[9] Frances Cobbe, 'Female Charity—Lay and Monastic', *Fraser's Magazine*, Dec. 1862, p. 776.

[10] Law Reports, *The Times*, 4 Feb. 1869, p. 10. The element of anti-Catholic feeling in the anti-conventual fiction was not, of course, new (see, e.g. G. F. A. Best, 'Popular Protestantism in Victorian Britain', *Ideas and Institutions of Victorian Britain*, G. Bell & Sons, 1967). However, as we shall see, with the emergence of Protestant sisterhoods at this time a further element of hostility toward, and suspicion of, all-female communities also assumed prominence in the debate.

and detractors. Yet at the same time women were no longer merely victims of the pen, but were wielding it themselves. As George Lewes noted, the time had come when a 'new element' might emerge in literary discourse—a 'woman's view of life, woman's experience'.[11] Accordingly the *Victoria Magazine* declared that women had been 'too silent', and urged female writers to defend their sex against attacks like those from the *Saturday Review* by testifying to the positive value of women's friendships.[12] How, then, did female pens rally to the call, and how much was sisterly solidarity a virtue of women writers in the mid-nineteenth century? What sense of women's relationships emerged from this 'woman's view of life'?

One would scarcely expect a consensus of opinion from these female commentators, and a glance at Eliza Lynn Linton's work would be enough to suggest that women writing about women demonstrated about as much loyalty and mutual respect as Kilkenny cats. However, if the popularity of Linton's *Girl of the Period* essays was revealing in its way, so too was the success of Elizabeth Gaskell's *Life of Charlotte Brontë* (1857)—one a sustained and vitriolic attack on female capacities for friendship and communality, the other both an act and celebration of the same things. Despite the polarization of opinion, certain preoccupations and perspectives remained constant, regardless of the writer's sympathies. These included the conception of women's friendships within a conventional framework of heterosexual roles, the related notion of female friends compensating for the lack of a male and the recognition of a need for male authority. Underlying all was a continuing definition of women and women's friendships in relation to men.

As this study will show, Gaskell, Brontë, and Eliot were each touched in some ways by this general controversy. In addition, the biographical context sheds light on the literary depictions of female friendships and communities, both locally, as when Charlotte Brontë addresses to her girlhood friend Ellen Nussey the words Jane Eyre later speaks of Rochester, and more generally, when the central importance of motherhood in Gaskell's life is reflected in the unifying power she attributes to maternity in her fiction; or Charlotte Bronte's ambivalence to solitude is explored in the development in her heroines toward self-sufficiency; or the aloof severity of George Eliot's male-centred life is mirrored in her creation of male-dependent heroines.[13]

11 Lewes, 'The Lady Novelists', p. 131.
12 'Friendship', *Victoria Magazine*, Oct. 1871, p. 545.
13 See Chapter 4 below, p. 93.

In examining women writers' attitudes to, and depictions of, female friendships and communities, this study represents in some respects an extension of the concerns raised by Elaine Showalter in *A Literature of Their Own* and Ellen Moers in *Literary Women*. Drawing on new perspectives offered by inter-disciplinary studies of women in the nineteenth century, both critics have recharted territory too long and too complacently regarded as familiar, and have provided a 'reliable map' of a rich network of women writers interacting as a community. However, whereas Moers and Showalter are concerned with a general, primarily historical survey of relationships between authors, this work will offer a detailed investigation of the real and fictive attitudes to female friendships and communities of three women novelists, balancing the historical and the literary by examining 'both the experience that generates the metaphor, and the metaphor that creates the experience'.[14]

What sense of women's relationships, then, did the fiction of these three novelists offer? Did it create the models Anne Elliot looked for in vain in 1818, and Virginia Woolf claimed she still could not find in 'that vast chamber where nobody has yet been' in 1928?[15] This book sets out to answer those questions.

[14] Sandra Gilbert and Susan Gubar, *The Madwoman in the Attic: The Woman Writer and the Nineteenth-Century Imagination* (New Haven: Yale University Press, 1979), p. xiii.
[15] Virginia Woolf, *A Room of One's Own* (1928; rpt. Harmondsworth: Penguin, 1974), p. 84.

1

The Popular Debate over Female Friendships and Communities

Women Beware Women

I

In the middle of the nineteenth century an extraordinary public debate raged over women's capacities for friendship and communal activity. Controversy over women's relationships was not remarkable in itself —after all, women's fickleness and jealousy had long been targets for the satirist. However, this debate was particularly significant both because it was so sustained and because the rapid growth in female authorship in the first half of the century meant that women themselves for the first time made a substantial contribution to the public dispute.

The urgency of the debate and the extent of interest in it were much influenced by public preoccupation with the demographic imbalance in the population (with a natural excess of females exacerbated by the exodus of males to the colonies), and the inescapable conclusion which followed, that some women at least would have to be considered in their own right as wage-earners and independent participants in society. In 1855 Anna Jameson declared in her celebrated lecture *Sisters of Charity* that the subject of women's occupations had become 'one of awful importance when we consider, that in the last census of 1851, there appears an excess of the female over the male population of Great Britain of more than half a million.'[1] The next census was no more consoling, as Frances Power Cobbe's bald statement of the facts in 1862 in 'What Shall We Do With Our Old Maids?' made clear:

It appears that there is a natural excess of four or five per cent of females over males in our population. . . . There is, however, an actual ratio of thirty per cent of women now in England who never marry. . . . This proportion further

---

[1] Anna Jameson, *Sisters of Charity*, p. 61.

appears to be constantly on the increase. It is obvious enough that these facts call for a revision of many of our social arrangements.[2]

Women without men, then, became the pressing concern of many women writers. 'If in the multitude of counsellors there is safety,' Dora Greenwell wrote in 1862, the same year as Cobbe's essay, 'how blest must be the security of our single women! Everyone who has a little spare wisdom at command seems just now inclined to lay it out for their benefit.'[3]

This new-fated singleness was seen as an essentially female predicament, whereas the demographic figures clearly indicated that marriage was no longer the inevitable state of adult life for either sex. Thus Cobbe observed:

. . . we cannot but add a few words to express our amused surprise at the way in which writers on this subject constantly concern themselves with the question of *female* celibacy, deplore it, abuse it, propose amazing remedies for it, but take little or no notice of the twenty-five per cent old batchelors (or thereabouts) who needs must exist to match the thirty per cent old maids. Their moral condition seems to excite no alarm, their lonely old age no foreboding compassion, their action on the community no reprobation.[4]

Beyond the abstraction of census data, the social fact—born of necessity—of women in various spheres working, co-operating, and congregating together was apparent as never before. One group of women, for example, recognized the need for a periodical written by women for women and began the *English Woman's Journal* in March 1858. The rationale expressed by the *Journal*'s young editor, Bessie Parkes, seemed simple: 'if I wish to work especially for women, it is because I am a woman myself, and so able to appreciate their particular troubles.'[5] Such sentiments seem more significant when one considers the masculine dominance of periodical editorship in the period. Not only did male editors judge what was fit for female readers, but they often pretended to be women in the process. For example, Frederick Greenwood, the editor of Samuel Beeton's successful *Queen* magazine, freely offered readers 'sisterly' advice under the cover of

[2] Frances Power Cobbe, 'What Shall We Do With Our Old Maids?', *Fraser's Magazine*, Nov. 1862, p. 594.

[3] Dora Greenwell, 'Our Single Women', *Essays (North British Review*, Feb. 1862; rpt. London and New York: Alexander Strahan, 1866), p. 1.

[4] Cobbe, 'Old Maids', p. 598.

[5] Bessie Parkes, quoted in 'Miss Parkes' Essays on Women's Work', *Victoria Magazine*, June 1865, p. 174.

anonymity: 'as for our own liberties, or our political principles, they may be safely left to men . . . therefore our survey of foreign affairs and of politics generally will be recorded in a few notes.'[6]

This establishment of a women's press with the *English Woman's Journal* and its sturdy progeny, the *Victoria Magazine*, begun in May 1863, created a focus for a wide and varied community of women, whose energetic projects extended its influence well beyond the modest beginnings of the *Journal*. Bessie Parkes claimed that the *Journal* 'threaded separate parts of the movement [and] brought the thinkers and workers together.'[7] The group of women thus gathered were directly responsible for the Society for the Promotion of Employment for Women, established by Jessie Boucherett in 1859 with Lord Shaftesbury as its President; the Victoria Press, founded by Emily Faithfull in 1859 to train and employ female compositors for the first time in England; a book-keeping school begun by Boucherett in 1860 to train women in a new and 'suitable' field of employment, and a Law Engrossing Office started by Marie Rye in the same year to employ women to copy legal documents; and the Middle-Class Emigration Society established by Marie Rye in 1861 to help emigrating women with loans and advice.

The *Journal* was also the corporate venture which 'launched the women's movement on the stormy sea of print,' providing it with a continuous voice in print from 1858 to 1880, contrary to Cynthia White's claim in *Women's Magazines* that 'no periodical which espoused the women's cause survived for more than a year or two.'[8] Although the group never included the major female literary figures of the day, it dwelt in tantalizingly close relation to them. The endeavour brought a significant assembly of secondary figures together as workers and contributors—women such as Christina Rossetti, Anna Jameson, Adelaide Procter, Barbara Bodichon (Leigh Smith), Bessie Parkes, Mary Taylor, Isa Craig, Jean Ingelow, and Anna and Mary Howitt—and those women in turn numbered among their close friends George Eliot, Elizabeth Gaskell, Harriet Martineau, Elizabeth Barrett Browning, Mary Mitford, and Jane Carlyle. Eliot and Gaskell, in

---

[6] Frederick Greenwood, quoted in Cynthia White, *Women's Magazines 1693–1968* (London: Michael Joseph, 1970), p. 50.

[7] Bessie Parkes, 'The Use of a Special Periodical', *Alexandra Magazine and English-woman's Journal*, Dec. 1864, p. 257.

[8] Hester Burton, *Barbara Bodichon 1827–1891* (Edinburgh: T. A. Constable, 1949), p. 98; White, *Women's Magazines*, p. 47.

particular, had direct dealings with the venture, as we shall consider in later chapters.[9]

Another focus for collective action by women was provided by the agitation surrounding Lord Brougham's presentation of the Married Women's Property Bill in 1856. Through the discussion of the issues in newspapers in the spring and early summer of 1856 and the efforts to collect signatures for the petition that accompanied the Bill, 'the people interested in the question were brought into communication in all parts of the kingdom, and . . . the germs of an effective movement were scattered far and wide.'[10] Even before this some middle-class women had demonstrated a remarkable capacity for organization and a willingness to take united action. In 1853 a group calling themselves the Committee for the Ladies' Address to their American Sisters on Slavery, inspired by *Uncle Tom's Cabin*, collected 576,000 signatures for their anti-slavery petition.[11]

Increasingly, public bodies were preoccupied with the fate of women as individuals or within groups. At the annual congress of Lord Brougham's National Association for the Promotion of Social Science in London in 1862 women's employment, education, emigration, and 'all other rights and wrongs of women were urged.'[12] As early as 1854 Parliament concerned itself with the growing movement for the establishment of nunneries, and in 1862 the Anglican convocation at Canterbury formally considered the subject of Protestant sisterhoods and deaconesses, approving the proposal that women adopting the vocation of charity should receive the sanction of the Church. In the same year the Church Congress at Oxford offered enthusiastic support for the scheme.

In dealing with the problem of the Superabundant Woman the initiative was 'taken by women themselves', as Louisa Hubbard claimed in looking back in 1888.[13] F. K. Prochaska, describing the enormous growth in women's involvement in philanthropic activity in the nineteenth century, refers to 'the explosion of charities managed exclu-

[9] For a full account of the venture and related undertakings see Pauline Nestor, 'A New Departure in Women's Publishing: The *English Woman's Journal* and *The Victoria Magazine*', *Victorian Periodicals Review*, XV. 3 (1982), 93–106.

[10] Bessie Parkes, 'A Review of the Last Six Years', *English Woman's Journal*, Feb. 1864, p. 361.

[11] Mary Howitt, *Mary Howitt: an Autobiography* (London: Isbiter, 1889), II. 93.

[12] Cobbe, 'Old Maids', p. 594.

[13] Louisa M. Hubbard, 'Englishwomen and Their Work in Queen Victoria's Reign', *The Englishwoman's Year-book*, VIII (London: Hatchards, 1888), 25.

sively by women'.[14] One such charity, the Governesses' Benevolent Institution, was very much a sign of the times, responding to the plight of the self-supporting gentlewoman. Formed in 1845 and hailed by Bessie Parkes as the 'true precursor' of the collective action of her group, the Institution was extending its aid by the 1860s in various directions:

It has given during the last year [1861], temporary assistance to the struggling, the invalid, and the aged governess, to the amount of £16,882. It has established a Provident Fund, enabling ladies, through their own earnings and savings, to purchase annuities. This fund now possesses a capital of £169,041; and in 1860, 427 ladies became entitled to annuities.[15]

In 1860 the Parochial Mission Women's Association was formed and became a striking example of organized support and self-help among women. Designed to establish habits of saving and economy, the organization collected 55 million pennies from working-class homes in its first twenty years. Beyond its practical, financial achievements, the Association also functioned as a network of communication: 'the lay superintendents may often find out from the mission woman's story of her week's work a great many cases of material or spiritual destitution which could otherwise have remained undiscovered, and towards which the proper channels of help can be directed.'[16]

The Englishwoman's Year-book, intended as a directory to the societies, institutions and organizations 'projected and managed by women' ran to several hundred pages when it first appeared in 1881. Writing of the *Year-book*, the Countess of Aberdeen challenged anyone to find traces of such organizations at the beginning of the century, claiming that 'nothing of the sort' existed until the mid-century. In the face of the emergence of women's co-operative endeavour, she argued, 'We must assume that the old prevailing idea that women could not work together in harmony and to good effect must surely be exploded, when we view the formidable array of women's organizations doing noble service on every hand.'[17]

[14] F. K. Prochaska, *Women and Philanthrophy in Nineteenth-Century England* (Oxford: Clarendon Press, 1980), p. 32.

[15] Greenwell, 'Our Single Women', p. 21.

[16] Lady Maud Hamilton, 'Mission Women', *Nineteenth Century*, Dec. 1884, p. 988.

[17] The Countess of Aberdeen, 'The International Council of Women in Congress', *Nineteenth Century*, July 1899, p. 19.

II

It was against this background of what Frances Cobbe called 'the modern principle of association' and Dora Greenwell characterized similarly as the '*principle of combination* in which [women] might find encouragement and protection' that female writers took up the question of women's relations to each other.[18] To ask what kind of friendship these women saw themselves and their sisters capable of, though, is to ignore a prior question which could not readily be taken for granted—more simply, whether women were actually capable of friendship. The *Saturday Review*, for example, offered a common view of women's relationships in two articles, 'Friendship' and 'The Exclusiveness of Women', published in 1870. The first claimed that female friendships were notoriously shallow, most often a 'rehearsal'. for the 'serious business' of relationships with men. Admitting the occasional 'very real' friendships, the article claimed these could only occur when both women were 'verging towards middle age, when neither [was] a wife or a mother, and when one [had] a stronger character than the other, so that they impact better together, and bring into their relations the charm of protection on the one side and of reliance on the other'—in effect, only when the relationship conformed to conventional heterosexual roles. The second article depicted women as possessive, competitive, and untrusting, 'not ashamed to suspect their sisters of improper feelings', and it concluded, 'you seldom see any sense of the community of sex.'[19]

Such observations were not new, although the unparalleled opportunities for women to respond were. The result, however, was not a simple and unified outcry on behalf of the sex. On the one hand, for example, the *Victoria Magazine* indignantly refuted the *Saturday Review*'s charges with a forthright statement of the potential and value of female friendships. Claiming that there was 'necessarily more sympathy, and therefore more true tenderness [and] more gentle charity' between women, the *Magazine* article concluded that women were capable of a distinctive chivalry toward each other:

We hear a great deal . . . as to the harsh judgment of women about their sex as contrasted to the leniency they show to men's sins. . . . There has been too much said on one side which shows them in one of the worst lights in which

18 Greenwell, 'Our Single Women', p. 19.
19 'Friendship', *Saturday Review*, 15 Jan. 1870, pp. 77–8; 'The Exclusiveness of Women', *Saturday Review*, 19 Feb. 1870, pp. 242–3.

they can be shown, while far too little has been said on the other side. We have been too silent, we women, in this matter, those among us at least who have experience in it, and on the bad side many men and women have been ready enough to cry together, the men in some cases through gratified contempt, and the women in a short-sighted pitiable indifference to the needs of those who have none to fight for them and none to help them. . . . There is then, with even a small portion of such a chivalrous spirit, a much greater capability in a woman of friendship with another woman than with a man. A friend is to her, if unmarried, in the place of what she would gain by marriage, indeed if each single woman could find, and be worthy of one true friend, we should have no need to pity that large class commonly called 'old maids'.[20]

Similarly, other women took up their pens to defend their sex. Frances Cobbe wrote in *Fraser's Magazine* in 1862 that single women were by nature far more happy than men in the same position:

If she have no sister, she has yet inherited the blessed power of a woman to make true friendships, such as not one man's heart in a hundred can ever imagine; and while he smiles scornfully at the idea of friendship meaning anything beyond acquaintance at a club or the intimacy of a barrack, she enjoys one of the purest of pleasures and the most unselfish of all affections. Nor does the 'old maid' contemplate a solitary age as the batchelor must usually do. It will go hard but she will find a *woman* ready to share it.[21]

On the other hand, not all women, of course, were inclined to defend their sex. Eliza Lynn Linton, for example, became the arch-antagonist of her sisters, and enjoyed remarkable success with her misogynistic *Girl of the Period* essays, which appeared anonymously in the *Saturday Review* beginning in March 1868. The *Victoria Magazine* found the essays remarkable for their 'uniformity of virulence . . . on the subject of women', and the *Magazine*'s opposition to the essays themselves became tinged with a sense of betrayal when it was discovered that a feminine pen lay behind the male persona: 'We feel sorry—but contempt is mingled with sorrow—for the woman who launches against women . . . such gross libel.'[22]

Ironically, rather like a liar protesting the demise of honesty, Linton consistently depicted women as divided and competitive. While she claimed that a 'faithful sisterhood' was possible, such concessions had little credence in the face of her contentions that no woman's

---

[20] 'Friendship', *Victoria Magazine*, Oct. 1871, pp. 545–6.

[21] Frances Cobbe, 'Celibacy v. Marriage. Old Maids, their Sorrows and Pleasures', *Fraser's Magazine*, Feb. 1862, p. 233.

[22] 'The Women of the Day', *Victoria Magazine*, Oct. 1868, pp. 551–64; 'Mrs. Lynn Linton on Women', *Victoria Magazine*, July 1876, p. 17.

friendship 'ever existed free from jealousy' and that much female be-haviour was determined by rivalry.[23] In Linton's view women were 'always more or less antagonistic to each other', and womanhood was divided by 'gynecian war' in which the emancipated women 'cannot combine . . . never support their weak sisters . . . shrink from those who are stronger than the average; and if they would speak the truth boldly . . . would confess to a radical contempt for each other's intellect.'[24] In her detailed accounts of women's facility for viciousness, Linton's own writing exemplified the venomousness she was allegedly diagnos-ing. Persistently scoffing at any notion of *esprit de corps*, Linton in-stinctively sided with men. For example, whereas the laws concerning married women's property united many women in opposing them, Linton conceded some injustice in the law, but declared that 'a great part of the sorry success' achieved by the agitators was due to the 'monstrous fictions', 'apocryphal crimes', and 'slanderous inven-tions' told of 'men's dealings with the women under consideration'.[25]

Such diversity of opinion amongst female commentators was not surprising. Indeed, what was far more rare than a polemical stance was any confident assumption that there was no real issue of gender, as Anne Mozley suggested in her simple conclusion to an article en-titled 'Some Aspects of Friendship' in *Blackwood's Magazine* in 1876: 'All that has been said of friendship in general, applies, of course, to female friendships.'[26] As for the severity of some female critics, it was a common feature of the debate to see women as their own harshest critics—the *Victoria Magazine* had indicated as much; Charlotte Yonge observed that women were 'severer censors' of their own sex, and Sarah Ellis lamented the fact that self-knowledge gave women a sure-ness of 'exactly where to wound'.[27] Perhaps this tendency was related to the severity of women's criticism of female authors which was evi-dent, for example, in the reviews of the *English Woman's Journal* and the *Victoria Magazine* and, as will be discussed further, in George Eliot's response to her sister authors. It has been suggested that such

[23] Eliza Lynn Linton, 'Our Small Sins', *Ourselves: A Series of Essays on Women* (London: Routledge & Son, 1870), p. 78; 'Men's Favourites', *The Girl of the Period* (London: Richard Bentley & Son, 1883), II. 101.

[24] Linton, 'Female Amenities', *Girl of the Period*, I. 184.

[25] Linton, 'Modern Man-Haters', *Girl of the Period*, II. 179.

[26] Anne Mozley, 'Some Aspects of Friendship', *Blackwood's Magazine*, Mar. 1876, p. 310.

[27] Charlotte Yonge, *Womankind* (Leipzig: Bernard Tauchnitz, 1878), p. 263; Sarah Ellis, *The Women of England: Their Social Duties and Domestic Habits* (London: Fisher & Son, 1839), p. 225.

severity was one way in which women became caught up in a critical double standard, requiring more of their sisters for fear of being suspected of a feminine lack of rigour and exactingness.[28] Clearly, though, the severity of many women commentators on the subject of female friendship cannot be entirely attributed to a chauvinistic defensiveness and suggests more simply an acceptance of prevailing, often derogatory assumptions about women.

The single woman was the focus for most definition of women's capacity for friendship. Dinah Mulock, for example, prefaced her *A Woman's Thoughts about Women* with the proviso: 'these thoughts do not concern married women.'[29] Writers such as Emily Faithfull, Frances Cobbe, and Mary Taylor attempted to dispel the sense of anomaly or failure surrounding this 'supernumary' class of single women. None the less, the beliefs that 'no woman [was] single by choice', and that single life was 'an unnatural condition of being' were widely held even amongst sympathetic commentators, and women without men were thought to be in particular need of guidance and advice.[30]

If it were possible to offer a composite picture of the 'true friend' from the wealth of women's writing on the subject, she would be a single, elderly woman who provided consolation to some other 'old maid'. At its simplest, singleness was seen as the state of something lacking, and female friendships were an appropriate solution for those who were losers in the demographic lottery. Pity was unnecessary, the *Victoria Magazine* urged, 'if each single woman could find, and be worthy of, one true friend.' Similarly Emily Winkworth, moved by the plight of Charlotte Brontë, wrote: 'Oh dear, if the single sisters in this world were but banded together a little . . . they could help each other as well as other people.'[31] Thus, in the absence of men, it was agreed that women had each other, even if this meant second best:

But to see two women, whom providence has denied nearer ties, by a wise substitution making the best of fate, loving, sustaining, and comforting one another, with a tenderness often closer than that of sisters, because it has all

[28] See Elaine Showalter, 'Women Writers and the Double Standard', *Woman in Sexist Society: Studies in Power and Powerlessness*, eds. Vivian Gornick and Barbara Moran (New York: Basic Books, 1971), p. 329.

[29] Dinah Mulock (Craik), *A Woman's Thoughts about Women* (London: Hurst & Blackett, 1858), p. 1.

[30] Dora Greenwell, 'Our Single Women', p. 5; Mulock, *A Woman's Thoughts*, p. 1.

[31] Susanna and Catherine Winkworth, *Memorials of Two Sisters: Susanna and Catherine Winkworth*, ed. M. J. Shaen (London: Longmans, Green & Company, 1908), p. 60.

the novelty of election which belongs to the conjugal tie itself—this, I say, is an honourable and lovely sight.[32]

In addition to having a need for friends, unmarried women were seen as having the space in their lives for other women.

Although the *Victoria Magazine* took exception to the *Saturday Review*'s assumption that male–female relationships were the defining norm for which attachments between young women were merely a 'rehearsal', it was a view shared by many women writing on the subject. First friendships, in Mulock's terms, were 'not the real thing . . . but rather a kind of foreshadowing of love', or, according to Linton, 'unconsciously rehearsing for the real drama to come by and by'.[33] A similar sense of that norm lay behind Mulock's 'wonderful law of sex', which ensured that in any deep and lasting friendship 'we can usually trace a difference—of strong or weak, gay or grave, brilliant or solid—answering in some measure to the difference of sex'.[34] The same constructs for understanding female friendships were offered in Annie Ireland's 'A Monograph on Miss Jewsbury', where she argued that the memorable and touching friendships of mature women for each other were too well known to need proof of their existence:

If they are, in a sense, a compromise, what then? In these undying, clinging attachments, it may sometimes be noted that one of the women is masculine in her very womanhood, dominating in intellect or will, or possessed of some subtle force of which we know nothing, and the other is 'a woman indeed'— defenceless, tender, instinctively craving after that 'shadow of a substance' for which she was made to long.[35]

III

The prolonged discussion of women's capacity for friendship was not the only manifestation of the growing concern with women's place in a demographically imbalanced society. The widespread contemporary controversies over the formation of sisterhoods, and the development of nursing as a profession were not simply concurrent debates, but were inextricably linked to the contemporary controversy over women's relationships, for they turned in part on the same issues—on respec-

---

[32] Mulock, *A Woman's Thoughts*, p. 174.
[33] Mulock, *A Woman's Thoughts*, p. 168; Linton, 'Our Small Sins', *Ourselves*, p. 80.
[34] Mulock, *A Woman's Thoughts*, p. 179.
[35] Annie Ireland, *Selections from the Letters of Geraldine Endsor Jewsbury to Jane Welsh Carlyle* (London: Longmans, Green & Company, 1892), p. v.

tive estimations of women's influence on one another and on the
female capacity for communal activity.

In 1863, for example, the *Victoria Magazine* appealed to the formation
of sisterhoods as a way of countering negative attitudes toward
women's capacity. In a review of the Revd. F. D. Maurice's *On
Sisterhoods* it declared: 'We ought to labour diligently for the establishment of Sisterhoods among us, as a chief instrument of combating the
notion that it is not good for women to be alone.'[36] However, as
might have been anticipated, this 'chief instrument' proved to be
very much a double-edged sword. On the one hand, the irrefutable
good works, courage, selflessness, and devotion of nuns were offered
as proof of what women united might achieve in works such as Anna
Jameson's *Sisters of Charity* and Miss Stanley's *Hospitals and Sisterhoods*.
On the other hand, however, if good works could be claimed as proof
of the positive force of female communities, the scandals that emerged
could be appealed to by detractors like Melanie Libri in her *Quarterly
Review* article in 1856, which offered a condensed history of the scandals and excesses of the nuns of Port-Royal.[37]

The negative case against sisterhoods was already being advanced
in 1854. As John Stuart Mill noted in his diary, in that year the
House of Commons voted twice on whether to set up a parliamentary
inquiry 'to ascertain whether young women are not detained in [re-
ligious communities] against their will'.[38] However, in 1868 the whole
issue of women in communities attracted sensational public attention
with the court case before the Queen's Bench of *Saurin* v. *Starr and
Others*. It involved the action of a nun against her Mother Superior,
claiming unfair dismissal from the convent and requiring damages
for defamation. As the longest case ever heard by the Queen's Bench,
and coming 'just at a time when the innovation [of Protestant sister-
hoods] coincided with an external curiosity on the subject of their
revelations', *Saurin* v. *Starr* attracted widespread press attention, including lengthy daily reports in *The Times*.[39] The nature of the
'revelations' was guaranteed to fascinate the uninitiated as accusation
was followed by counter-accusation. Charges of broken vows, undue
attention to the chaplain and assignations with an elderly gentleman

---

[36] Review of F. D. Maurice, *On Sisterhoods*, in the *Victoria Magazine*, Aug. 1863,
p. 290.

[37] Melanie Libri, 'Nuns of Port-Royal', *Quarterly Review*, Sept. 1856, pp. 491–521.

[38] John Stuart Mill, *The Letters of John Stuart Mill*, ed. Hugh Elliot (London:
Longmans, Green & Co., 1910), II. 138.

[39] Anne Mozley, 'Convent Life', *Blackwood's Magazine*, May 1869, p. 607.

in the convent tower (an allegation which dissolved in the face of the unprepossessing and decrepit appearance of the unfortunate gentleman in court) were met with claims of the tyranny of the Superior and of the energy she devoted to inventing more and more excessive penances. Beyond 'a rude shock' to the 'romance of the British cloisters', it was unmistakably 'a woman's squabble', and detractors lost no opportunity in seizing upon this fact.[40] In an absolute rebuttal of the hopes with which the *Victoria Magazine* began the decade, Eliza Lynn Linton closed it declaring that,

The revelations of conventual life which we have had of late . . . will never be forgotten. They proved the whole question as to the capacity of peace and fair-dealing among a community of women unchecked by masculine influence; and *they proved it against ourselves.*[41]

There were women who would not accept Linton's view of 'proof', nor that of the predominantly male outcry about the case. Penelope Holland challenged both the substance and the tone of the criticism in an article in *Macmillan's Magazine* in April 1869:

When men talk of women they often talk like silly women catching the folly they attribute to their subject.

Such an exhibition of feeling has lately been made during the long trial of Saurin *v.* Starr, and the contagion has spread beyond the press. When will people learn the folly of exaggeration and know that every time they overstep the bounds of accurate truth they are working so much for the opposite side. It is because men have done this on the present occasion, and because I think it probable that the harsh and ignorant ridicule that has lately been levelled against convents may cause a revulsion of feeling in their favour, that I venture to say a few words about them.[42]

What was particularly significant about Penelope Holland's argument, and a similar case put the next month by Anne Mozley in *Blackwood's Magazine*, was that they reoriented the terms of the controversy. Unlike Linton, these women refused to see the issue in terms of female incapacities, locating culpability, rather, in the system itself, which was blameworthy because it had built into it procedures which actually militated against the potential for true friendship and community of which women were ordinarily capable. Both Mozley and Holland objected to the restraints placed on natural

[40] Mozley, 'Convent Life', p. 607.
[41] Linton, 'Tact and Temper', *Ourselves*, p. 179.
[42] Penelope Holland, 'A Few More Words on Convents and on English Girls', *Macmillan's Magazine*, Apr. 1869, p. 534.

affections. Substantiating her case, Holland quoted from a document called 'The Religious Life Portrayed', which, although Roman Catholic in its origin, had been 'adopted without reserve' by a clergyman of the Church of England:

'You must love all [your sisters], and I would have you love them *equally*. Avoid special preferences, they are fatal to the true charity of the religious life, and do great harm to communities. If you have any preference let it be for such amongst them as show you least affection, who bring most humiliation upon you and to whom you have most natural disinclination.'

Under this 'barbarous rule', Holland protested, 'even the affection between friends is to be cut off.'[43]

This view of the anti-communal nature of sisterhoods was substantiated by two books by Margaret Goodman, an ex-member of the best-known and most extensive sisterhood, Miss Sellon's Sisters of Mercy. In her account Goodman claimed:

One of the strictest rules of a nun's life is, that she walk loose to all human friendships; she must consider all ties of relationship severed when she becomes a recluse. . . . Whether at Miss Sellon's or any other nunnery, if a friendship between two of the members be discovered, they are at once carefully separated.[44]

Like Mozley and Holland, Goodman found this 'artificial' imposition of the system intolerable.

It is not surprising that, as in the debate on friendship, women writers were by no means unanimous on the subject of sisterhoods. Opinion was simply polarized on certain points, such as the issue of whether convents were merely a refuge for single women. However, beyond such polarities it is possible to isolate certain telling assumptions which ran through arguments on both sides. The most convincing defence of sisterhoods, before which even the most sceptical seemed to bow, was an appeal to their efficacy as agents of practical philanthropy. Anna Jameson, Barbara Bodichon, Frances Cobbe, and Florence Nightingale all gave voice to the belief that the drift of so many women into the Catholic Church was due to the fact that Catholicism offered them the opportunity 'to throw their energies into a sphere of definite utility'.[45] Revealingly, behind a repeated insistence

---

[43] Holland, 'A Few More Words', p. 539.

[44] Margaret Goodman, *Experiences of an English Sister of Mercy* (London: Smith, Elder & Company, 1862), p. 12.

[45] Jameson, *Sisters of Charity*, p. 101.

in these arguments that 'the absolute law of the ideal sisterhood must be work', there lay not simply the bias of a Victorian work ethic or the sectarian desire to distinguish the Protestant sisterhoods from the suspect medievalism of the Catholic contemplative orders.[46] There was, it seems, a deep mistrust of leaving any woman unoccupied. In *Sisters of Charity* Anna Jameson actually made the equation of activity with mental and spiritual health explicit:

I conceive that any large number of women shut up together in one locality, with no occupation connecting them actively and benevolently with the world of humanity outside, with all their interests centred within their walls, would not mend each other, and that such an atmosphere could not be perfectly healthy spiritually, morally or physically. There would necessarily ensue, in lighter characters, frivolity, idleness, and sick disordered fancies; and in superior minds, ascetic pride, gloom and impatience. But it is very different with the active orders, and I should certainly like to see amongst us some institutions which, if not exactly like them, should supply their place.[47]

And similarly Dinah Mulock hinted at the grim consequences of any disregard for the 'absolute law' of work:

It is a strange thing to say—yet I dare to say it, for I believe it to be true—that entering a Sisterhood, almost any sort of Sisterhood *where there was work to do, authority to compel the doing of it*, and companionship to sweeten the same, would have saved many a woman from a lunatic asylum.[48]

All this amounted to more than a conventional view of the devil making work for idle hands, whether male or female. Underlying the prospect of 'sick disordered fancies' envisaged by Jameson, or the potential for 'a pack of unhappy women' to be rendered 'morbid, sensitive and undevout' suggested by Frances Taylor, or the spectre of the asylum held up by Mulock, was the common conviction that the feminine temperament was particularly vulnerable, and that women's tenuous grasp on rationality and control was dependent on proper occupation and supervision.[49] There was, then, an inherent danger in any community which might paradoxically leave its female members too completely to themselves, and the constitutional vulnerability of women could, it seemed, be exacerbated by the potential for 'contagion' in a community.[50]

---

[46] Dinah Mulock, *About Money and Other Things* (London: Macmillan & Co., 1886), p. 164.   [47] Jameson, *Sisters of Charity*, p. 51.

[48] Mulock, *About Money*, p. 160 (my italics).

[49] Frances Taylor, 'Works of Charity', *Dublin Review*, Mar. 1857, p. 136.

[50] Nina Auerbach introduces this idea in her discussion of female education in *Communities of Women* (Harvard: Harvard University Press, 1978). Contrasting the 'salutary

Thus, as one might expect, the question of the exercise of authority in sisterhoods occupied a prominent place in these discussions. It was, though, an issue complicated by sectarian considerations. There was, for example, the fairly general disapproval of the absolutism of vows taken by Roman Catholic nuns, especially the vow of obedience, offending as it did the belief in the primacy of the individual conscience. Yet there was also an almost universal acknowledgement of the need for firm control. A community of women without men was 'unstable as water' Anna Jameson claimed; Dora Greenwell stated the need for *'the habit of working in concert and subordination'*; Charlotte Yonge diagnosed the 'absolute need of the feminine nature for discipline and obedience'—and so it went on.[51]

And if it was generally assumed that control was necessary, it was also assumed that women were not to be trusted with the exercise of it. The exploits of Miss Starr and Miss Sellon had provided ample ammunition for women such as Eliza Lynn Linton, who wrote of the 'restless, all-pervading tyranny' of women invested with power.[52] Yet even women who took a more sanguine view of female capacity seemed unable to avoid similar conclusions. In one article Frances Cobbe could satirize the paternalism of the Convocation of Canterbury, who had decided,

. . . that it was extremely desirable that all these lady guerillas of philanthropy should be enrolled in the regular army of the Church, together with as many new recruits as might be enlisted. To use a more appropriate simile, Mother Church expressed herself satisfied at her daughters 'coming out,' but considered her chaperonage was decidedly necessary to their decorum.

while in another she conceded:

Enough has been revealed to us of the secrets of convents, to leave no doubt that the possession of unnatural authority by the superiors has continually proved too strong a temptation; and the woman who in her natural domestic sphere might have been the gentlest of guides, has become in a convent the cruellest of petty despots.[53]

microcosm of men and manly boys' celebrated by Thomas Hughes in *Tom Brown's Schooldays* with the 'shameful taboo attached to "knots of young women"', she quotes a 'choice slice of Victorian misogyny' from the *Imperial Review* as the most extreme expression of the belief that the 'effect of young women on each other must invariably be a subtle sexual contagion' (p. 14).

[51] Jameson, *Sisters of Charity*, p. 124; Greenwell, *Essays*, p. 51; Yonge, *Womankind*, p. 16.

[52] Linton, 'Tact and Temper', *Ourselves*, p. 179.

[53] Cobbe, 'Old Maids', p. 594; 'Female Charity', p. 786.

Margaret Goodman too argued for the necessity of 'episcopal superintendence' for sisterhoods in order to guarantee the 'care and oversight of men of years and judgement': 'Let not Bishops, or any other men, trust that women will certainly be merciful to each other: like the tender mercies of the wicked, the tender mercies of women, when they deal with each other, are too often cruel.'[54] The fiercely Catholic reviewer, Frances Taylor, arguing for 'submission to priestly office', quoted from an 'extremely just' work which claimed ' "not rarely you will have the Lady Superior go crazy, because of the unlimited indulgence of her talent for governing.' "[55] It was, of course, an extreme view, but it differed only in degree from many of the arguments advanced by other women, and it betrayed once again a deep mistrust of the stability of women's characters—a stability which these women saw as strained in some ways by the test of community.

IV

In this period the debate over nursing was closely connected with the controversy over sisterhoods, although the discussion of nursing generally unified women more and gave rise to a more favourable view of women's relationships. The two issues were interconnected as much in practice as in theory. Many of Florence Nightingale's nurses in the Crimea, for example, were drawn from Miss Sellon's Sisters of Mercy and Pusey's community at Park Village. Sisterhoods provided the more educated, socially superior class of women that nursing needed to attract in order to improve its image and practice, while nursing in turn offered suitable occupation for communities of women. Each in a sense lent respectability to the other, with the result that 'female celibacy became defined as a role which might be consciously chosen, and thus lost some of its negative valuation.'[56]

However, the two issues were not simply inseparable in terms of their effect on the controversy over women's communities and collective action. To begin with, the discussion of nursing was not so fraught with divisive sectarian prejudices. Nor was it so liable to the damage that scandalous revelations had done to the general estimation

[54] Goodman, *Experiences*, pp. 111 and 28.

[55] Taylor, 'Works of Charity', p. 136.

[56] As suggested by Michael Hill, *The Religious Order: A Study of Virtuoso Religion and its Legitimation in the Nineteenth-century Church of England* (London: Heinemann, 1973), pp. 289, 274.

of women's religious communities, for the simple reason that the public opinion of the nursing profession was already so low. Dickens's portrait of the slatternly midwife, Sarah Gamp, in *Martin Chuzzlewit* was scarcely challenged by the reality as described, for example, in Miss Stanley's *Hospitals and Sisterhoods*.

In a sense, then, the reputation of nursing could only improve, and for this the figure of Florence Nightingale was crucial. Against the backdrop of the Crimean War, Nightingale and her fellow workers provided nursing with an outstanding model of achievement, something that Protestant sisterhoods patently lacked. Whereas Miss Starr and even Miss Sellon were subject to deep suspicion and press vilification, Nightingale and her nurses emerged from *The Times*'s coverage of the Crimean War as the heroines of the nation. Women writers found in them the exemplars for which they yearned. Caroline Cornwallis, for example, wrote in 1857 in the *Westminster Review* that the female nurses in the Crimea

. . . won for themselves what they had not sought—an everlasting remembrance in the annals of their country, and the affectionate admiration of the whole nation. . . . It is no small advantage to our argument, when claiming for women a more independent position than they had hitherto occupied in this country, that we can point to such an instance as a proof of female capability and tact.[57]

Seeing in those women a 'proof' so different from the one that Eliza Lynn Linton offered as verification of the incapacity 'of peace and fair-dealing among a community of women', Cornwallis concluded:

. . . as we are not without experience of what well-educated women can do when allowed to act, we have a right to point to the band of self-devoted ladies in our Eastern hospitals, and say to the Legislature, 'Give the freedom of action, and await confidently the result, in improved institutions and purer morals.'[58]

Similarly Frances Cobbe, who remained unreconciled to communities of religious women, appealed to the example of the Crimea as a vindication of women's capacities for united action. In fact the very terms of Cobbe's argument put aside the division of nationality in favour of the unity of gender:

. . . in the history of the Crimean War and its results . . . [lay] the origin of a movement whose limit it is hard to calculate. The hospital of Scutari was the

[57] Caroline Cornwallis, 'The Capabilities and Disabilities of Women', *Westminster Review*, Jan. 1857, p. 43.

[58] Cornwallis, 'Capabilities', p. 55.

cradle of a new life for the women of England . . . till the cry of agony from the Crimea came to call forth Miss Nightingale's band and their sister nurses in the hostile camp, the 'public function of women' was still to be sought. A thousand prejudices did that gallant little army break down forever.

Since the birth of that 'new life', Cobbe claimed, nursing was no longer the work of half a dozen exceptional women 'labouring unaided save by men; it [was] the chosen life-task of hundreds—perhaps we should say thousands—of women seeking to co-operate with one another.'[59]

The restrictions on personal friendships, which a number of female commentators, including Cobbe, found so unacceptable in sisterhoods, did not apply to nursing communities. On the contrary, Florence Nightingale drew attention to the potential of the nursing community to encourage friendship in her annual address to probationer-nurses of the Nightingale School at St. Thomas's Hospital in 1873: 'the friendships which have begun at this School may last through life, and be a help and strength to us. For may we not regard the opportunity given for acquiring friends as one of the uses of this place.'[60] In that and subsequent addresses Nightingale stressed the supportive power of communal living: 'Although we know how many and serious faults we have, ought we not also be able to find here some virtues which do not equally flourish in the larger world?'[61]

Further, the question of the exercise of authority in sisterhoods did not present the same problem in the nursing debate. Whereas an 'incipiently feminist conception of the role of women' seemed to lie behind the insistence on the right of women to organize their own activities in religious communities, the nursing community could be reassuringly envisaged as operating within a wider framework of predominantly masculine medical authority.[62] Furthermore, nursing was less controversial because the occupation itself was more in accordance with accepted norms of womanly behaviour, although this in turn made some women writers hesitate in any celebration over the effects of the nursing debate on the Woman Question. For example, Elizabeth Barrett Browning wrote to Anna Jameson in 1855:

If a movement at all, it is retrograde, a revival of old virtues! Since the siege of Troy and earlier, we have had princesses binding wounds with their hands;

[59] Cobbe, 'Female Charity', pp. 774–5.
[60] Florence Nightingale, *Florence Nightingale to her Nurses* (London: Macmillan & Co., 1914), p. 33.
[61] Nightingale, *Florence Nightingale to her Nurses*, p. 106.
[62] Hill, *The Religious Order*, p. 271.

it's strictly the woman's part, and men understand it so, as you will perceive by the general adhesion and approbation on this late occasion of the masculine dignities. Every man is on his knees before ladies carrying lint, calling them 'angelic she's,' whereas if they stir an inch as thinkers or artists from the beaten line (involving more good to general humanity than is involved in lint), the very same men would curse the impudence of the very same women and stop there. I can't see on what ground you think you see here the least gain to the 'woman's question,' so called. It's rather *the contrary*, to my mind . . .[63]

However, there was a further dimension to this 'womanly' aspect of nursing beyond the disturbingly conservative element that Barrett Browning perceived. Many women writers, whose opinions otherwise differed substantially, were united in the view that nursing was not only appropriately feminine, but ought to be exclusively so. In fact the whole question of medical practice aroused appeals to the 'community of the sex' which the *Saturday Review* claimed was so seldom seen, and a wide spectrum of female opinion seemed to merge in agreement that women should tend women and that medical treatment particularly in the areas of gynaecology and obstetrics needed to be improved and reclaimed by women. So, for example, Frances Cobbe represented doctoring as 'one of the "rights of women", which albeit theoretically denied is practically conceded.'[64]

The pioneering female doctors, Elizabeth and Emily Blackwell, agreed that an exclusively masculine medical profession was detrimental to proper care: 'At present, when women need medical aid or advice, they have at once to go out of their own world, as it were.'[65] Even Mrs Oliphant, a woman not given to feelings of *esprit de corps* as her writings on her sister authors indicated, claimed that the advantage to women of having a woman doctor to refer to was incalculable: 'To discuss the peculiar ailments of their mysterious frames with a man is always a trial and pain to the young.'[66]

Dinah Mulock went well beyond this concession to sexual reticence in her demand that women should resume their traditional place as midwives:

[63] Elizabeth Barrett Browning, *Letters of Elizabeth Barrett Browning*, ed. F. G. Kenyon (London: Smith, Elder & Co., 1897), II. 189.

[64] Cobbe, 'Old Maids', p. 607.

[65] Elizabeth and Emily Blackwell, 'Medicine as a Profession for Women', *English Woman's Journal*, May 1860, p. 153.

[66] Margaret Oliphant, 'The Grievances of Woman', *Fraser's Magazine*, May 1880, p. 707.

Obstetric practice once did belong, and still ought to belong, exclusively to capable, carefully trained, and experienced medical *women*. . . . I believe the number of women, especially poor women, who have been actually murdered through having male attendance in their hour of need, would, if known, be enough argument for our sex to hold its own.[67]

Various sources substantiated Mulock's dramatic claim that female attendants could actually save lives. Sophia Jex-Blake, one of Britain's first female physicians, for example, detailed cases of women leaving serious gynaecological disorders untreated because of a reluctance to submit to male doctors.[68] Similarly the *English Woman's Journal* printed an essay in 1862 by Samuel Gregory, the Secretary of the New England Female Medical College, which claimed that the statistics proved that 'the attendance of male practitioners has often a very embarrassing, disturbing effect, causing disastrous and not infrequent fatalities to mothers or infants, when there is not the least necessary occasion for such a result.'[69] Two years earlier the *Journal* printed extensive quotations from Gregory's 'Letter to Ladies' because it wished to disseminate important facts and 'to sow the seed of a revolution which shall exclude the male practitioner from the lying-in chamber—and hand over the science of obstetrics and the diseases of women and children to the duly trained and qualified female physician.'[70]

Annie Thomas sounded much the same call in fiction when she wrote *New Grooves* in 1871. Her heroine Ethel declares that '*women* ought to be about women that are ill', and she recovers from her own near-death more than ever convinced: 'There was ever ringing in her ears the sound of the unuttered cry of her sister-women, asking for leave and power to seek aid from, and give aid to, one another.'[71] However, Sophia Jex-Blake, looking back in 1893, noted how little the female medical controversy was reflected in the fiction of the period.[72] Nevertheless, as we shall see, it was against this background of widespread reconsideration of woman's social role and expanding possibilities for women's association with women that Elizabeth

[67] Dinah Mulock, *Concerning Men and Other Papers* (London: Macmillan, 1888), p. 17.

[68] Sophia Jex-Blake, *Medical Women: Two Essays* (Edinburgh: William Oliphant, 1872), p. 41.

[69] Samuel Gregory, 'Female Physicians', *English Woman's Journal*, Mar. 1862, p. 6.

[70] Samuel Gregory, 'Letter to Ladies', quoted in *English Woman's Journal*, Nov. 1860, p. 278.

[71] Annie Thomas, *New Grooves* (London: Charlton Tucker, 1871), pp. 94, 131.

[72] Sophia Jex-Blake, 'Medical Women in Fiction', *Nineteenth Century*, Feb. 1893, pp. 261–72.

Gaskell, Charlotte Brontë, and George Eliot had the opportunity of 'telling their own story'. All three not only were touched by the issues, but themselves deepened the whole consideration in this period of women's relationships with each other.

2

Elizabeth Gaskell's Endorsement of Female Communality

A Great Capacity for Friendship

I

Elizabeth Gaskell's contemporary reputation was appropriately more modest than either Charlotte Brontë's or George Eliot's. However, the very limitations of her success and achievement contributed to make her relations with other women writers more fruitful and less problematic. On the one hand Gaskell's female colleagues were not overawed and resentful of her in the ways they tended to be with Brontë and Eliot, and even the prickliest of her contemporaries responded to Gaskell's considerable personal charm. Mrs Oliphant, for example, described her as 'a sensible and considerate woman' and Eliza Lynn Linton wrote of her 'gracious graciousness and feminine dignity'.[1] On the other hand Gaskell herself was not overwhelmed by success, and her relatively modest self-image allowed her to be frankly admiring of more gifted women writers and generously tolerant of those less talented. Whereas celebrity proved a trial in many ways for Brontë and Eliot, Gaskell participated in the world opened up to her by literary success with enthusiasm and enjoyment.

Gaskell's letters reveal a woman who identified herself as one of a community of women writers, linked by virtue of gender and endeavour, and who was temperamentally prepared for what Eliza Lynn Linton characterized as 'the give and take of equality'.[2] For example, she exchanged new works with other women such as Charlotte Brontë, Anna Jameson, and Geraldine Jewsbury, and she frequently sought advice on her writing. She sent outlines of *Ruth* to Charlotte Brontë for discussion, asked Brontë and Jameson for their opinions on the

---

[1] Margaret Oliphant, 'Modern Novelists—Great and Small', *Blackwood's Magazine*, May 1855, p. 559; Eliza Lynn Linton, *My Literary Life* (London: Hodder & Stoughton, 1899), p. 93.

[2] Eliza Lynn Linton, 'George Eliot', *Women Novelists of Queen Victoria's Reign* (London: Hurst & Blackett, 1897), p. 77.

idea of serializing *North and South*, and enlisted the help of her Manchester friend Catherine Winkworth to discover practical information about business failures for that novel. Unlike Brontë and Eliot, who jealously guarded their work in composition, Gaskell ingenuously solicited judgements: 'What do you think of a fire burning down Mr. Thornton's mills *and house* as a help to failure? Then Margaret would rebuild them larger and better and need not go and live there when she's married.'[3]

In the same spirit Gaskell was prepared to offer advice to those who asked. One long letter survives, for example, in which she took considerable care to give comfort and direction to an unknown woman writer who had sent a manuscript. Signing the letter 'Your sincere and unknown friend', Gaskell concluded her reply with an expression of willingness to write again: 'If this letter has been of *any* use to you, do not scruple to write to me again, if I can help you.' It is clear that the occurrence was not unusual for Gaskell, for in warning the aspiring authoress of the difficulties of finding a publisher she wrote: 'I can only judge of it from a number of MSS. sent me from time to time; and only *one* of these writers has ever succeeded in getting her writings published, though in several instances I have used my best endeavours on their behalf' (*GL* 693–4). That willingness to use her position to help other women writers is evident, too, in her approach to Richard Bentley on behalf of the Winkworth sisters and their translation of *The Life of Niebuhr* (*GL* 251) and in her successful petition to obtain a grant from the Literary Fund for 'a poor authoress . . . a *lady* whom I picked up in Knutsford' (*GL* 829).

Gaskell took a lively interest in news of her sister authors. At times it amounted to little more than personal curiosity, as in her 'always lik[ing] to hear news of' Harriet Beecher Stowe (*GL* 767) or her entreaty to her publisher George Smith for information about George Eliot: 'send us PLEASE a long account of what she is like etc. etc. etc. . . . your impression of her,—which we won't tell anybody' (*GL* 587). However, it was also frequently a professional interest. So, for example, on seeing an advertisement for a new book by Dinah Mulock in 1851 she wrote: 'I wish she had some other means of support besides writing; I think it bad in its effects upon her writing, which must be pumped up instead of bubbling out; and very bad for her health, poor

[3] Elizabeth Gaskell, *The Letters of Mrs. Gaskell*, eds. J. A. Chapple and Arthur Pollard (Manchester: Manchester University Press, 1966), p. 310. All further references to this work appear in the text, abbreviated as *GL*.

girl' (*GL* 167). Similarly, when contemplating some biographical sketches, she enquired of her publishers: 'knowing that Miss Kavanagh wrote on those subjects I wanted to know how far she had forestalled me, or how far I should interfere with her' (*GL* 676).

Gaskell's sense of herself as a member of a community of women writers is further evident in her inclination to measure herself against other authors. In contrast to George Eliot who, as we shall consider in Chapter 6, deeply resented comparisons with her sister authors and never praised other writers in terms of contrast with herself, Gaskell wrote: 'Is Miss Jewsbury's review shallow? It looked to me very deep, but then I know I'm easily imposed upon in the metaphysical line, and could no more attempt to write such an article than fly—' (*GL* 91). Yet when Gaskell compared herself with Charlotte Brontë and George Eliot, the comparisons that women writers of the period were 'compulsively drawn' to make, she did so without the 'resentment' that so often accompanied the 'adulation' Brontë and Eliot inspired.[4] When she wrote to Charles Norton: 'Not a line of the book is written yet,—I think I have a feeling that it is not worth while \ trying / to write, while there are such books as Adam Bede and Scenes from Clerical Life—I set "Janet's Repentance" above all, still' (*GL* 581), it was not with the bitter competitiveness of a woman like Mrs Oliphant, but in a genuine spirit of 'humbl[e] admiration', such as that in which she later wrote to Eliot herself (*GL* 592).[5] Gaskell was less dogged by a competitive spirit because although she was not unconcerned with the fruits of literary success, as her hard-headed negotiations with publishers made clear, nor was she careless of her craft, she had nothing of that sense of near-sacred artistic vocation that made Eliot so stern with herself and with other women writers. Retaining more of the spirit of an amateur, she claimed never to have 'cared for literary fame' (*GL* 694). Thus, she could more composedly entertain the idea of her 'inferior vehemence of power and nature' in relation to Charlotte Brontë and suggest: 'she puts all her naughtiness into her books and I put all my goodness. I am sure she works off a great deal that is morbid *into* her writing, and *out* of her life; and my books are so far better than I am I often feel ashamed of having written them as if I was a hypocrite' (*GL* 229).

In return, Gaskell was the recipient of generous consideration from other women writers. Elizabeth Barrett Browning offered support

[4] As suggested by Elaine Showalter, *A Literature of Their Own*, p. 105.

[5] See Margaret Oliphant, *Autobiography and Letters of Mrs. Oliphant*, ed. Mrs Harry Coghill (Edinburgh: Blackwood & Sons, 1899), pp. 4–10.

amid the outcry caused by the publication of *Ruth*: 'I am grateful to you as a woman for having so treated such a subject.'[6] And George Eliot accepted Gaskell's admiration graciously, in spite of the fact that Gaskell had felt compelled to allude to her disapproval of Eliot's private life: 'your letter . . . has brought me the only sort of help I care to have—an assurance of fellow-feeling. . . . I shall always love to think that one woman wrote to another such sweet encouraging words —still more to think that you were the writer and I the receiver.'[7]

The most explicit and practical gesture of fellowship came from Charlotte Brontë and was recounted by Gaskell with 'sad, proud pleasure' in *The Life of Charlotte Brontë*. In the biography Gaskell tells of Brontë's willingness to delay the publication of *Villette* in order to give precedence to *Ruth* and quotes Brontë's 'words of friendship':

> I dare say, arrange as we may, we shall not be able wholly to prevent comparisons; it is in the nature of some critics to be invidious, but we need not care: we can set them at defiance; they *shall* not make us foes, they *shall* not mingle with our mutual feelings one taint of jealousy: there is my hand on that; I know you will give clasp for clasp.[8]

In fact Gaskell neglects to make clear that Brontë's gesture came in response to Gaskell's own request—or so at least Charlotte Brontë claimed to Ellen Nussey: 'Mrs. Gaskell wrote so pitifully to beg that it should not clash with her "Ruth" that it was impossible to refuse to defer publication a week or two.'[9] Nevertheless Brontë does suggest to Gaskell that the initial thought was hers: 'Before receiving yours, I had felt, and expressed to Mr. Smith, reluctance to come in the way of "Ruth"' (*Life*, II. 276).

In any case, the friendship between Gaskell and Brontë was important for both women. At a simple personal level Gaskell offered Brontë the comfort of consistent support and took an almost motherly interest in her:

> Miss Brontë has been ill. . . . I wrote to her directly—though I don't know that *that* did much good—only one felt how lonely and out of the world she must be, poor creature. I've a great mind to go and see her uninvited some

---

[6] Elizabeth Barrett Browning in *Bulletin of the John Rylands Library Manchester*, XIX. 1 (1935), 141.

[7] George Eliot, *The George Eliot Letters*, ed. Gordon Haight (London: Oxford University Press, 1954), III. 198.

[8] Elizabeth Gaskell, *The Life of Charlotte Brontë* (London: Smith, Elder & Co., 1857, II. 277. All further references to this work appear in the text, abbreviated as *Life*.

[9] Charlotte Brontë, *The Brontës: Their Lives, Friendships and Correspondence* (Oxford: Blackwell, 1932), IV. 36.

day. I could (that's to say if I'd the money stay at the inn so as not to be in Mr. Brontë's road). (*GL* 219)

Correspondingly, her solicitude was received by Brontë with a gratitude that went beyond mere politeness: 'If anybody would tempt me from home you would . . . the feeling expressed in your letter— proved by your invitation—goes *right home* where you would have it go, and heals as you would have it heal.'[10]

In professional terms, Gaskell probably received more than she gave in the friendship. Most directly, Brontë offered advice on writing, as we shall consider further in Chapter 4. Less tangibly, though, it is arguable that the actual experience of bearing witness to the friendship in *The Life of Charlotte Brontë* was significant for Gaskell as a writer. Edgar Wright, for example, contends that 'the sustained psychological interest' required by the task altered the nature of Gaskell's later work, replacing earlier 'melodrama and excitement' with a new depth.[11] Furthermore the endeavour meant that Gaskell was exposed to new ways of seeing the problems of women's authorship. It is unlikely that she would have characterized Brontë's objections to critical double standards so penetratingly—'praise mingled with pseudo-gallant allusions to her sex, mortified her far more than actual blame' (*Life*, II. 127)—had she not first confronted Brontë's own protest: 'I wish you did not think me a woman. . . . You will, I know, keep measuring me by some standard of what you deem becoming to my sex; where I am not what you consider graceful, you will condemn me' (*Life*, II. 126), and had she not immersed herself in a sense of the injustice of the Brontë household, where Branwell's alleged genius was afforded such unquestioned priority.

The biography itself is a testimony to Gaskell's sense of communality. In one sense it is simply an act of friendship, a fervent desire to create 'a right understanding of the life of my dear friend' (*Life*, I. 10). Time and again the urgency of an advocate breaks through the narrative composure. For example, Gaskell declares: 'all I can say is, that never, I believe, did women, possessed of such wonderful gifts, exercise them with a fuller sense of responsibility for their use' (*Life*, II. 51), or similarly: 'Think of her home . . . think of her father's sight hanging on a thread . . . and then admire as it deserves to be admired, the steady courage which could work away at *Jane Eyre*' (*Life*, II. 7).

---

[10] Charlotte Brontë, *The Brontës*, III. 286.
[11] Edgar Wright, *Mrs. Gaskell: The Basis for Reassessment* (London: Oxford Univ. Press, 1965), p. 151.

More broadly, the biography can be seen not just as a sisterly act but as a celebration of sisterhood in which the bonds between Charlotte, Emily, and Anne are treated with a kind of reverence. Professional and personal spheres become inseparable as Gaskell endeavours to 'make the world (if I am but strong enough in expression) honour the woman as much as they have admired the writer' (*GL* 345). Appropriately, too, Gaskell extended the sense of the interconnection between women writers by choosing the book's epigraph from *Aurora Leigh*, Elizabeth Barrett Browning's poetic tribute to female creative genius:

> Oh my God,
> —Thou hast knowledge, only Thou,
> How dreary 'tis for women to sit still
> On winter nights by solitary fires,
> And hear the nation's praising them far off.[12]

II

Given the extent to which successful authors were 'lionized' in the mid-nineteenth century, it is not surprising perhaps to discover these connections between Gaskell and other major women writers. However, Gaskell also maintained associations with many less celebrated women who were active in the broader literary and political subculture, which linked her with many of the interests and concerns discussed in Chapter 1.

For example, on her first trip to London as the acclaimed author of *Mary Barton* in May 1849, Gaskell took advantage of her celebrity to make the acquaintance of Anna Jameson, who was the mentor of the young women at the *English Woman's Journal* and one of the most renowned contributors to the debate on women's communities and friendship with her two lectures *Sisters of Charity* and *Communion of Labour* (*GL* 78). It was the beginning of a friendship of some significance for Gaskell's professional life. She found Jameson's sympathy during the furore over *Ruth* 'a comfort and a pleasure' (*GL* 226), and it was Jameson's '*very* valuable opinion' that she sought on the

---

[12] In the epigraph Gaskell substituted 'God' for the original 'Father'. Although appropriate in most senses, the choice of epigraph is ironic in so far as Brontë disliked Barrett Browning, whom she characterized as a 'word-twister' with a style 'wordy, intricate, [and] obscure' (*The Brontës*, III. 174). Barrett Browning in return, condemned *Jane Eyre* as 'savage and free-thinking' (in Margot Peters, *Unquiet Soul: A Biography of Charlotte Brontë*, London: Hodder & Stoughton, 1975, p. 367).

question of alterations to *North and South*. The details and spirit of Jameson's frank reply were well received by Gaskell: 'you have not been a bit too abrupt. I wanted just what you tell me. . . . So I have sent today since receiving your letter to stop the press' (*GL* 330).[13] Similarly Jameson's general injunction, 'do not with your powers engage to write periodically', echoing the same advice from Charlotte Brontë, was also well absorbed, if Gaskell's later views are any indication: 'But half a dozen papers are all I ever wrote for any periodical as I dislike and disapprove of such writing \ for myself / as a general thing' (*GL* 699).

Gaskell's new associations in London brought her within the circle of young proto-feminists who were to work so strenuously to advance the women's cause in print. Anna Jameson's protégée Bessie Parkes, for example, the originator and first editor of the *English Woman's Journal*, counted Gaskell among her friends. Indeed, as Ellen Moers suggests in her *Literary Women*, we can trace an influential link between the two women:

For just as every woman knew conservative women who urged her toward convention and silence, she also knew active feminists, who prodded her pen from the other, radical side of the Woman Question.
George Eliot knew Barbara Leigh-Smith. . . . Mrs. Gaskell knew Bessie Parkes; and Charlotte Brontë knew Mary Taylor.[14]

The young Parkes was virtually inseparable from her friend Barbara Bodichon, herself an enthusiastic writer and worker for the women's cause and financial supporter of the *Journal*, and so it is not surprising to find that she and Gaskell were acquainted. Rather less expectedly Gaskell had shown uncharacteristic timidity in making an overture of friendship in 1850 to the then twenty-three-year-old Bodichon: 'Do you know I've a great fancy for asking Barbara Smith [Bodichon] to come and pay us a visit. *Do* you think she'd come?' (*GL* 121). However, by the end of the decade, when Bodichon's radical credentials were more apparent, it was clear that it was reserved respect rather than fellow-feeling that Gaskell felt for Bodichon:

She is—I think in consequence of her birth, a strong fighter against the established opinions of the world,—which always goes against my—what shall I call it?—*taste*—(that is not the word,) but I can't help admiring her noble bravery, and respecting—while I don't personally *like* her. (*GL* 606)

[13] For Jameson's reply see Elizabeth Haldane, *Mrs. Gaskell and her Friends* (London: Hodder & Stoughton, 1931), p. 113.

[14] Ellen Moers, *Literary Women* (New York: Doubleday & Co., 1976), p. 19.

Another friend and fellow worker of Parkes and Bodichon was the poet Adelaide Procter, who stayed as a guest of the Gaskells in Manchester in 1851. Procter's parents were frequently hosts of literary gatherings which Gaskell attended, beginning with her London début in May 1849. When in 1861 Adelaide Procter edited *Victoria Regia: a Volume of Original Contributions in Poetry and Prose*, designed as 'a choice specimen of the skill attained' by the female artists and compositors of the Victoria Press, Gaskell was among the 'first authors of the day' who promised contributions.[15]

Procter was also promised a contribution to the anthology from Mary Howitt, a long-standing friend of Gaskell. It was Gaskell's visit to the Howitts on vacation in Heidelberg in 1841 that, according to Winifred Gérin, provided 'the first contact of the uninitiated amateur with the successful professional'.[16] They 'urged this promising new writer to "use her pen for the public benefit"' after recognizing merit in the description of Clopton House, which Gaskell provided for William Howitt's *Visits to Remarkable Places* in 1840, and Gaskell's first three stories were published in *Howitt's Journal* in 1847 and early 1848. The Howitts' daughter Anna Mary was a colleague of Parkes and Bodichon as one of the original workers in the *Journal* community and as a member of their Portfolio Club, which was formed with Christina Rossetti among others to offer mutual encouragement in their artistic projects. Not only had Mary Howitt consented to offer these women a contribution for *Victoria Regia*, but she was eager to provide a worthwhile piece:

I had been very anxious to write the poem I had promised Adelaide Procter for the 'Victoria Regia.' I was afraid I could not manage it. However, in the night my mind was filled with a subject which came very clearly, and yesterday I wrote it. I hope it is good, for I have a great desire to stand well amongst the women.[17]

In the published work a number of other women friends of Gaskell appeared such as Bessie Parkes, Anna Jameson, Geraldine Jewsbury, Dinah Mulock, and Harriet Martineau. Gaskell's own 'contribution', however, never materialized. Its absence is puzzling, but one possible

[15] Adelaide Procter, Introduction, *Victoria Regia* (London: Victoria Press, 1861), p. vii; Emily Faithfull, 'Women Compositors', *English Woman's Journal*, Sept. 1861, p. 37.

[16] Winifred Gérin, *Elizabeth Gaskell: A Biography* (London: Oxford University Press, 1976), p. 68.

[17] Mary Howitt, *Mary Howitt: An Autobiography*, ed. Margaret Howitt (London: Isbiter, 1889), II. 144.

explanation is that Gaskell, like Howitt, had difficulty in 'managing' to get something written. The need to do so came at one of the most difficult times in her creative career, as she struggled with *Sylvia's Lovers*, and only months after the appearance of *Victoria Regia* in September 1861, for example, she wrote to an unknown correspondent: 'I am extremely sorry that I must decline your offer of writing a set of papers such as you name for the Daily News, for my hands are already overfull with literary engagements' (*GL* 677).

A further link with the wider literary subculture existed for Gaskell in Manchester, where she maintained a close and supportive friendship with the Winkworth sisters, who brought Gaskell 'the double compensation of understanding for her work and the emotional outlet she needed'.[18] Although they lacked the radicalism of Barbara Bodichon, or even of Bessie Parkes, and were wary of being identified unequivocally with the cause of 'Women's Rights', the five sisters were directly involved in the women's movement, especially Emily, who was a close friend of Frances Cobbe, an important champion for the single woman, as we have seen, and Susanna, who contributed to Emily Faithfull's *Victoria Magazine*.[19]

III

Gaskell's association with this wider circle of women writers and activists was not based simply on personal friendship, for she also shared many of their public concerns. Indeed, in various ways Gaskell was touched by every major aspect of the debate on women's place in the changing society of mid-nineteenth-century England. As the mother of four daughters, for example, she was keenly aware of the problems facing the 'superabundant' woman. She anticipated the psychological strain—the 'time of trial' and 'sudden feeling of *purposelessness*' (*GL* 117)—of single life, and she sought to alleviate the practical difficulties for her unmarried daughters as far as possible:

. . . but really the residents at the Lakes *are* all women I think; and once upon a time we thought of buying land and building a house there as a future home for our girls, because there is a kind of old-fashioned chivalrous respect paid to women in all that country, which we thought would be a pleasant surrounding for brotherless women. (*GL* 571)

[18] Gérin, *Elizabeth Gaskell*, p. 92.
[19] M. J. Shaen, ed., *Memorials of Two Sisters: Susanna and Catherine Winkworth* (London: Longmans, Green & Co., 1908), p. 292. See, e.g., review of Frances Cobbe's *Broken Lights*, in the *Victoria Magazine*, July 1864.

When Gaskell finally accomplished her plan of buying a house away from Manchester shortly before her death in 1865, she wrote: 'The house is large . . . and in the middle of a pretty rural village, so that it won't be a lonely place for unmarried daughters who will inherit' (*GL* 775).

Gaskell was similarly well acquainted with the issues relating to women's employment. Her residence in a major industrial city, her involvement with emigration schemes and the Establishment for Invalid Gentlewomen and, not least, her friendship with Charlotte Brontë, all contributed to Gaskell's understanding of the difficulties and limitations faced by the would-be independent woman. So she was prepared to support her daughter in her desire to take up nursing:

I have told Meta she may begin to prepare herself for entering upon a nurse's life of devotion when she is thirty or so, by going about among the sick now, and that all the help I can give in letting her see hospitals, etc. if she wishes she may have. (*GL* 320)

Her positive attitude to nursing was undoubtedly reinforced by her admiration for Florence Nightingale whom she met in October 1854. However, the publication of *Ruth* in January 1853 suggests, as we shall discuss, that Gaskell's sympathy pre-dated the friendship. Predictably, the one 'grand quarrel' Gaskell had with Nightingale arose from the latter's contention that all children should be brought up in crèches. Despite Gaskell's deep respect for Nightingale, she believed that the pioneer nurse was 'too much for institutions, sisterhoods and associations' (*GL* 320).

In some senses, however, this objection was an immediate response to Nightingale's anti-maternal pronouncements. More generally, Gaskell was interested in, and tolerant of, the activities of communities of women, such as Miss Sellon's Sisters of Mercy (*GL* 116) and the nursing sisterhood at Kaiserswerth (*GL* 731). Like many of the female commentators already considered, Gaskell saw sisterhoods as offering refuge to single women and was prepared to acknowledge the positive value of the mutual support they could offer:

. . . but do you not think many single women would be happier if, when the ties of God's appointment were absolved by death, they found themselves some work like the Sisters of Mercy? I feel sure you do—I do not think they need to be banded together, or even to take any name, unless indeed such forms strengthen their usefulness. (*GL* 116)

Although Gaskell was closely connected with many women who participated in the public debate over women's nature and capacities, she was never tempted to do so herself. Nevertheless her early fiction was more consciously and purposefully topical than either Charlotte Brontë's or George Eliot's and made obvious contributions to the controversy. For example, the subjects treated in *Mary Barton* and *Ruth* were undertaken with a careful determination to influence public opinion by veracity and fairness. Of *Mary Barton* Gaskell claimed: 'those best acquainted with the way of thinking and feeling among the poor acknowledge its *truth*; which is the acknowledgement I most of all desire, because evils being once recognized are half way on towards their remedy' (*GL* 827); and similarly after writing *Ruth* Gaskell declared, like a woman who had accomplished a mission: 'I think I have put the small edge of the wedge in, if only I have made people talk and discuss the subject a little more than they did' (*GL* 226).

Clearly the plight of the fallen woman was Gaskell's primary interest in *Ruth*. In addition, though, the novel addresses the issue of the rehabilitation of nursing, not only through Ruth's saintly role as a nurse, which provides a considerable advance on that of her literary predecessor Sarah Gamp, but by an explicit challenge to prevailing opinions:

'Still, you can't say that any knowledge of any kind will be in my way, or will unfit me for my work.'

'Perhaps not. But all your taste and refinement will be in your way, and will unfit you.'

'You have not thought so much as I have, or you would not say so. Any fastidiousness I shall have to get rid of, and I shall be better without; but any true refinement I am sure I shall find of use, for don't you think that every power we have may be made to help us in any right work, whatever that is? Would you not rather be nursed by a person who spoke gently and moved quietly about, than by a loud bustling woman?'[20]

The novel, written before Gaskell was personally influenced by her friendship with Florence Nightingale, came before the impact of Nightingale's experience in the Crimea had aroused widespread sympathy. So it can appropriately be seen more as a challenge to public opinion than a reflection of it.

In Gaskell's fiction more generally women take on medical practice as their rightful domain, substantiating Frances Cobbe's contention in 'What Shall We Do with Our Old Maids?' that doctoring was one of 'the "rights of women", which albeit theoretically denied is practically conceded.'[21] In *Mary Barton*, for example, Alice Wilson 'in addition to her invaluable qualities as a sick nurse . . . added a considerable knowledge of hedge and field simples', and the loyal French maid in 'Crowley Castle' had 'a certain cupboard where she kept medicine and drugs of which she alone knew the properties'.[22] In 'Christmas Storms and Sunshine' it is a female neighbour who saves the life of a young child seized by a 'croup-fit', and when the physician finally arrives, he concedes: ' "It has been a sharp attack, but the remedies you have applied have been worth all the Pharmacoepia an hour later." '[23]

Further, in *Mary Barton* Gaskell seems to amplify the widespread call for female attendance at childbirth. Thus, when Mrs. Barton goes into labour in Chapter 3, Gaskell juxtaposes the immediate response of the working-woman called by John Barton to assist his wife against the tardiness of the male doctor, suggesting that only the women fully understand the critical urgency of birth:

While the woman hastily dressed herself, leaving the window still open, she heard cries of agony, which resounded in the little court in the stillness of the night. In less than five minutes she was standing at Mrs. Barton's bedside, relieving the terrified Mary, who went about, where she was told, like an automaton; her eyes tearless, her face calm, though deadly pale, and uttering no sound, except when her teeth chattered for very nervousness.

The cries grew worse.

The doctor was very long in hearing the repeated rings at his night bell, and still longer in understanding who it was that made this sudden call upon his services; and then he begged Barton just to wait while he dressed himself, in order that no time might be lost in finding the court and house. Barton absolutely stamped with impatience, outside the doctor's door, before he came down; and walked so fast homewards that the medical man several times asked him to go slower.

'Is she so very bad?' asked he.[24]

[21] Cobbe, 'What Shall We Do with Our Old Maids?', p. 607.

[22] Elizabeth Gaskell, *Mary Barton*, (1848), *Works*, I. 15; 'Crowley Castle', (1863), *Works*, VII. 701.

[23] Elizabeth Gaskell, 'Christmas Storms and Sunshine' (1848), *Works*, II. 202.

[24] Gaskell, *Mary Barton*, *Works*, I. 19.

As we have seen in Chapter 1, the campaign for female midwives made direct appeals to solidarity amongst women. Some women writers extended this call for solidarity, arguing that the general improvement of women's lot depended on widespread co-operation between women. For example, the *Victoria Magazine* declared on the plight of seamstresses: 'It is impossible to acquit ladies of blame in this matter; both the short notice they give, and the long credit they expect, operate most mischievously upon the interests of all employed'; and Dinah Mulock advanced a similar argument in *A Woman's Thoughts about Women*:

> . . . every woman, be she servant or mistress, sempstress or fine lady, should receive the 'protection' suitable to her degree. . . . Let us, at least, hold the balance of justice even, nor allow an over-consideration for the delicacy of one woman to trench over the rights, conveniences, and honest feelings of another.[25]

A similar preoccupation is evident on Gaskell's part in the opening chapters of *Ruth*, where the scenes in which Mrs. Mason's apprentices work through the night to meet orders for the hunt ball and Ruth is treated so cavalierly by Bellingham's partner as she mends her dress at the ball seem carefully designed to illustrate this need for mutual and class responsibility.

Furthermore, Gaskell's conviction that 'there is . . . moral advantage [in] uniting mistresses and maids in a more complete family bond', expressed in 'French Life' in 1864 echoes the thinking of her 'nice little friend' Dinah Mulock in *A Woman's Thoughts about Women*: 'servants are of like passions and feelings. . . . [We are] all "sisters" together.'[26] In fact, on the question of responsibility among women Gaskell consistently demonstrates the deep and important bonds between mistress and servant. Repeatedly the servant is depicted as an integral part of the family, 'more like [a] friend' than an employee, and often the economic bond is broken and the roles reversed with the servant offering financial support and protection to the erstwhile mistress, as Martha does to Miss Matty in *Cranford* and Sally to the Bensons in *Ruth*.[27] Serving women such as Nancy in *The Moorland*

[25] 'The Manufacture of Wearing Apparel', *Victoria Magazine*, June 1865, p. 178; Mulock, *A Woman's Thoughts*, p. 33.

[26] Elizabeth Gaskell, 'French Life' (1864), *Works*, VII. 609; Mulock, *A Woman's Thoughts*, p. 93.

[27] See also, Miss Mours in 'A Dark Night's Work', Amante in 'The Grey Woman', and Alice in 'The Manchester Marriage'.

Cottage and Natee in *Lois the Witch* also offer an alternative source of emotional nourishment where family ties have failed.

Gaskell's interest in sisterhoods is also reflected in her fiction. Eight months after receiving from Anna Jameson a copy of her celebrated lecture *Sisters of Charity: Catholic and Protestant*, Gaskell published the short story 'The Poor Clare' (*GL* 338). The story, like Jameson's lecture, conveys a sense of the unfailing piety and mercy of the nuns and stresses the love they inspire in the townspeople. However, for all Gaskell's tolerance, she cannot overcome an antipathy towards Roman Catholicism. So the Jesuit confessor Father Bernhard is gratuitously revealed to be a Jacobite conspirator, and many of the macabre details—the nuns as veiled grey figures wading across the battlefield 'their feet all wet with blood' and starving to death in silence within the enclosure of the convent—have more in common with Gaskell's ghost stories or indeed with the sensational 'anti-sacerdotalist fiction' discussed in G. F. Best's 'Popular Protestantism in Victorian Britain' than with any sympathetic consideration of religious community.[28] However, in 1853, before the controversy over sisterhoods really took hold Gaskell depicts the choice of the master's daughter to enter a convent in 'My French Master' as sound and reasonable:

So she pleaded with her father to allow her to become a Sister of Charity. She told him that he would have given a welcome to any suitor who came to offer to marry her, and bear her away from her home, and her father and sister; and now, when she was called by religion, would he grudge to part with her? He gave his consent, if not his full approbation.[29]

V

Given the extent to which Gaskell willingly interacted with her sister authors, the number of friendships she maintained with women in the wider literary subculture, and her apparent sympathy towards women on many of the issues involved in the general controversy, it is surprising perhaps to find in an undated letter: 'I wish I could help taking to men so much more than to women (always excepting the present company, my dear!) and I wish I could help men taking to me, but I believe we've a mutual attraction of which Satan is the

---

[28] Elizabeth Gaskell, 'The Poor Clare' (1855), *Works*, V. 387; G. F. A. Best, 'Popular Protestantism in Victorian Britain', *Ideas and Institutions of Victorian Britain*, ed. Robert Robson (London: G. Bell & Sons, 1967), pp. 115–42.

[29] Elizabeth Gaskell, 'My French Master' (1853), *Works*, II. 528.

originator' (*GL* 808). Balanced against that, however, her letters in general reveal that she wrote to women with a frank confidentiality and a sense of *esprit de corps*, which, as we shall see, is also evident in her fiction.

Admittedly, the freedom with which she expressed herself to Eliza Fox, for example, while testifying to the ease of that friendship, indicates as much about Gaskell's general frankness as about any more specifically feminine confidentiality:

> . . . I believe I've been as nearly dazed and crazed with this c——, d—— be h—— to it, story as can be. I've been sick of writing, and everything connected with literature or improvement of the mind; to say nothing of deep hatred to my species about whom I was obliged to write as if I loved 'em. . . . Seriously it has been a terrible weight on me and has made me have some of the most felling headaches I ever had in my life. (*GL* 325)

At the same time a more partisan feeling emerges on occasion, as for example in a letter to her sister-in-law, Mrs Charles Holland: 'the sort of consciousness that Wm may at any time and does generally see my letters makes me not write so naturally and heartily as I think I should do' (*GL* 34). Such feeling is particularly apparent in letters in which she discusses motherhood, like that to another sister-in-law Anne Robson:

> . . . one can't help having 'Mother's fears'; and Wm I dare say kindly won't allow me ever to talk to him about anxieties, while it would be SUCH A RELIEF often. . . . Now you know that dear William feeling most kindly towards his children, is yet most reserved in *expressions* of either affection or sympathy—and in the case of my death, we all know the probability of widowers marrying again,—would you promise, dearest Anne to remember MA's peculiarity of character, and as much as circumstances would permit, watch over and cherish her. . . . Still let me open my heart sometimes to you dear Anne, with reliance on your sympathy \ and secrecy / .

The conviction that women can properly make special claims on each other is typical of Gaskell, and, as we shall see in the following chapter, anticipates the representation in her fiction of fundamental bonds between women.

3

Elizabeth Gaskell's Fiction

A Sanctuary in the Eleusinian Circle

I

The spirit both of Gaskell's dealings with her sister authors and of her letters to women friends suggests a feeling of female camaraderie. Her representation in fiction of women's relationships goes further still, exploring a more radical and complex sense of female solidarity. Repeatedly in her novels and short stories Gaskell depicts women united by circumstance and by choice and celebrates their talent for friendship and mutual support. Underlying this is a conception of fundamental bonds between women, both natural and political. These are seen primarily in terms of shared maternal feelings and a common lot as victims of the social and sexual passivity to which women are inevitably subjected.

For Elizabeth Gaskell there is no love more sacred than that of a mother, no notion more totemic than motherhood. Significantly, her first writing ventures were made in its name. Shortly after her daughter Marianne's birth in 1834 she began *My Diary*, 'a token of her Mother's love, and extreme anxiety in the formation of her little daughter's character', in which she claims that the dear and tender tie between mother and daughter is the 'love which passeth every earthly love'.[1] Two years later she wrote 'On Visiting the Grave of my Stillborn Little Girl', pledging never to forget the lost child:

> I think of thee in these far happier days,
> And thou, my child, from thy bright heaven see
> How well I keep my faithful vow to thee.[2]

In a sense she kept that promise as a writer by introducing the spectre of the lost child repeatedly in her work. There is scarcely a mother in Gaskell's fiction who has not known the grief of losing a child, or at

[1] Elizabeth Gaskell, *My Diary: The Early Years of my Daughter Marianne* (London: privately printed, 1923), p. 5.
[2] Elizabeth Gaskell in Gérin, *Elizabeth Gaskell*, p. 53.

least the threat of loss. And this vulnerability to grief is akin to Sarah Ellis's 'sisterhood of shared pain'. In *Cranford* she writes of 'those strange eyes, that I've never noticed but in mothers of dead children', and even in this lightest of works, she accords a solemnity and urgency to the tale of the flight across India by Mrs. Brown, the conjuror's wife: '"if this baby dies too, I shall go mad; the madness is in me now."'[3] Similarly in 'Christmas Storms and Sunshine' the two feuding women put aside their grievances as they come together at the sick-bed of the croup-stricken child, and in the opening chapters of *Mary Barton* the pregnant Mrs. Barton, haunted by the earlier death of her infant son, is soothed by 'the unburdening of her fears and thoughts to her friend' Mrs. Wilson, who herself nurses her 'little, feeble twins'.[4]

This union of women by virtue of their peculiar vulnerability to grief in the mother–child relationship is felt conversely by daughters who have lost their mothers. When Hazel Mews argues in *Frail Vessels* that nineteenth-century women writers show surprisingly little interest in motherhood and that mothers are 'quietly accepted without emotional over-valuation', she fails to take account of the paradoxical importance of the absence of mothers.[5] Significantly that absence was a reality for all three of the major women writers under consideration, who each lost their natural mother at an early age—Gaskell in infancy, Brontë in girlhood, and Eliot in adolescence. In February 1849 Gaskell wrote: 'I think no one but one so unfortunate as to be early motherless can enter into the craving one has after the lost mother' (*GL* 614). Accordingly, her heroines often feel, like Barrett Browning's Aurora Leigh, the sharp pain of 'a mother-want about the world'.[6]

Mary Barton's real trials begin when she loses her mother and, indeed, she identifies this in court in her own defence: '"For, you see, sir, mother died before I was thirteen, before I could know right from wrong about some things"' (I. 377). Ruth likewise lacks the maternal guidance which might prevent her seduction by the unscrupulous Bellingham. The old servant, Thomas, longs 'to give her a warning

[3] Elizabeth Gaskell, *Cranford* (1853; rpt. London: Smith, Elder & Co., 1906), *Works*, II. 131. All further references to this work appear in the text, abbreviated as II.

[4] Elizabeth Gaskell, *Mary Barton* (1848; rpt. London: Smith, Elder & Co., 1906), *Works*, I. 11. All further references to this work appear in the text, abbreviated as I.

[5] Hazel Mews, *Frail Vessels: Women's Role in Women's Novels from Fanny Burney to George Eliot* (London: Athlone Press, 1969), p. 160.

[6] Elizabeth Barrett Browning, *Aurora Leigh*, Bk.1, l. 40.

of the danger that he thought she was in and yet he did not know how', and he plans vaguely to '"put my missus up to going to town and getting speech of her, and tell her a bit of her danger."'[7] In the scenes immediately before Ruth's fall her vulnerability is underscored by various references to motherhood which reinforce the fact of Ruth's orphan status: the young servant girl soothes her mother's headache with strong tea, Bellingham joins his mother in Paris, and the setting reminds Ruth of the garden beneath her mother's window.

The death of the mother is particularly traumatic. In *North and South*, for example, Margaret is unable to respond to Dixon's attempts to comfort her when Mrs. Hale dies: 'this seemed a loss by itself; not to bear comparison with any other event in the world', and in *Sylvia's Lovers* Sylvia is entirely absorbed by the excitement of her infatuation with Kinraid until her perspective is radically altered when she first perceives that her mother's life is threatened: 'No thought of company or gaiety was in Sylvia's mind as long as her mother's illness lasted; vehement in all her feelings, she discovered in the dread of losing her mother how passionately she was attached to her.'[8] Molly Gibson in *Wives and Daughters* instinctively seeks out the Squire's wife to satisfy that 'mother-want', for although 'she had been too young to be conscious of it at the time', Gaskell represents the loss of her mother as 'a jar to the whole tenour of her life'.[9] That pervasive hold of the mother's image on the unconscious, as well as the conscious, mind is evident, too, in the delirium of both Mary and Alice in *Mary Barton*, in which each 'thinks she's with her mother at home' (I. 391).

Gaskell consistently upholds the primacy of the maternal bond. In her terms it acquires a sacrosanctity and is placed ahead of other frequently conflicting claims and impulses. So in *North and South*, for example, it takes precedence over personal and class antagonism, linking Mrs. Hale with Mrs. Thornton, who agrees to watch over Margaret after her mother's death. In the short story 'Half a Life-Time Ago' a tension is played out between the heroine's sexual desire and her familial and maternal impulses toward her orphaned brother.

[7] Elizabeth Gaskell, *Ruth* (1853; rpt. London: Smith, Elder & Co., 1906), *Works*, III. 50. All further references to this work appear in the text, abbreviated as III.

[8] Elizabeth Gaskell, *North and South* (1855; rpt. London: Smith, Elder & Co., 1906), *Works*, IV. 299; *Sylvia's Lovers* (1863; rpt. London: Smith, Elder & Co., 1906), *Works*, VI. 137. All further references to these works appear in the text, abbreviated as IV and VI respectively.

[9] Elizabeth Gaskell, *Wives and Daughters* (1865; rpt. London: Smith, Elder & Co., 1906), *Works*, VIII. 2. All further references to this work appear in the text, abbreviated as VIII.

The two males in her life precipitate the necessity of choice, with the brother jealously demanding: ' "Which on us do you like best?" ' and the lover finally insisting: ' "Choose between him and me, Susy, for I swear to thee, thou shan't have both." ' [10] Although there is no doubt that the maternal claim should take precedence, Gaskell removes the choice from the realm of the simplest moralism by demonstrating that Susan, having chosen in favour of her ward, feels natural resentment: 'It might have been right; but, as she sickened she wished that she had not instinctively chosen the right. How luxurious a life haunted by no stern sense of duty must be!' (V. 313). This opposition between sexual and maternal feelings in the female psyche is also touched upon in *Ruth*. At the birth of her child Ruth feels 'a strange yearning kind of love for the father' (III. 190), and when Bellingham appears at Earl's Crag, Ruth is torn: ' "I do believe Leonard's father is a bad man, and yet, oh! pitiful God, I love him" ' (III. 271). However, at the decisive moment Gaskell sets up a revealing and characteristic opposition:

'I am so torn and perplexed! You, who are the father of my child!'

But that very circumstance, full of such tender meaning in many cases, threw a new light into her mind. It changed her *from the woman into the mother*— the stern guardian of her child [my italics]. (III. 270)

Motherhood forms the corner-stone for Ruth's redemption. Her response to the news of her pregnancy, ' "Oh, my God, I thank Thee!" ' is regarded by Faith Benson as 'very depraved' (III. 117). Yet in the novel's terms it is evidence of Ruth's goodness, an instinctive affirmation of the most positive impulses in a way reminiscent of the Ancient Mariner's 'And I blessed them unaware'.

The primacy of the maternal bond is also affirmed in *Ruth* when Mrs. Bradshaw's maternal loyalty is tested against her obedience to her husband. Her priorities are uncompromisingly clear: ' "If I'm to choose between my husband and my son, I choose my son; for he will have no friends unless I am with him" ' (III. 404), and in 'Lizzie Leigh' Mrs. Leigh makes a similar choice of child over husband: 'she had rebelled against her husband as against a tyrant, with a hidden, sullen rebellion, which tore up the old landmarks of wifely duty and affection, and poisoned the fountains whence gentlest love and reverence had once been for ever springing' (II. 207).

---

[10] Elizabeth Gaskell, 'Half a Life-Time Ago' (1855), *Works*, V. 304. All further references to this work appear in the text, abbreviated as V.

It is consistent, then, that when Gaskell contemplated the difficulties and pain of unmarried life, she did so not in terms of the forfeit of conjugal love, but of the absence of children: 'I think an unmarried life may be to the full as happy *in process of time* but I think that there is a time of trial to be gone through with *women*, who naturally yearn after children' (*GL* 598). However, in keeping with Anna Jameson's sense of a 'maternal organization common to all women', Gaskell saw mothering love as a potential in every woman, the exercise of which was not simply guaranteed by the act of giving birth.[11]

This is clear in one respect from the number of failed mothers in Gaskell's fiction. Their failure takes different forms, just as the gravity of the inevitable consequences varies. At one end of the spectrum is the complacent neglect of Lady Cumnor in *Wives and Daughters*, who remains oblivious to any causal connection between the 'clever, heedless' nature of her daughter and her own failings as a mother. More seriously, some mothers betray their children by emotional defection. Mrs. Bradshaw in *Ruth* acts as an informant against her children to her husband in a 'system of carrying constant intelligence to headquarters' (III. 221). When Mr. Bradshaw seeks to enlist Ruth into his network of supervision, her loyalty to Jemima provides a neat counterpoint to Mrs. Bradshaw's weakness: 'there was something indefinably repugnant to her in the manner of acting which Mr. Bradshaw had proposed, and she was determined not to accept the invitations which were to place her in so false a position' (III. 225). In a sense Ruth is fittingly rewarded by Jemima's loyalty when Mr. Bradshaw discovers the truth about her past. Mrs. Bradshaw, however, suffers for her betrayal, hating the husband who requires such maternal disloyalty and alienating her daughter, 'who long ago felt it as an insurmountable obstacle to any free communication with her mother' (III. 221).

In *The Moorland Cottage* and 'The Crooked Branch' maternal affection is exclusively focused on the male child, to the consequent neglect of the female. Recalling Mrs. Rivers's fate in *Jane Eyre*, the unfairness rebounds on the mothers in the form of ill-treatment suffered at the hands of their sons, who in each case have become desperately embroiled in financial dishonesties. In *The Moorland Cottage*, the more satisfactory of the two stories and the one that anticipates *The Mill on the Floss* in ways we shall examine in Chapter 6, there are moments of genuine pathos. Gaskell explores the stress under which the heroine,

[11] Anna Jameson, *Anna Jameson*, p. 333.

Maggie, acts as she moves further and further into 'drawn battle'
with her brother, Ned, and searches for alternative sources of affection from the servant, Nancy, and the invalid neighbour, Mrs. Buxton:
'Maggie, in all her yearning to become Joan of Arc, or some great
heroine, was unconscious that she had showed no little heroism in
bearing meekly what she did every day from her mother' (II. 296).
The real sadness stems from Maggie's desperate need to believe her
mother loves her. Even at the point of reconciliation when Mrs.
Browne offers a vague apology and Maggie takes 'her short slumber
by her mother's side with her mother's arms around her, and . . .
[feels] that her sleep had been blessed', the mother's mind reverts to
'her darling son' and 'to this day it is the same. She prizes the dead
son more than a thousand living daughters' (II. 382).

Gaskell's last novel, *Wives and Daughters*, provides the most extended
and penetrating study of a failed mother in the figure of Mrs. Gibson.
The first indications of doubt about her character come when she
takes Molly's food at the picnic, withholding nourishment contrary to
all maternal impulses, and when Mary Cumnor expresses reservations
because of her treatment of Cynthia: ' "The only thing that makes me
uneasy now is the way in which she seems to send her daughter away
from her so much" ' (VIII. 103). A poisonous rivalry emerges in
which the mother–daughter relationship is subsumed in the threat the
ageing woman feels from the beautiful girl: 'she had felt how dis-
agreeable it would be to have her young daughter flashing out her
beauty by the side of the faded bride, her mother' (VIII. 138). One of
the most chilling moments in the novel comes when Cynthia breaches
the shallow decorum between them to ask: ' "Do you look forward
to the consequences of my death, mamma?" ' (VIII. 497). The consequences of Mrs. Gibson's failure to provide maternal love are felt
more generally in the psychological scarring of the brilliant daughter,
who in never knowing love never feels it.

Just as the failure of these mothers challenges any narrowly biological definition of motherhood, so too does the example of a number
of successful, surrogate mothers in Gaskell's fiction. In cases such as
Miss Galindo's in *My Lady Ludlow* or Susan's in 'Lizzie Leigh' circumstances force the mothering role onto the women concerned. In
others—Mrs. Hamley's in *Wives and Daughters* or Mrs. Buxton's in
The Moorland Cottage—a combination of kindness and need (both
women have lost daughters) inspires each woman to provide the emotional nourishment lacking in the child's home. In 'Libbie Marsh's

Three Eras', Gaskell's first published short story, the heroine is drawn into sharing the mothering role with the natural mother, and the two women are united in that sharing to such an extent that they set up house together after the child's death. In all these examples the love that surrogate mothers bear for their charges is as strong and valuable as any more strictly natural link.

II

Despite the central importance of mothers in Gaskell's fiction, it is her community of spinsters in *Cranford* that has provided the most obvious focus for consideration of Gaskell's thinking about women. Nina Auerbach takes it as a central example for her book *Communities of Women*, and other critics divide with polemical readings of the novel. On the one hand, Martin Dodsworth argues that *Cranford* is 'a kind of trimmed and tidied dream, in which Mrs. Gaskell's unconscious hostility to the male struggles with her awareness of the pointlessness of such hostility in the predominantly masculine society of her day', and an 'elegy to the insufficiency of the female in a world of the two sexes' concerned 'not with the wrongs of the female at the hands of the male, but with the consequences of attempting to repress sexual needs under the cover of feminism.'[12] On the other, Coral Lansbury claims that the novel depicts 'women who choose to live together, creating "families" of their own devising', and its delight is 'that a group of middle-aged and old women can order a society to their own pleasure.'[13] Of the two extremes Lansbury's reading seems more convincing, although she is inclined to celebrate the 'women who choose' without really questioning the nature of the choice. However, it is necessary to recognize in any case that *Cranford* represents only one aspect of Gaskell's treatment of female friendships and communities.

To begin with, we might usefully broaden the consideration of the novel by examining an earlier work, 'Mr. Harrison's Confession', which appeared in 1851. Stylistically it marks a witty departure from the earnestness of Gaskell's work up to this point, and in its setting, the Duncombe of 'Mr. Harrison's Confession' directly anticipates Cranford: '"You will find it is a curious statistical fact, but five-sixths

---

[12] Martin Dodsworth, 'Women without Men at Cranford', *Essays in Criticism*, XIII (1963), 138–45.

[13] Coral Lansbury, *Elizabeth Gaskell: The Novel of Social Crisis* (London: Elek, 1975), pp. 87–93.

of our householders of a certain rank in Duncombe are women. We have widows and old maids in rich abundance"' (V. 414).[14] The Misses Tomkinson are the first of Gaskell's pairs of sisters who function together in a way that offers an emotional and psychological substitute to heterosexual unions. Mr. Harrison, the young male narrator, observes that '"Miss Tomkinson . . . did not strike me as remarkably requiring protection from any man. She was a tall, gaunt, masculine-looking woman, with an air of defiance about her, naturally"' (V. 414) and that her sister, Miss Caroline, '"was as soft and sentimental as Miss Tomkinson was hard and masculine"' (V. 415). This begins a pattern which is repeated in many ways with Miss Jenkyns and Miss Matty in *Cranford* and Miss Browning and Miss Phoebe in *Wives and Daughters*, even in the detail of the stronger character claiming the patronym in each case, and is very much in accordance with the tendency in the theoretical discussion of female friendship, discussed in Chapter 1, to define female relationships in terms of a heterosexual norm, as typified by Dinah Mulock's 'wonderful law of sex'.[15]

One of the most significant changes in the development from 'Mr. Harrison's Confession' to *Cranford* is the switch from a male narrator in the story to a female in the novel. It allows for a deeper, more sympathetic exploration of female community in the later work. In 'Mr. Harrison's Confession' the interpreting presence of the male narrator transforms each incident into a male–female interaction, regardless of the numerical supremacy of the Duncombe women. Mr. Harrison is seen as an alien besieged, locking himself in his room to avoid the relentless romantic pursuit of Miss Caroline, Miss Bullock, and Sophy. This opposition of interests between the narrator and the town inhabitants, which allows for certain simple, comic opportunities, could not have accommodated the gentler irony and deeper understanding of *Cranford*.

Although *Cranford* differs stylistically from earlier novels, it is nevertheless as topical in its own way as *Mary Barton* or *Ruth*. Its serialization began in December 1851 at a time when, as we have seen, 'Everyone who ha[d] a little spare wisdom at command seem[ed]

---

[14] Gaskell herself saw the short story as a new departure. After several years of publishing with Chapman & Hall and with Dickens in *Household Words*, she offered the story to a new women's periodical, the *Ladies' Companion*. However, it seems more likely that this was due to a sense of the story's limited, even frivolous, appeal rather than to a desire to secure a more politically sympathetic audience.

[15] Mulock, *A Woman's Thoughts*, p. 179.

. . . inclined to lay it out for the benefit of single women.'[16] However, the very nature of the Cranford community, 'in possession of the Amazons' as it is, challenges one of the underlying attitudes which stimulated the wider debate. Rather than treat singleness as a grim affliction to be remedied where possible, *Cranford* suggests an alternative way of life by portraying not simply one character's unmarried life amid a norm of adult couples, but a largely self-sufficient community of unmarried women.

Within that community there are self-pronounced spokeswomen for the alternative in the aggressive and separatist brand of feminism espoused by Miss Jenkyns and Miss Pole. Miss Jenkyns, for example, 'would have despised the modern idea of women being equal to men. Equal indeed! she knew they were superior' (II. 15), and Miss Pole proclaims:

. . . sitting down with the decision of a person who has made up her mind as to the nature of life and the world . . . 'Well, Miss Maddy! men will be men. Every mother's son of them wishes to be Samson and Solomon rolled into one —too strong ever to be beaten or discomfited—too wise ever to be outwitted. If you will notice, they have always forseen events, though they never tell one for one's warning before the events happen, my father was a man, and I know the sex pretty well.' (II. 115)

Given the dictatorial force of Miss Jenkyns in the community, it is not surprising that even a much gentler soul, Miss Matty, should express the prevailing feeling: ' "we had almost persuaded ourselves that to be a man was to be 'vulgar' " ' (II. 8)—'a tremendous word in Cranford' (II. 4).

However, Gaskell exposes a real element of rationalization in the characters' motives. When Miss Jenkyns declares at her mother's funeral that ' "if she had a hundred offers, she never would marry and leave [her] father" ' (II. 70), she is forsaking one relationship of devotion to a male in order to take up another and embracing the very role she ostensibly rejects:

His eyes failed him, and she read book after book, and wrote, and copied, and was always at his service in any parish business. She could do many more things than my poor mother could, she even wrote a letter to the Bishop for my father. But he missed my mother sorely. (II. 70)

All that she fails to take on, of course, is the sexual role of the wife, and that is symptomatic of a more general fear which prevails among

---

[16] Greenwell, *Essays*, p. 1.

Cranford women. In any case the force of Deborah's conviction is undercut by Miss Matty's comment further to the 'hundred offers': ' "It was not very likely she would have so many—I don't know that she had one; but it was not less to her credit to say so" ' (II. 70). The moment provides a good example of the tact and warmth of Gaskell's humour in the novel. Miss Matty's opinion is offered so genuinely without malice and with a readiness to give credit for the partial generosity of Deborah's resolve that it enables Deborah's character to be touched by the irony without being transformed by it.

Furthermore, despite Deborah's separatist claims, her sense of superiority is founded largely on satisfaction at participating in a male world and beating men at their own game. Hence in the passage that outlines Deborah's notions of female superiority, Gaskell observes with gentle irony the details of Deborah's mannish dress: 'Miss Jenkyns wore a cravat, and a little bonnet like a jockey-cap' (II. 15). The actual significance of Deborah's disagreement with Captain Brown over the relative merits of Johnson and Dickens lies in the contest for authority, and Deborah's first impulse on hearing of Captain Brown's death is, as Dodsworth points out, to assume control over the Brown household.[17]

Miss Pole's rantings against marriage are scarcely more than comic. She does less harm than Miss Jenkyns, for she lacks the power to sway the inhabitants of Cranford with her opinions. As the narrator, Mary Smith, points out: 'If I had been inclined to be daunted from matrimony, it would not have been Miss Pole to do it; it would have been the lot of poor Signor Brunoni and his wife' (II. 129). At the same time even Miss Pole is not simply made a figure of fun, as she might have been in 'Mr. Harrison's Confession', and there remains something poignant in Mary's observation:

I don't know whether it was a fancy of mine, or a real fact, but I have noticed that just after the announcement of an engagement in any set, the unmarried ladies in that set flutter out in an unusual gaiety and newness of dress, as much to say, in a tacit unconscious manner, 'We are also spinsters.' (II. 140)

The feminist element of the novel is further qualified by the general sense that the Cranford women's reaction against men is largely motivated by fear. In a world so rigidly regulated, where codes of conduct entrench the known, the Cranford inhabitants retreat from the threat of otherness. In agreeing to open a shop for the sale of tea

[17] Dodsworth, 'Women without Men', p. 133.

Miss Matty takes into account: 'One good thing about it . . . she did not think men ever bought tea; and it was of men particularly she was afraid' (II. 171). Similarly Mary Smith is reassured to find that Captain Brown 'joked quite in the way of a tame man' (II. 5).

Nevertheless the unknown also holds some attraction for Cranford women. It is symptomatic of this ambivalence that the arrival of the exotic Signor Brunoni causes so much excitement at the same time as it unleashes hysterical exaggerations about the threat of intruders. Clearly the prospect of robbery is a manifestation of the threat Brunoni offers to their carefully guarded private worlds. It is only after he has been 'tamed', when he is ill and thus less forcefully masculine, that the Cranford inhabitants calm down:

Somehow we all forgot to be afraid. I dare say it was finding out that he, who had first excited our love of the marvellous by his unprecedented arts, had not sufficient every day gifts to manage a shying horse, made us feel as if we were ourselves again. (II. 125)

From Signor Brunoni he becomes simply Mr. Brown, and in a neatly emblematic moment Miss Matty covers with coloured felt the ball she has brought to roll under her bed in order to check for hidden prowlers and gives it to one of Brown's children as a plaything.

However, the comic aspect of the women's fear does not simply invalidate the fear itself. Even in this town of 'Amazons' the male has a power which cannot be resisted. If it is potentially protective, leading Miss Pole to hang a man's hat in her hall to deceive intruders into believing that there is a male resident, it is at the same time the very source of the threat. The two aspects are suggested in the figure of Captain Brown. He is undoubtedly a benevolent presence in the town, but his is 'a loud, military voice', his arrival is represented as an 'invasion of their territories', and he is employed by the 'obnoxious railway', an irresistible force against which the Cranford residents have unsuccessfully petitioned and at the mercy of which Captain Brown loses his life. That moment shocks Cranford as only one other moment, the public flogging of Peter Jenkyns by his father, does:

'My dear! that boy's trick, on that sunny day, when all seemed going straight and well, broke my mother's heart, and changed my father for life. It did, indeed. It did, indeed. Old Clare said, Peter looked as white as my father; and stood as still as a statue to be flogged; and my father struck hard! When my father stopped to take breath, Peter said, "Have you done enough, sir?" quite hoarsely, and still standing quite quiet. I don't know what my father said—or if he said anything. But old Clare said, Peter turned to where the people outside the railing were, and made them a low bow, as grand and grave as any gentleman; and then walked slowly into the house.' (II. 64)

It is significant that this violence is also male-centred, and although Deborah Jenkyns in some senses replaces her father as the patriarch of Cranford, she is incapable of such violence. Under the 'Amazons' Jessie Brown has good cause to exclaim: '"what a town Cranford is for kindness!"' (II. 18).

Perhaps the most serious challenge of all to the doctrines of male exclusion advanced by Miss Jenkyns and Miss Pole comes from the sense of waste surrounding Miss Matty's unfulfilled life. Her refusal, at Deborah's insistence, to marry Holbrook shadows the rest of her life. She is condemned at his death to covert mourning and, sadder still, to the tension in her feelings between respect for her sister and natural resentment toward her. She is also conscious of the sadness of wasted opportunity:

'My father once made us . . . keep a diary, in two columns; on the one side we were to put down in the morning what we thought would be the course and events of the coming day, and at night we were to put down on the other side what really happened. It would be to some people rather a sad way of telling their lives.' (II. 128)

After refusing Holbrook, Miss Matty's life becomes progressively more sterile in some ways, and through her recurring dream of having a child, a sadly unreal fate, Miss Matty's lot is connected with a more general sense of Cranford sterility. As Miss Pole acknowledges: 'As most of the ladies . . . were elderly spinsters, or widows without children, if we did not relax a little, and become less exclusive, by-and-by we should have no society at all' (II. 77). As we might expect of Gaskell, she seems more regretful of the loss of maternal, rather than marital, fulfilment. The story of Mrs. Brown's trek through India, for example, introduces a sober note of admiration for the courage and sacrifice of motherhood. Similarly a telling juxtaposition is offered between the image of the fruitful mother joyously holding her child, and the 'withered' spinster that child has become: '"Dear mother, I wish you could see her! Without any parshality, I do think she will grow up a regular bewty!" I thought of Miss Jenkyns, grey withered, and wrinkled; and I wondered if her mother had known her in the courts of heaven' (II. 54).

The unnecessary element of Miss Matty's wasted life is highlighted by the parallel story of Lady Glenmire, the widow who forsakes her title to marry the socially inferior and awkward surgeon, Mr. Hoggins, and by the depiction of Martha's and Jem's relationship. Indeed, the very terms of Martha's complaint against Miss Matty's early prohibition on visits from suitors recall Miss Matty's own mistake: ' "many a one has as much as offered to keep company with me; and I may never be in such a likely place again, and it's like wasting an opportunity" ' (II. 45).

Significantly, the criticism within Cranford of any unbending doctrine of female self-sufficiency is self-generated, and not the imposition of a heterosexual status quo. The women of Cranford are reassured in their singleness by their sister spinsters and widows, and any external threat or criticism is quickly suppressed. Thus Peter is harshly beaten for the charade which drew attention to his sister's spinsterhood, and Mr. Holbrook, who is inadvertently a disruptive force in his pursuit of Miss Matty, is quickly outcast on the seemingly disinterested grounds of class. The criticism that does emerge, then, comes more tellingly from within and stems from a sense of lack:

'. . . don't be frightened by Miss Pole from being married. I can fancy it may be a very happy state, and a little credulity helps one on through life very smoothly,—better than always doubting and doubting, and seeing difficulties and disagreeables in everything'. (II. 129)

Yet for all this, it is true that one of the delights of the novel is 'that a group of middle-aged and old women can order a society to their own pleasure.'[18] Although Gaskell does not endorse a Cranfordian dismissal of the desirability of the married state, neither does she discount the viability and worth of those single women's lives. Cranford may lack a sense of perspective which would enable it to perceive its own ridiculousness, and the choice of its single inhabitants 'to live together' may be conditioned by circumstance, fear, and communal pressure. Nevertheless, while the novel is no Utopian justification for female separatism, neither is it reducible to 'an elegy to the insufficiency of the female'.[19] Cranford establishes that it is possible to imagine a community of women without men, in which marriage is not

[18] See Coral Lansbury, *Elizabeth Gaskell*, p. 93.
[19] See Martin Dodsworth, 'Women without Men at Cranford', p. 136.

regarded, as Emily Faithfull lamented, 'as the sole and inevitable destiny of any woman' and which has value and honour despite its shortcomings.[20]

Like Jane Austen, Gaskell explores the way in which manners, Cranford's 'strict code of gentility' (II. 77), function. On the one hand they can reinforce a meaningless hierarchy and provide the means for Mrs. Jamieson's social bullying. On the other, they provide a framework in which the best impulses of the characters can find formal expression. For example, the generosity of the Cranford women in rallying around Miss Matty when she is financially ruined is complemented by the tact of their secret arrangements, which demonstrate the finer aspect of their habitual, at times slavish, respect for discretion. Even within this strictest and most eccentric of hierarchies, the fundamental priorities of the Cranford women are sound. So the elaborate precautions in laying protective paper paths on the new carpet are forgotten when the workman brings news of Captain Brown's death: 'she brought the affrighted carter, sleeking down his hair, into the drawing room, where he stood with his wet boots on the new carpet and no one regarded it' (II. 19).

Cranford also offers mutual support for its inhabitants. It may be only Miss Pole's deluded rationalizations of spinsterhood or the swapping of hysterical tales of robbery, but it is the stuff that sustains individuals in their daily living. Also, individuals willingly take responsibility for others, as for example in the community's treatment of the Misses Brown after the Captain's death, and of the unfortunate Brunoni family, and of Miss Matty when her stocks crash.

In the end Gaskell makes it clear that it would be a mistake to dismiss Cranford for its quaintness. When Mary Smith's father scorns Miss Matty's honouring of the worthless £5 bank note and declares that 'such simplicity might be very well in Cranford, but would never do in the world', the failure in clear-sightedness is his. Indeed, Gaskell cannot resist having the last laugh at the male outsider, who would dismiss the values that Cranford has to offer: 'And I fancy the world must be very bad, for with all my father's suspicion of every one with whom he has dealings, and in spite of all his many precautions, he has lost upwards of a thousand pounds by roguery only last year' (II. 174).

---

[20] Emily Faithfull, 'Open Council', *English Woman's Journal*, Sept. 1862, p. 70.

III

Both the exceptional self-enclosed nature of the community depicted in *Cranford* and the comic nature of that depiction ensure that the novel's outlook is not too disturbing, as Gaskell's own lingering sense of the work attests:

> It is the only one of my own books that I can read again;—but whenever I am ailing or ill, I take 'Cranford' and—I was going to say *enjoy* it! (but that would not be pretty!) laugh over it afresh! And it is true too, for I have seen the cow that wore the grey flannel jacket—and I know the cat that swallowed the lace, that belonged to the lady that sent for the doctor, that gave the emetic &c!!! (*GL* 747)

It remains more a place where Alderney cows wear grey flannel than a model for a separatist existence—a fact which has probably contributed to its lasting popularity. However, as I have argued, *Cranford* ought not be offered as a complete indication of Gaskell's thinking on women's friendship and community, and there is much in her fiction to suggest a more disturbing sense of women's place and a more challenging view of female relationships than has usually been recognized. This more radical view is a product of Gaskell's sense of women as victims, sharing a fate of social and sexual passivity.

This may seem a curious claim to make of a novelist who so consistently creates strong female characters such as Mary Barton, Margaret Hale, and Molly Gibson, women who assume control within their worlds. However, personal strength in itself is no safeguard against the victimization of the female. Women are consistently portrayed in situations of relative powerlessness in their interaction with men, as the extensive list of unsuccessful and very often unwelcome suitors in her novels suggests. The earliest example of such masculine imposition comes in *Mary Barton* in the incidental mention of Jem stealing a kiss from Mary in Green Heys Fields. As a child, free from sexual pressures and constraints, Mary resolves the matter, summarily: '"Take that for old acquaintance sake, then," said the girl, blushing rosy red, more with anger than shame, as she slapped his face' (I. 10). However, when Jem proposes marriage later in the novel, Gaskell underlines, in rather simple and unsophisticated terms at this point, the stress that is involved for Mary in the situation: 'Her voice was calm, although she trembled from head to foot' (I. 148). In what is to become a recurring concern, Mary's feelings are compounded by parental, and more especially paternal, pressure. John Barton has 'upbraided her with the loss of Jem Wilson' just before the proposal scene, and when Jem innocently touches on this, '"And Mary! think how glad your father would be!"', he inadvertently provides Mary with the resolve to refuse him utterly. Mary unsuccessfully attempts to deflect the sexual element in the confrontation: '"I will always be your friend, Jem, but I can never be your wife"' (I. 148), and the scene ends with her weeping hysterically.

It is a fairly conventional scene, but it contains elements which are more interestingly reworked in later novels. Possibly the best example of the vulnerability of the female in being subjected to a proposal occurs in *North and South* when Lennox comes by train from London to Helstone in order to propose. His sophisticated intrusion into Margaret's simple country life parallels his worldly-wise intrusion upon her innocence. The proposal takes place in the tranquil, but fading, evening light in the parsonage garden, the locale of Margaret's childhood. Margaret's instinctive reaction is to retreat to her parents, wishing herself 'back with her mother—her father— anywhere away from him' (IV. 28), and her impulse to deflect the sexual pressure of Lennox's proposal recalls Mary's: '"I have always thought of you as a friend,—and please, I would rather go on think- ing of you so. I don't like to be spoken to as you have been doing"' (IV. 30). After Lennox leaves, Margaret feels 'guilty and ashamed of having grown so much into a woman as to be thought of in marriage' (IV. 34) and worried that her father might be displeased that she has taken it upon herself to refuse Lennox.

Further, while Margaret is left to sit by herself at the fire and assimi- late what has happened, Lennox can go just as he chose to come, intruding upon her world and then returning to his own sphere of action:

How different men were to women! Here was she disturbed and unhappy, because her instinct made anything but a refusal impossible; while he, not many minutes after he had met with a rejection of what ought to have been the deepest, holiest proposal of his life, could speak as if briefs, success and all its superficial consequences . . . were the sole avowed objects of his desires. (IV. 33)

Gaskell returns to a similar point in *Sylvia's Lovers* when she writes: 'Even with the most domestic and affectionate men, their emotions seem to be kept in a cell, distinct and away from their actual lives' (VI. 377).

When Thornton proposes to Margaret later in the novel she is more able to cope in terms of social poise and sexual maturity. None the less she is fundamentally disturbed, and once again she has had no control over the sexual component of the interaction. She has never been more than civil to Thornton and is shocked to find her courage during the riot construed as an indication of her attachment to Thornton. Not surprisingly, she is disconcerted by the apparent arbitrariness of male and female relations: 'Margaret began to wonder whether all offers were as unexpected beforehand; as distressing at the time of their occurrence, as the two she had had' (IV. 234).

The obvious exception to this vulnerability is Cynthia Kirkpatrick's sexual exploitativeness in *Wives and Daughters*. Yet even the 'natural coquette' in Cynthia has no adequate defence against the sexual threat of Preston. When Cynthia comes under his power, she is a child of sixteen whose mother provides only rivalry, not support or affection, and from this position of inequality she can never regain the advantage. There is something particularly ominous in the combination of entreaty and threat Preston offers: ' "If you will but keep your word, and marry me, I'll swear I'll make you love me in return" ' (VIII. 538), especially in retrospect when we learn that Cynthia ' "hated his way of showing what he called his 'love' for me" ' (VIII. 548). It is no accident that when Molly demands the letters from Preston, her power comes not simply from her righteousness, but from the fact 'that Molly was unconscious that he was a young man, and she a young woman' (VIII. 561), a detail which strikes Preston himself. For that interview at least Molly escapes the terms of reference which so often render women passive and vulnerable.

The example of the woman who accepts a proposal she neither seeks nor wants provides a further variation on that female vulnerability. In 'The Manchester Marriage' the heroine, Alice, is an orphan who lives without guidance in an unsympathetic household. Her decision to marry is, in effect, a non-choice:

So when her cousin, Frank Wilson, came home from a long absence at sea, and was first kind and protective to her; secondly, attentive; and thirdly, desperately in love with her, she hardly knew how to be grateful enough to him. It is true, she would have preferred his remaining in the first and second stages of behaviour; for his violent love puzzled and frightened her. (V. 493)

Her terms of reference are naïve and non-sexual: 'liking him better than anyone in the world except her uncle (who was at this time at sea), she went off one morning and was married to him' (V. 494). In her innocence and unprotectedness Alice is as much a victim as Ruth has been in her seduction, even if the terms of Alice's victimization are more socially acceptable. She is similarly coerced into her second marriage, and in both unions the conduct of the relationship is entirely dictated by her husbands:

As for Alice's own life, it was happier than it had ever been before. Mr. Oppenshaw required no demonstration, no expression of affection from her. Indeed, these would rather have disgusted him. The perpetual requirements of loving words, looks and caresses, and misconstruing their absence into absence of love, had been the great trial of her former married life. (V. 503)

In 'The Grey Woman' the heroine, Anna Scherer, has allowed the ritual of courtship to go too far, and in remaining passive in a situation in which women are positively encouraged to be simply the recipients of male initiatives, she pays a huge price: 'I was bewitched,— in a dream,—a kind of despair. I had got into a net through my own timidity and weakness, and I did not see how to get out of it. I clung to my own home-people that fortnight as I had never done before.'[21] When Anna appeals to her father for help, he takes the side of her fiancé, 'as if, after the ceremony of betrothal, no one had any right over me but my future husband' (VII. 313).

In *Sylvia's Lovers* not only the circumstances, but the consequences, of such forced acceptance are explored. Sylvia suffers because of her passivity in two ways—in waiting upon the whims of Kinraid's affection, and then more grievously in enduring Philip's unwelcome attention. When Sylvia has the security of home and family, she does not even consider accepting his advances. However, as Sylvia's security is relentlessly undermined—her father imprisoned and hanged, the farm sold, her mother distracted with grief—Gaskell shows Philip gradually insinuating his way into her life and dependence:

'Maester Hall had sent a notice to quit . . . and Philip had ta'en it in hand to answer.'
    'Without asking thee?'
    Sylvia went on without minding the interruption. (VI. 342)

She marries Philip out of desperation for she can see no alternative and is drained of energy and will:

She did not see what else she could have done but marry so true a friend, and she and her mother so friendless, but at the same time, it was like lead on her

---

[21] Elizabeth Gaskell, 'The Grey Woman' (1861), *Works*, VII. 312. All further references to this work appear in the text, abbreviated as VII.

morning spirits when she awoke and remembered that the decision was made, the deed done, the choice taken which comes to most people but once in their lives. (VI. 370)

The cost of Sylvia's choice is distressingly high. Part of the tragic irony in the novel is that in forcing Sylvia to marry him, Philip stifles the very things in her that originally attracted him. Sylvia obeys him out of 'gentle indifference', in a 'spirit of obedience' and 'duty', and he longs for 'the old Sylvia back again; captious, capricious, wilful, haughty, merry, charming' (VI. 349). The 'sense of estrangement' which Kester feels on visiting Sylvia after her marriage goes further than the awkwardness between them, for in marrying Philip Sylvia has become more fundamentally estranged from the naturalness and vitality of her life at the farm and her peace of mind.

In the tale *Lois the Witch* the heroine resists what Sylvia has succumbed to and refuses to be coerced into marriage. Lois recognizes the danger of Manasseh's appeal to prophecy, and she will not humour him by entertaining the possibility of divine direction: ' "I may take a dream to be truth, and hear my own fancies, if I think about them too long. But I cannot marry any one from obedience" ' (VII. 146). The pressure on Lois is perhaps the most extreme that Gaskell considers. She is motherless, like many of Gaskell's women, and an outsider within a strange and severe New England community. Her suitor, Manasseh, is deeply disturbed, as the initial image of him staring vacantly at Lois while ignoring the open Bible on his knee suggests. It foreshadows a more insidious complication of sexual and religious feelings, in which Manasseh represents his obsession with Lois as respectable and necessary: ' "It is borne on me—verily, I see it as in a vision—that thou must be my spouse, and no other man's. Thou canst not escape what is foredoomed" ' (VII. 145).

Lois finds Manasseh physically repellent once she is forced by his declaration to consider him as a potential husband: 'He might be good, and pious—he doubtless was—but his dark fixed eyes, moving so slowly and heavily, his lank black hair, his grey coarse skin, all made her dislike him now—all his personal ugliness and ungainliness struck on her senses with a jar' (VII. 142). The pressure on Lois is heightened further by the need to live in the same house with Manasseh. Indeed, within the Hickson household there is no likely ally, for Manasseh is 'esteemed a hero by most of those around him, simply because he was the only man in the family' (VII. 147). Far from protecting Lois, Mrs. Hickson shamelessly manipulates her in an attempt to maintain control over her increasingly disturbed son. Mrs. Hickson's betrayal of Lois and her belated contrition link her with the failed mothers discussed earlier. Appropriately Lois is represented as being 'brought to bay' (VII. 143) in her final confrontation with Manasseh, recalling the hunted aspect of Anna Scherer's having 'got into a net' (VII. 312) in 'The Grey Woman'.

As a condemned witch Lois is a victim not just of Manasseh, but of the religious fathers of that New England community, who orchestrate the female hysteria. Lois has already expressed sympathy for witches in their position as outcasts before she herself comes under suspicion: ' "They are fearful creatures, the witches! and yet I am sorry for the poor old women" ' (VII. 121). Beyond mere kindliness, there is a point of prophetic connection in her sympathy: ' "her eyes met mine as they were glaring with fury—poor, helpless, baited creature! . . . I used to dream that I was in that pond, that all men hated me with their eyes because I was a witch" ' (VII. 122). The old woman in Lois's past has lived a solitary existence on the outskirts of the village, ' "always talking and muttering to herself" ', and she is put to death as a witch after ' "many a one fell sick in the village, and much cattle died one spring" ' (VII. 122). A similar pattern is repeated in 'The Poor Clare', where Bridget's existence inspires suspicion and hostility:

She had got into the habit of perpetually talking to herself; nay more, answering herself, and varying her tone according to the side she took at the moment. It was no wonder that those who dared to listen outside her door at night believed she held converse with some spirit; in short, she was unconsciously earning for herself the dreadful reputation of a witch. (V. 339)

And in 'The Heart of John Middleton' Gaskell notes the common connection between healing power and suspicion of witchcraft: 'my father used to curse her, under his breath, for a witch, such as were burnt long ago on Pendle Hill top; but I had heard that Eleanor was a skilful sick nurse' (II. 386). In all, the fear of deviance and of strange power in women is met with determination to make them victims.[22]

Although Phillis Holman is not subjected to unwelcome proposals in *Cousin Phillis*, she suffers from the same powerlessness and vulner-

---

[22] The plight of the witch was also considered by Eliza Lynn Linton in *Witch Stories* in 1861. She, like Gaskell, notes the connection between healing powers and accusations of witchcraft: 'To be skilful in healing, too, was just as dangerous as to be powerful in sickening' (London: Chapman & Hall, 1861, p. 3). The use of witchcraft trials as a means of victimizing women has been an area of continuing interest to feminist scholars such as Margaret Murray in *The Witch-Cult in Western Europe* (1921) and *The God of Witches* (1931) and Mary Daly in *Beyond God the Father* (1973).

ability in sexual politics as her fictional predecessors. Phillis's innocence, like Margaret's and Sylvia's, is imaged in the details of her
simple rural existence, and her lover, like theirs, comes from a more
sophisticated world into the rural idyll. However, the connection
between character and environment is extended in this tale to provide
a sustained parallel between the natural and emotional worlds, deep-
ening the sense of disturbance to each. Both Phillis's world and the
world of Hope Farm are powerless against Holdsworth's intrusion,
which is once again associated with the power of the railway, this time
in a fundamental way, for as an engineer Holdsworth is responsible
for its construction. Thus the thunderstorm that breaks over Phillis,
Holdsworth, Holman, and Paul, when Phillis first recognizes her love
for Holdsworth, mirrors the way in which he has overwhelmed
Phillis's life and that simple, natural world.

Holdsworth is never emotionally vulnerable in the way Phillis is.
He has his 'other world' of work, like Lennox in *North and South*. In
departing for Canada without leave-taking, he allows his work to
displace thoughts of Phillis, who has just been as bold as she dares in
offering him the bouquet as a token of affection. His view that the
proposal can wait—'"she lives in such seclusion, almost like sleeping
beauty"' (VII. 64)—is presumptuous and complacent, made by a
man who need not deal with the pain and waste of waiting and whose
view of the farm is arrogant and sentimental. The march of the
seasons makes the passage of time clear enough for Phillis.

Phillis is ill equipped to deal with the awakening of her feelings for
Holdsworth. Her parents have deliberately striven to keep her young
and thereby ignore any issue of emerging sexuality, as Betty makes
explicit: ' "They've called her 'the child' so long . . . that she's grown
up to be a woman under their very eyes, and they look on her still as if
she were a baby in long clothes. And you ne'er heard on a man falling
in love wi' a babby in long clothes!" ' (VII. 88). It is not simply, as
the narrator suggests, that her parents are unaware of her progress
towards womanhood. More particularly, like John Barton, Phillis's
father wants to arrest or deny it. He is incensed that Phillis might
have taken an active part by falling in love without explicit encouragement and sanction: ' "I could not have believed it," said he, in a
hard voice' (VII. 99). Similarly he accuses Paul of spoiling Phillis's
' "peaceful maidenhood with talk about another man's love"' (VII.
98). In such a world, where female sexual passivity is normative, but
not, as Gaskell recognizes, natural, women are inevitably condemned

to feelings of guilt. So Phillis moves toward total collapse, declaring: ' "I am so sick with shame! . . . She hung her head, and leant more heavily than before on her supporting hand" ' (VII. 99), just as the heroine of an earlier work, 'Six Weeks at Heppenheim', announces: ' "My shame and my reproach is this: I have loved a man who has not loved me" ' (VII. 374).

The Reverend Ebenezer Holman's response is conditioned by jealousy and a sense of betrayal, felt all the more strongly because of marked similarities between himself and Phillis's lover. There is a necessary opposition in his mind between his daughter's love for him and for another: ' "Phillis! did we not make you happy here? Have we not loved you enough?" ' (VII. 99). His failure to perceive Phillis's tortured expression betrays a deeper lack of understanding. He pushes Phillis to the point where even Paul, the male narrator, 'could have struck him for his cruelty' (VII. 99). Significantly, when Phillis does collapse, her father is terrified and uncertain, whereas her mother instantly reacts with purpose and sympathy: 'I remember I was surprised at the time at her presence of mind, she seemed to know so much better what to do than the minister, in the midst of the sick affright which blanched her countenance, and made her tremble all over' (VII. 100). While her father is 'so unmanned', the women in the house 'were putting her to bed, still unconscious, still slightly convulsed' (VII. 101). In *Sylvia's Lovers* too there is a comparable sense of the effective protectiveness of the mother. Bell Robson perceives the attraction between Sylvia and Kinraid before anyone else, and her instinctive response is to guard Sylvia: 'No one saw the real motive of all this inhospitable haste to dismiss her guest, how the sudden fear had taken possession of her that he and Sylvia were "fancying each other" ' (VI. 111). When Bell discovers that Daniel Robson is jeopardizing his adolescent daughter's reputation by taking her drinking, she accepts her husband's thoughtlessness:

She really believed her husband to have the serious and important occupation for his mind that she had been taught to consider befitting the superior intellect of the masculine gender; she would have taxed herself severely if, even in thought, she had blamed him. (VI. 132)

But like Phillis's mother, Bell acts decisively to remedy the situation: ' "I'll ask her father to leave her a bit more wi' me" ' (VI. 133).

It is not surprising that Phillis Holman breaks down under the pressure of her emotional turmoil and guilt. More generally, such breakdown is a common occurrence in Gaskell's fiction. Although the device is too frequently used, in some cases it does provide the logical end to a sequence of stress and pain in which the sufferer is necessarily passive, allowing for the ultimate withdrawal into complete passivity.

IV

The Reverend Ebenezer Holman's reaction is characteristic of the proprietorial nature of the father–daughter relationship as portrayed by Gaskell. It is a factor, as we have seen in both John Barton's and Mr. Hale's relationships with their daughters, and it lies behind the insistence of Anna Scherer's father in 'The Grey Woman' that only her fiancé has 'any right' over her. It is evident too in the strength of Dr. Gibson's reaction when he intercepts a love letter intended for Molly in *Wives and Daughters*. Insisting that at seventeen she is 'a mere child', Gibson himself later recognizes 'he had got an idea that all young men were wolves in chase of his one ewe-lamb' (VIII. 61). In 'A Dark Night's Work' Gaskell states her view with blunt resignation:

It was the usual struggle between father and lover for the possession of love, instead of the natural and graceful resignation of the parent to the prescribed course of things; and, as usual, it was the poor girl who bore the suffering for no fault of her own. (VII. 449)

The parallel in a mother–son relationship exists in Mrs. Thornton's jealousy in *North and South* when her son announces his love for Margaret Hale. There, Mrs. Thornton recognizes clearly the usurpation of her place and her claim on her son: ' "after tonight, I stand second" ' (IV. 224). Yet if the parallel exists, the difference is marked. Unlike Mr. Holman, Mrs. Thornton does not precipitate any confrontation, but rather accepts the painful situation, exhorting her son to take courage in his proposal to Margaret. 'And she went slowly and majestically out of the room. But when she got into her own, she locked the door, and sate down to cry unwonted tears' (IV. 225). Her behaviour approaches more closely to the 'natural and graceful resignation' of which Gaskell wrote, and in her acquiescence it is she who absorbs the pain rather than her son 'suffering for no fault of [his] own'. It is true, of course, that in the end Mrs. Thornton has no choice. She cannot forbid her son to propose to Margaret, nor compel Margaret to refuse him. The assumption of a right of 'possession' arises only in an individual or group accustomed to power and is not, then, an assumption that women make in Gaskell's fiction. Without power or an assumed right of 'possession', the very question of competitiveness and rivalry between women is altered, and the consequences are manifest in the differences that Gaskell suggests between male and female sexual jealousy.

While Gaskell does not see sexual jealousy as the exclusive domain of the male sex, she does challenge any stereotype of female rivalry such as that offered by Eliza Lynn Linton:

I doubt if any woman's friendship ever existed free from jealousy. If we are not jealous about men we are about other women, and guard our rights against division with the vigilance of a house dog guarding his domain. No man can understand the unresting pettiness of jealousy that exists between woman-friends: no man knows it for his own part, and no man would submit to it from his friend.[23]

On the contrary, in Gaskell's work female jealousy is finally much less disruptive and divisive than male jealousy. The difference is nowhere more marked than in her extended consideration of the powerful and arbitrary nature of sexual attraction in *Sylvia's Lovers*. In that novel Philip's obsessive love for Sylvia gives rise to a jealousy which is more violent and poisonous than anything felt by the women in the story. Witnessing a tender exchange between Kinraid and Sylvia, for example, Philip 'watched it all greedily as if it gave him delight' (VI. 150). In the end that jealousy undermines his integrity, leading him to conceal his knowledge of Kinraid's fate and to coerce Sylvia into marriage. It is significant that Philip is reconciled with Sylvia when he is disfigured and near death, so the question of sexual desire is not resolved so much as put aside. In contrast to Philip's jealousy, Sylvia's reaction when she imagines that her friend, Molly, is to marry her 'hero', Kinraid, is one of sympathetic excitement. In fact she is 'disappointed' to discover that Molly's suitor is a middle-aged Newcastle shopkeeper: 'it was a coming-down from the romance with the speckioneer for its hero' (VI. 122). There is something girlish and innocent about such camaraderie, but that does not discount the spirit it suggests. And in any case the same reservation does not apply to Hester's feelings towards Sylvia, her rival for Philip's affection. In many ways Hester has reason to see herself as more deserving of Philip's love. She shares his faith, has served him loyally in the business, and holds him in far higher esteem than Sylvia does. Yet Hester accepts her lot, like Mrs. Thornton, with pained resignation: 'Hester Rose, who met Sylvia on rare occasions came back each time with a candid, sad acknowledgement in her heart that it

---

[23] Linton, *Ourselves*, p. 78.

was no wonder that Sylvia was so much admired and loved' (VI. 101). There is no doubt that Gaskell admires this capacity in women for self-abnegation. Of Hester's agreement to help Philip prepare the house for Sylvia as his new wife, Gaskell writes: 'Never was such a quiet little bit of unconscious and unrecognized heroism' (VI. 357). Similarly in *Wives and Daughters* she admires as Molly's 'humility and great power of loving' that she can acknowledge Roger's straightforward attraction' to Cynthia 'to be the most natural thing in the world. She would look at Cynthia's beauty and grace, and feel as if no one could resist it' (VIII. 401).

To conclude from this, however, that Gaskell at least implicitly ascribes a moral superiority to women in their relations with each other would be at once too simple and too partisan. To begin with, Gaskell's view comes in part from a very conventional sense of women as devoid of libidinous feeling. She is well aware that 'like men, women have their affections', but she sees females as incapable of the kind of obsessive or desperate love that men such as Philip, Manasseh, Preston, or even Roger Hamley demonstrate. And in its most negative aspect that 'conquest of self' can involve an element of self-gratification, even masochism, as her sense of Molly's feelings suggests: 'She would have been willing to cut off her right hand, if need were, to forward this attachment to Cynthia; and the self-sacrifice would have added a strange zest to a happy crisis' (VIII. 401).

Nevertheless, more positively, Gaskell's women demonstrate a degree of imaginative projection and fellow-feeling in which divisiveness is not the necessary consequence of a shared object of affection. So in *Mary Barton* Gaskell uses the image of Ruth and Naomi, the archetypal example of women united through loving, to describe Mary's feelings for Jem's mother: 'And then came up the old feeling which first bound Ruth to Naomi; the love they both held towards one object' (I. 308), and Gaskell returns to the image in 'The Manchester Marriage' when she describes the decision of the heroine, Alice, to stay by her mother-in-law on the death of her son: 'Alice's heart was touched, and she drew near to Mrs. Wilson with un-wanted caresses, and, in a spirit not unlike to that of Ruth, entreated that, come what would, they might remain together' (V. 497). It is also implicit in the assumptions of solidarity which her female characters frequently make. In 'Lizzie Leigh', for example, the contrast is made between Lizzie's brother, who assumes that his sister's shame must be kept a secret from the woman he loves: 'would not Susan shrink away from him with loathing', and Lizzie's mother, who cannot doubt Susan's sympathy: ' "if she's so good as thou sayst, she'll have pity on such as my Lizzie" ', and determines to 'go and see Susan Palmer . . . and tell her the truth about Lizzie' (II. 220). When Hester appeals to Sylvia to forgive Philip, it is on the grounds of a shared womanhood: ' "if you have any love for me because of your dead mother's love for me, or because of any fellowship, or daily breadliness between us two" ' (VI. 470). Similarly it is the disappointment of that expectation of solidarity that forms part of Margaret Hale's distress after her interview with Mrs. Thornton: 'it is hard to think that anyone—any woman—can believe all this of another so easily. It is hard and sad' (IV. 383).

The example of Gaskell's women challenges the notion that where women do stand by each other it is from 'instinctive or personal affection' and not any broader basis of solidarity.[24] There is no love lost between Mrs. Thornton and either of the Hale women, but Mrs. Hale appeals to Mrs. Thornton as a mother, and Margaret expects sympathy from her because of a shared sense of woman's honour. In *North and South*, as in 'Lizzie Leigh', a bond of nature transcends the more fickle links of shared interest.

These bonds between women are evident in the differences between the sense of communality amongst men and amongst women in Gaskell's industrial novels. We have noted the association of the male with the intrusive force of the railway in a number of works. That implied connection between masculine power and the machinery of the industrial world, with its energy and its ruthlessness, is made explicit in the world of Milton in *North and South*:

> . . . there was something dazzling to Mr. Hale in the energy which conquered immense difficulties with ease; the power of the machinery of Milton, the power of the men of Milton, impressed him with a sense of grandeur, which he yielded to without caring to inquire into the details of its exercise. But Margaret went less abroad, among machinery and men; saw less of power in its public effect, and, as it happened, she was thrown with one or two of those who, in all measures affecting masses of people, must be acute sufferers for the good of many. (IV. 79)

The difference in response between Margaret and her father is stressed again when Mr. Hale listens attentively to Thornton describe 'the magnificent power' of the steam hammer: ' "this imagination of power, this practical realization of a gigantic thought, [that] came out

[24] Linton, *The Girl of the Period*, I. 184.

of one man's brain"' (IV. 93), while Margaret 'rearranged her mother's worsted-work, and fell back into her own thoughts' (IV. 92). There is more at stake in this than the simple confirmation of conventional male and female roles. Margaret's detachment and exclusion from that world of power is indicative of Gaskell's sense of women's function in industrial communities as custodians of humanity. As such, for example, Margaret marks the day Milton 'became a brighter place for her' from the beginning of her involvement with the Higgins family: 'It was not the long, bleak sunny days of spring, nor yet was it that time was reconciling her to the town of her habitation. It was that she had found a human interest' (IV. 84). While Thornton characterizes the rioting mob generally as an assembly of 'wild beasts', Margaret singles out the individual in the assembly: 'she read it all in Boucher's face, forlornly desperate and livid with rage' (IV. 210). The difference in perception remains a source of tension between them: 'Margaret's whole soul rose up against him while he reasoned in this way—as if commerce was everything and humanity nothing' (IV. 180).

Gaskell does not see that female detachment from the power of the industrial world as a sign of female weakness. It is Margaret who is required to inform her mother of her father's decision to leave the clergy, who must tell Mrs. Boucher of her husband's death when both Hale and Higgins are reluctant to do so, who keeps the secret of her mother's illness and her brother's whereabouts, and who sends Thornton to confront the strikers. More generally, women act as a strong, cohesive force in the industrial community, as we have seen, in their supportive presence at the scenes of birth and death and in their role as ministers of folk medicine. Like the factory girls in the opening chapters of *Mary Barton*, the young women in *North and South* create an atmosphere of spirited camaraderie:

The girls, with their rough, but not unfriendly freedom, would comment on her dress, even touch her shawl or gown to ascertain the exact material; nay, once or twice she was asked questions relative to some article which they particularly admired. There was such simple reliance on her womanly sympathy with their love of dress, and on her kindliness, that she gladly replied to these inquiries, as soon as she understood them; and half smiled back at their remarks. She did not mind meeting any number of girls, loud spoken and boisterous though they might be. (IV. 81)

Nor is that fellowship lost in the older women in the community: 'The women who lived in the court were busy taking in strings of caps,

frocks and varied articles of linen, which hung from side to side. . . .
Many greetings were given and exchanged between the Wilsons and
these women, for not long ago they had also dwelt in this court'
(I. 12). In ways comparable to those of Eliot's women, as we shall
see, their memories and their shared domestic tasks unite the community in the present and give it continuity with the past.

The solidarity of trade unionism, which prompts Barton and
Wilson to nurse a plague-stricken fellow worker, offers some parallel
in the male world of factory workers. Yet there is a significant difference, for even in the nursing of the sick man, it is the solidarity of
workers, not of males, that prevails. The ties of unionism are bonds of
interest rather than of nature, and as such they are liable to break
down, as they clearly do in the ruthlessness of the closed shop. In the
face of the ostracism that can come of such 'union', Boucher commits
suicide and Jem Wilson emigrates to Canada. Once again, as non-
participants in the struggle for power, political or sexual, women can
transcend the divisions in which men are entrenched. Thus Margaret
challenges Thornton:

'I beg your pardon, but is not that because there has been none of the equality
of friendship between the adviser and the advised classes? Because every man
has had to stand in an unchristian and isolated position, apart from and
jealous of his brother-man: constantly afraid of his rights being trenched
upon?' (IV. 142)

V

We have examined the irrational fear of men in Cranford's inhabitants and the way in which that sense of threat is largely self-generated.
However, as suggested, the world of *Cranford* does not represent
Gaskell's total vision. In other less sheltered environments male
violence is seen not simply as a possibility but as a fact. While
Gaskell's work offers an assortment of comparatively two-dimensional
villains, the character of John Barton, for example, provides a more
disturbing study.[25] Essentially a good man, he becomes gradually
more desperate and violent, eventually beating Mary and accepting
the mission to murder Carson. Gaskell views Barton's violence more
as a consequence of the conditions of his working-class existence than
as a characteristic of his gender. None the less, even if born of desper-

[25] See, e.g. 'French Life', 'The Grey Woman', 'The Doom of the Griffiths', 'The
Crooked Branch', and 'The Squire's Story'.

ation and drunkenness, such violence exists and very often claims as its victims the least powerful, women and children. Gaskell takes up this concern in one of her earliest stories 'Libbie Marsh's Three Eras'. When Libbie's young friend jokes about the drinking habits of her fiancé, Libbie protests: '"you don't know yet what it is to have a drunken husband. I have seen something of it. . . . God above only knows what a wife of a drunken man has to bear"' (I. 484). It emerges that Libbie's father has killed his youngest child 'in one of his bouts' and, significantly, once again Gaskell depicts the mother and child uniting against the father: '"mother never looked up again, nor father either, for that matter, only his was in a different way. Mother will have gotten to little Jemmie now, and they'll be so happy together"' (I. 484).

Violence erupts again in *North and South* when Margaret is struck by the stone thrown by rioters. Although one can argue that the missile was meant for Thornton, to rest there is to ignore the sexually charged atmosphere of the scene, and the shock that Margaret feels when forced to confront the fact that in the face of that crowd of men she is not inviolable: 'If she thought her sex would be a protection . . . she was wrong' (IV. 212). In fact this connection between sexual power and potential violence lightly, but effectively, underscores much of her interaction with Thornton. So Thornton thinks of Margaret as an 'unwilling slave' and wants her to perform 'what he saw her compelled to do for her father, who took her little finger and thumb in his masculine hand, and made them serve as sugar-tongs' (IV. 91). Similarly he later feels he 'could have struck her before he left, in order that by some strange overt act of rudeness, he might earn the privilege of telling her the remorse that gnawed at his heart' (IV. 401). A corresponding feeling takes on a more sinister aspect in Gaskell's portrayal of Preston in *Wives and Daughters*:

As she turned a corner in the lonely path, she heard a passionate voice of distress; and in an instant she recognized Cynthia's tones. . . . So Molly left the path, and went straight, plunging through the brown tangled growth of ferns and underwood, and turned the holly bushes. There stood Mr. Preston and Cynthia; he holding her hands tight, each looking as if just silenced in some vehement talk by the rustle of Molly's footsteps. . . . Mr. Preston let go Cynthia's hands slowly with a look that was more of a sneer than a smile. (VIII. 534)

In 'Half a Life-Time Ago' the potential for violence is in fact realized. As the story unfolds, it becomes clear that the heroine, Susan, is surrounded by concealed violence. On her death-bed Susan's mother, eliciting a promise from Susan to take care of her brother, reveals that the father has struck the son 'before now'. She explains her secrecy simply: ' "I did not want to make a stir" ' (V. 283). After Susan's lover, Michael, lashes out and kicks the young brother, Susan endeavours to make the peace, but she is not in a position to understand her brother's reluctance to be conciliated: 'for he remembered many a harsh word and blow of which his sister knew nothing' (V. 294). Michael later abandons Susan because of her refusal to institutionalize her brother, who has been left deranged after a fever which has killed her father. She discovers the violent nature of her ex-lover only accidentally when she observes him making his drunken way home to his new wife. After he drops his whip attempting to open the gate latch, Michael strikes his horse 'with his closed fist' and on finding the whip 'his first use of it was to flog his horse well, and [Susan] had much ado to avoid its kicks and plunges' (V. 315). Further, Susan's brother, although generally docile, suffers from violent convulsions, and in a manner reminiscent of her mother's concealment, Susan keeps 'their very existence hidden and unknown' (V. 315). The fits usually occur at night 'and, whatever had been their consequence, Susan had tidied and redded up all signs of aught unusual before morning' (V. 316). With her brother's death the third, and final, masculine element is removed from her life, and from thence Susan herself assumes complete control:

She was regularly present in Conniston market with the best butter and the earliest chickens of the season. Those were the common farm produce that every farmer's wife about had to sell; but Susan, after she had disposed of the more feminine articles, turned on the man's side. A better judge of a horse or cow there was not in all the country round. Yorkshire itself might have attempted to jockey her, and would have failed. (V. 318)

This seems a natural conclusion for the story, yet Gaskell adds a further dimension, announcing: 'But there was a third act in the drama of her life' (V. 317). That 'third act' sees Susan's union with the wife of her ex-lover following her decision to take 'Michael Hurst's widow and children with her to live there [at Yew Nook Farm]' (V. 327). After Michael's death Susan has discovered his wife, Eleanour, living in poverty and neglect. The awkward device of a timely paralysing stroke extends the encounter, as Eleanour nurses Susan 'like a sister', and Gaskell cursorily concludes: 'And so it fell out that the latter days of Susan Dixon's life were better than the former' (V. 327). However, if the actual details of the ending are not especially interesting, the idea is, for Susan and Eleanour are just two of a number of women who band together, united in the face of their powerlessness and ill-use.[26]

The most extreme example of this is provided by the gruesome tale of 'French Life', the story of the French noblewoman, Madame de Gange, and her marriage to a ruthless opportunist who is intent on murdering his new wife and squandering her fortune. The terms of the story are crudely categorical. Madame de Gange is a helpless victim: 'It gives one an awful idea of the state of society in those days . . . to think of this helpless young woman, possessed by a too well-founded dread, yet not knowing of any power to which she could appeal for protection' (VII. 667). And the details of the attempts on her life are nightmarishly graphic. After being forced to drink poison, for example, she pushes her hair down her throat to induce vomiting, then jumps from her window and flees to the protection of an assembled group of townswomen. This is all to no avail, for the pursuing husband stabs her 'five times before his weapon [breaks] in her shoulder' (VII. 672). Nevertheless the women put on a spirited show of solidarity:

Then the ladies burst in to the assistance of Madame, who was lying on the floor bathed in blood. Some ran to her help; others called through the window to passers-by to fetch the surgeon quickly. . . . brave Mademoiselle Brunel caught hold of his arm, and hung all her weight upon it. He struck her over and over again, to make her let go; but she would not; and all the women flew upon him 'like lionesses', and dragged him by main force out of the house, and turned him into the village street. One of the ladies, who was skilled in surgery, returned to the room where Madame de Gange lay; and at her desire she put her knee against the wounded shoulder of Madame, and pulled out the broken point of the sword by main force. Then she staunched the blood, and bound up the wounds. (VII. 672)

If in the face of the sympathetic treatment Gaskell affords the principal male characters in *Cranford*, Martin Dodsworth can perceive 'unconscious hostility to the male', one hesitates to think what he would make of such extreme polarization of the sexes, culminating in

---

[26] *Aurora Leigh*, published in 1857, a year after 'Half a Life-Time Ago', provides an interesting parallel when Aurora declares: 'The man had baffled, chafed me, till I flung/ For refuge to the woman' (Bk. IV, ll. 347–8), and Marian alleges: 'man's violence,/ Not man's seduction, made me what I am' (Bk. VI, ll. 1226–7). Christina Rossetti's 'Goblin Market', published in 1862, also deals in its fantastic way with sexual violence and the union of two sisters against that threat.

the women's thirst for vengeance: 'The ladies of Avignon and Mont-pellier were indignant that the Marquis de Gange was not to be broken on the wheel as well as his brothers' (VII. 675). Obviously, in terms of its literary merit, it would have been no loss if Gaskell had never written 'French Life'. But in a way the sensationalism and extremism of the story distil elements that exist and have been over-looked in Gaskell's more important work.

An episode in *Sylvia's Lovers*, for example, when Bell tells Sylvia the story of 'crazy Nancy', draws together many of the issues already discussed. Bell's awareness of the attraction between Kinraid and her daughter elicits her maternal protectiveness and in relating the tale, she intends the 'threat of danger' to act as a warning to Sylvia. The narrative gives a sense of Bell's gentleness toward Sylvia and her transparent simplicity in suggesting that Nancy's lover, like Kinraid, had some connection with the sea:

'Sylvie,' she began at length, 'did I e'er tell thee on Nancy Hartley as I knew when I were a child? I'm thinking a deal on her to-night; maybe it's because I've been dreaming on yon old times. She was a bonny lass as ever were seen, I've heard folk say; but that were afore I knew her. When I knew her she were crazy, poor wench . . . allays crying out for pity, though never a word she spoke but "He once was here." Just that o'er and o'er again, whether she were cold or hot, full or hungry, "He once was here," were all her speech. She had been farm-servant to my mother's brother—James Hepburn, thy great-uncle as was; she were a poor, friendless wench, a parish 'prentice, but honest and gaum-like, till a lad, as nobody knowed, came o'er the hills one sheep-shearing fra' Whitehaven; he had summat to do wi' th' sea, though not rightly to be called a sailor; and he made a deal on Nancy Hartley, just to beguile the time like; and he went away and ne'er sent a thought after her more. It's the way as lads have; and there's no holding them when they're fellows as nobody knows. . . . It were a caution to me again thinking a man t' mean what he says when he's a talking to a young woman.'
(VI. 199)

Like so many of Gaskell's women, Nancy is 'a motherless wench', vulnerable in her sexual relationship and powerless in the Keswick workhouse, where she is beaten 'till she were taught to be silent and quiet' (VI. 199). Significantly, Sylvia does not recoil from Nancy's story, as her mother had hoped, but responds with pity and fellow-feeling: 'Her mother's story had taken hold of her; but not as a "caution", rather as a parallel case to her own' (VI. 200). In the event, her fellow-feeling is not misplaced, for Sylvia finds herself declaring to Hester: ' "I'm speaking like a woman; like a woman who finds out she's been cheated by men as she trusted; and who has no help for it" ' (VI. 468). When Sylvia discovers that Hester has also suffered in unrequited love, she strives to resolve the tension between them, and later comforts Hester, 'sitting on the ground holding her, and soothing her with caresses and broken words' (VI. 469). After Philip's desertion Sylvia and Hester live together, and the novel concludes with the report that after Sylvia's death Hester takes on the upbringing of her daughter.

It is, as we have seen, a familiar motif, and one that challenges the notion that a happy marriage provides the neat and inevitable conclusion for all works of fiction in the nineteenth century. Even Gaskell's earliest story, 'Libbie Marsh's Three Eras', departs from that 'norm', as Libbie and Margaret unite in adversity: ' "Mrs. Hall, I should like—would you like me to come for to live here altogether . . . I could sleep with you, and pay half, you know: and we should be together in the evenings; and her as was home first would watch for the other" ' (I. 487). In 'Lizzie Leigh' Lizzie retires in the end with her mother to the seclusion of a country cottage. Throughout the story women react against the harshness of men. So Lizzie's mother rebels 'against her husband as against a tyrant' (II. 207) and defies her son in appealing to Susan for pity on Lizzie, and Susan rears Lizzie's illegitimate child in spite of the unsympathetic presence in the house of her drunken uncle. In *Ruth* the heroine refuses Bellingham's renewed offers of marriage and continues to live in the matriarchal Benson household, the integrity of which is clearly contrasted against the repression and hypocrisy of the patriarchal Bradshaw home. Further, *My Lady Ludlow*, like 'Mr. Harrison's Confession' and *Cranford*, deals with an almost exclusively female community. Lady Ludlow rears her group of young women ' "who are to me as daughters" ' (V. 11), in a house which is removed both geographically and psychologically from the heterosexual world: ' "I dress my young friends myself. . . . I reserve to myself the option of paying their travelling expenses—disliking gadding women. . . . They have but few opportunities for matrimony, as Connington is far removed from any town" ' (V. 12). In this tale too Lady Ludlow's clerk, Miss Galindo, risks social disapproval in order to take into her care the illegitimate daughter of a London barrister, her sometime lover. Thus Gaskell repeatedly depicts women living happily and quietly together, united by their shared suffering as women.

VI

This union of women can, as we have seen, take many forms. It can provide compensation for the absence of men, offer support in adversity and foster sisterly solidarity. As a further final possibility, that love between women can become not simply a substitute for heterosexual relationships, but a positive alternative, in which it is not so much a case of women without men as women repudiating men. Gaskell's tale 'The Grey Woman' focuses most sharply on this kind of friendship. Initially, it appears to be just another of the suspense stories of which Gaskell was so fond. The young heroine marries the mysterious nobleman and discovers too late that he is the leader of a desperate group of bandits. She subsequently flees to safety aided by her faithful maid-servant. Certainly aspects of the horror story are evident in the prolonged chase sequence and such macabre details as the bandits roasting their victims' feet. However, the tale rewards closer attention: the heroine, Anna Scherer, feels trapped into her marriage and her father is deaf to her appeals for help, insisting that once the ceremony, like a business transaction, is completed, 'no one had any right over [her] but [her] future husband' (VII. 313). Anna is initially attracted to her fiancé's almost effeminate features, 'so elegant' and 'delicate as a girl's' (VII. 309). His manner provides a welcome contrast to that of her earlier suitor, the 'rough-spoken and passionate' Karl, whose insistent masculinity repels Anna: 'The more Karl advanced, the more I disliked him' (VII. 306). As the story unfolds, sex roles are gradually merged in ways that substantiate the claim that Gaskell 'never saw sex as being identified simply by gender.'[27] A deliberate contrast is built up between the strength of Anna's maid and companion, Amante, and her husband, Tourelle. Amante is 'tall and handsome, though upwards of forty, and somewhat gaunt' (VII. 318), whereas Tourelle is associated with more conventionally feminine characteristics: 'I remember the sweet perfume that hung in the air, the scent bottles of silver that decked his toilet-table, and the whole apparatus for bathing and dressing, more luxurious than even those which he had provided for me' (VII. 325). From the outset Tourelle is 'jealous of [Anna's] free regard' for Amante, although in fact the early friendship between Anna and Amante is seen in terms of ordinary devotion between servant and mistress.

[27] See Coral Lansbury, *Elizabeth Gaskell*, p. 8.

The figurative 'net' which draws Anna into the marriage is given physical dimension as she is held captive in her husband's house: 'I was becoming tame to my apparent imprisonment in a certain part of the great building, the whole of which I had never yet explored' (VII. 319). Even the flower garden below her window is her husband's, 'for he was a great cultivator', and 'the only access . . . was through his rooms' (VII. 324). Anna suspects that it is designed 'in order to give me exercise and employment under his own eye' (VII. 324), and with the servants acting as spies, she feels 'trammelled in a web of observation, with unspoken limitations, extending over all my actions' (VII. 325). Her imprisonment is psychologically suggestive. She is kept 'tame' within a strictly defined part of the 'great' and 'unexplored' building. Within those confines she and Amante settle their own space: 'mov[ing] the furniture in the rooms, and adjust[ing] it to our liking' (VII. 319). When Amante accidentally discovers that Tourelle is withholding Anna's mail, the two women plot together to trespass into the forbidden area to take back what is rightfully Anna's. This act of daring, undertaken together, provides the knowledge of her husband's villainy, which inspires the plan to escape.

In order to facilitate their flight Amante disguises herself as a pedlar and Anna poses as a pedlar's wife. Obviously, though, beyond simple devices for escape, the disguises are in themselves a manifestation of the roles that have begun to evolve in the partnership. When Anna faints in her husband's room, for example, Amante takes her 'in her vigorous arms' and bears Anna to her room. In all their encounters during their flight Amante, dressed as she is and with her low voice and charcoal-blackened face, is accepted as a man, and the two women share a 'marital' bed at night: 'We crept into our bed, holding each other tight' (VII. 349).

When they finally settle in a small German town, the lingering possibility of detection is mooted in order to establish the need for continued disguise, and Amante announces: ' "We will still be husband and wife" ' (VII. 354). However, by this point it is clear that the threat of discovery is much less relevant than the fact that the relationship has developed into one of mutual dependence and attachment, as valid in the love that nourishes it as any heterosexual relationship. Amante continues to act out a male role, working as a tailor, and Anna gives birth to the child conceived during her brief marriage. Before the birth she prays that it might be a girl: 'I had feared lest a boy might have something of the tiger nature of its father, but a little girl seemed all my own. And yet not all my own for the faithful Amante's delight and glory in the babe almost exceeded mine' (VII. 355). In a sense that replacement of the husband and the parent-like sharing have been present since the earliest months of the pregnancy, for Amante 'knew what I had not yet ventured to tell M. de la Tourelle, that by-and-by I might become a mother' (VII. 319).[28] Amante's devotion finally costs her her life as she is slain by her pursuers. It is perhaps as a gesture of deference to the value and importance of the story's central relationship that whereas with Amante Anna 'grew strong in time' (VII. 356), Gaskell represents Anna as somehow spent and reduced in her marriage at the end of the tale to Dr. Voss:

. . . there I lived in the same deep retirement never seeing the full light of day, although when the dye once passed away from my face my husband did not wish me to renew it. There was no need; my yellow hair was grey, my complexion was ashen-coloured, no creature could have recognized the fresh-coloured, bright-haired young woman of eighteen months before. (VII. 359)

The tale takes the form of a letter from Anna to her daughter, written to disclose that the daughter's fiancé is the son of one of Tourelle's victims. Thus, the damage done by the father extends to blight the daughter's life, and with that knowledge the daughter remains single for life.

It would be a distortion of 'The Grey Woman' to see its significance in terms of its daring as a depiction of a homosexual relationship. Gaskell depicts a comprehensive love between two women which goes beyond the simple logic of sexual attraction. Far from daring, there is if anything a quality of innocence about the tale, which comes in part from Gaskell's sense of the non-libidinous nature of women discussed earlier. However, such innocence is liberating in a sense, for it allows Gaskell to accept unselfconsciously the existence of a deep and abiding love between women.

In *Surpassing the Love of Men* Lillian Faderman argues more generally that the prevalent assumption in the nineteenth century that there

---

[28] We have seen a number of such partnerships between female couples in Gaskell's fiction, and once again the parallel with *Aurora Leigh* is marked. In Barrett Browning's poem, Aurora and Marian unite to raise Marian's illegitimate child:

> Come,—and, henceforth, thou and I
> Being still together, will not miss a friend,
> Nor he a father, since two mothers shall
> Make that up to him. (Bk. VII, ll. 122–5)

was no possibility of sexual desire between women permitted 'a lati-
tude of affectionate expression and demonstration that became more
and more narrow with the growth of the general sophistication and
pseudo-sophistication regarding sexual possibilities between women.'[29]
Similarly in 'The Female World of Love and Ritual' Carroll Smith-
Rosenburg suggests that an intense and sometimes sensual female
love was 'one very real behavioural and emotional option socially
available to nineteenth century women.'[30] From her study of
American women Smith-Rosenberg concludes that it was not 'homosocial ties' but rather heterosexual relationships that were inhibited:
'While closeness, freedom of emotional expression, and uninhibited
physical contact characterized women's relationships with each other,
the opposite was frequently true of male–female relationships.'[31]

Although in one sense such research has only an oblique bearing on
Gaskell's work, it does draw upon the same realities that are reflected
so strongly in her fiction—women living in 'emotional proximity',
friendships following 'the biological ebb and flow of women's lives',
and intense bonds of love and intimacy between women who 'shared
such stressful moments'.[32] Furthermore, Gaskell herself was writing
in a comparable atmosphere of unself-conscious acceptance of passionate attachment between women. Amid her circle of female friends
such bonds were valued and nourished. The relationship between
Geraldine Jewsbury and Jane Carlyle is perhaps the most celebrated
example of this, but it is by no means an isolated instance.[33] Anna
Jameson, for example, formed passionate attachments with Lady
Byron and Ottilie von Goethe. Another acquaintance, Frances
Cobbe, set up house with the girls' reformatory pioneer Mary
Carpenter in an oddly assorted ménage consisting of the two women,
Carpenter's adopted daughter, a serving girl, and two convicted
thieves from the girls' reformatory. Cobbe later established her home
in London with the sculptor Mary Lloyd, her 'Playmate, Friend,
Companion, Love' with whom she lived for 'thirty-four blessed

[29] Lillian Faderman, *Surpassing the Love of Men: Romantic Friendship and Love between
Women from the Renaissance to the Present* (London: Junction Books, 1981), p. 152.

[30] Carroll Smith-Rosenberg, 'The Female World of Love and Ritual: Relations
between Women in Nineteenth Century America', *Signs*, I. I (1975), 8.

[31] Ibid., p. 8.

[32] Ibid., p. 24.

[33] See Geraldine Jewsbury, *Selections from the Letters of Geraldine Endsor Jewsbury to Jane
Welsh Carlyle*, ed. Mrs Alexander Ireland (London: Longmans, Green & Co., 1892).

years'.[34] Yet another of Gaskell's friends, Mrs Procter, was devoted to Anna Jameson, to whom she wrote happily comparing Jameson's position in her affections with her husband's:

. . . pray write to me or I shall think that, like many ladies, my letter has lost me *my lover*; don't laugh at my vanity in giving you that name, for that is really what you are to me. I never had but two before; one I married and of course lost, and the other I did not love and therefore lost.[35]

The ease with which the comparison is made suggests the truth of Smith-Rosenberg's claim that the twentieth-century tendency to view love and sexuality 'within a dichotomized universe of deviance and normality, genitality and platonic love, is alien to the emotions and attitudes of the nineteenth century.'[36] Gaskell herself wrote playfully to her friend Eliza Fox, inviting her to 'come live with me and be my love' (*GL* 86), and as we shall see, both Charlotte Brontë and George Eliot wrote to female friends as their 'lovers'. And while Jameson, Jewsbury, and Charlotte Brontë fantasized in life about setting up house with their female friends, Gaskell, as we have seen, explores such possibilities repeatedly in her fiction.[37]

Against this background, then, it is not surprising to find that Gaskell's female characters are much freer and more overt in their physical and verbal expressions of love for each other than for their male partners. The point is well illustrated in *Ruth*, for example, in the contrast between Jemima's interaction with Ruth and that with her fiancé, Farquhar. Jemima's reconciliation with Ruth on the night before her wedding—'In an instant they were in each other's arms—a long, fast embrace' (III. 381)—is followed shortly after by their fulsome declaration of mutual regard:

'But I should come to you, love, in quite a different way; I should go to you with my heart full of love—so full that I am afraid I should be too anxious.'

'I almost wish I were ill, that I might make you come at once.'

'And I am almost ashamed to think how I should like you to be in some position in which I could show you how well I remember that day—that terrible day in the schoolroom.' (III. 386)

---

[34] Frances Cobbe, *Life of Frances Power Cobbe as Told by Herself* (London: Swan, Sonnenschein & Co., 1904), p. 393.

[35] Mrs Procter in Jameson, *Anna Jameson*, p. 76.

[36] Smith-Rosenberg, 'The Female World', p. 8.

[37] Jameson, *Anna Jameson*, p. 115; Jewsbury, *Letters*, p. 333; Charlotte Brontë, *The Brontës: Their Lives, Friendships and Correspondence* (Oxford: Blackwell, 1932), I. 146.

Against this, the proposal scene between Jemima and Farquhar is marked by a strained formality between the two characters—' "Will you call me Walter?" '—and a conventional reticence on Gaskell's part: 'She was as red as any rose; her looks dropped down to the ground. They were not raised, when, half-an-hour afterwards, she said, "you won't forbid my going to see Ruth, will you?" ' Furthermore, the scene is shadowed by Gaskell's recognition even here of the proprietorial aspect of masculine love, both in Farquhar's relish of 'right' of 'control' and in the suggested transfer of power from father to lover:

The arm around her waist clasped her yet more fondly at the idea, suggested by this speech, of the control which he should have a right to exercise over her actions at some future day.

'Tell me,' said he 'how much of your goodness to me, this last happy hour, has been owing to the desire of having more freedom as a wife than as a daughter?' (III. 371)

A similarly revealing contrast is provided in *Wives and Daughters*. The scene in which Molly comforts Cynthia after her confrontation with Mr. Gibson is unmistakably erotic:

She took Cynthia into her arms with gentle power, and laid her head against her own breast, as if the one had been a mother, and the other a child.

'Oh my darling!' she murmured. 'I do so love you, dear, dear Cynthia!' and she stroked her hair, and kissed her eyelids. (VIII. 639)

In contrast the scene of Roger's proposal to Cynthia is one of constrained emotion: ' "Pray don't invent stories about me! I have engaged myself to Mr. Roger Hamley, and that is enough" ' (VIII. 434), and when Roger protests: ' "I will not accept your pledge . . . you must not shackle yourself by promises" ' (VIII. 434), the very terms of his generosity introduce once more the idea of confinement and restraint.

Gaskell recognizes a clear element of infatuation in both Jemima's and Molly's attachments. So Jemima 'could have kissed her hand and professed herself Ruth's slave' (III. 182), and Molly 'was absorbed in the contemplation of Cynthia's beauty . . . [and] fell in love with her, so to speak on the instant' (VIII. 247). At the same time she accepts that power of attraction as perfectly natural and independent of any narrow preoccupation with gender: 'A woman will have this charm, not only over men but over her own sex' (VIII. 249).

In the end, Gaskell's tendency, by nature and in her fiction, is to acknowledge those things that unite individuals, and the common interests of a 'sisterhood of shared pain' lead her to see womanhood as perhaps the most fundamental bond of all.

4

Charlotte Brontë's Ambivalence towards Solitude and Society

'Content with Seclusion' or 'Craving Companionship'?

I

Elizabeth Gaskell can be more readily identified than Charlotte Brontë as a member of a community of writing women. Gaskell's gregarious nature, wide circle of acquaintance, and willingness to acknowledge bonds both of gender and endeavour with other authors all contributed to the easy and continuing associations she maintained with many women writers. Charlotte Brontë, on the other hand, was temperamentally less suited to such intercourse. With very few close friendships, she was deeply divided between conflicting impulses to seek out companions and to isolate herself from the stress of social contact. Even in simple geographical terms Brontë was cut off from society by residence at Haworth in ways that Gaskell was not in Manchester.[1] Consequently her most important literary and social interactions were familial rather than communal:

> Resident in a remote district where education had made little progress, and where, consequently, there was no inducement to seek social intercourse beyond our own domestic circle, we were wholly dependent on ourselves and each other, on books and study, for the enjoyments and occupations of life.[2]

The Brontës' deepest feelings of kinship 'appear to have been expressed . . . in literary collaboration'.[3] Accordingly, at various points Charlotte acted as agent, editor, advocate, and critic for her sisters, and provided assessments of their work which were often both

---

[1] For the sake of brevity Charlotte Brontë will sometimes be referred to as Brontë. Should other members of the family be mentioned, their names will be given in full.

[2] Charlotte Brontë, 'Biographical Notice of Ellis and Acton Bell', *The Brontës: Their Lives, Friendships and Correspondence in Four Volumes*, eds. T. J. Wise and J. A. Symington (Oxford: Blackwell, 1932), II. 48. All further references to this work appear in the text, abbreviated as *BL*.

[3] See Gilbert and Gubar, *Madwoman in the Attic*, p. 251.

clear-sighted and frank. Most notably she was receptive to the originality and moments of startling excellence in Emily Brontë's poetry:

> . . . I know no woman that ever lived ever wrote such poetry before. Condensed energy, clearness, finish—strange, strong pathos are their characteristics; utterly different from the weak diffusiveness, the laboured yet most feeble wordiness, which dilute the writings of even very popular poetesses. (*BL* II. 256)

The deaths of Emily and Anne Brontë, then, not only shattered Charlotte's sense of sisterly self-sufficiency: 'loving each other as we did—well—it seemed as if—might we but have been spared to each other—we could have found complete happiness in our mutual society and affection' (*BL* II. 317), but left her devoid of the literary companionship and support with which she had grown up. With 'the two human beings who understood [her] and whom [she] understood . . . gone', she wrote to W. S. Williams in September 1849 as an author 'who has shewn his book to none, held no consultation about plan, subject, characters or incidents, but fabricated it darkly in the silent workshop of his own brain' (*BL* III. 21). In her loneliness as a writer after her sisters' deaths she became more vulnerable to doubts in the process of composition, and to criticism of the finished product. For example, in response to an unfavourable review of *Shirley* in the *Daily News* she wrote: 'Were my sisters now alive they and I would laugh over this notice; but they sleep . . . and I am a fool to be so moved by what is not worth a sigh' (*BL* III. 30). And even during the composition of *Villette*, well after her literary celebrity had been established, Charlotte still lamented the solitary nature of her endeavour:

> I can hardly tell you how I hunger to hear some opinion beside my own, and how I have sometimes desponded, and almost despaired, because there was no one to whom to read a line, or of whom to ask counsel. 'Jane Eyre' was not written under such circumstances, nor were two thirds of 'Shirley.' I got so miserable about it, I could bear no allusion to the book. (*BL* IV. 13)

For all that, the literary renown that followed the publication of *Jane Eyre* and the discovery of the true identity of Currer Bell did bring outside contacts to Haworth. A visitor to the parsonage in October 1850, for example, noted that most of the books on the shelves were 'evidently the gift of the authors since Miss Brontë's celebrity' (*BL* III. 168). And in a paradoxical way Brontë's isolation made her relationship to the literary community particularly interesting because it provided her with a vantage point from which to assess how far, and in

what manner, her engagement with the literary world should progress. About this Brontë evidently felt deeply ambivalent. More ambitious than her sisters, she was, according to her close friend Mary
Taylor, drawn to the camaraderie that might come with successful
authorship: 'Of course artists and authors stood high with Charlotte,
and the best thing after their works would have been their company.
. . . This was her notion of literary fame—a passport to the society of
clever people' (*BL* I. 276). Yet this scarcely tallies with Brontë's own
declaration to Margaret Wooler that were she obliged to live in London
she should 'certainly go little into company—especially [she] should
eschew the literary coteries' (*BL* III. 76), or with her announcement to
W. S. Williams that she 'recoil [ed]' from literary coteries, despite
'long[ing] to see some of the truly great literary characters' (*BL* III.
17). However, Brontë's apparent rejection of literary society had as
much to do with fear as with distaste or disapproval. Thus she wrote
to Williams in July 1848:

. . . the experiment of an introduction to society would be more formidable
than you, probably, can well imagine. An existence of absolute seclusion and
unvarying monotony, such as we have long—I may say, indeed, ever—been
habituated to, tends I fear to unfit the mind for lively and exciting scenes, to
destroy the capacity for social enjoyment. (*BL* II. 242)

Similarly there is much more a sense of inadequacy than detachment
or scorn in her confession to Margaret Wooler:

You say you suspect I have formed a large circle of acquaintance by this time.
No: I cannot say that I have. I doubt whether I possess either the wish or the
power to do so. A few friends I should like to have—and these few I should
like to know well. . . . However, I have as yet scarcely been tried. During the
month I spent in London in the Spring—I kept very quiet—having the fear of
'lionizing' before my eyes. (*BL* III. 164).

In many ways Brontë's divided attitude to the literary community
is inseparable from a more fundamental ambivalence toward solitude
and society. At times she was 'content with seclusion' (*BL* III. 17),
prepared to see it as 'more congenial than publicity' (*BL* IV. 79), and
to put her faith in the 'voice we hear in solitude'.[4] However, in more
depressed moments her 'loathing of solitude grew extreme' (*BL*
III. 189), and she wrote to Ellen Nussey 'the deadly silence, solitude, desolation were awful—the craving for companionship—the

---

[4] Charlotte Brontë, *Shirley*, Clarendon edn. (1849; rpt. Oxford: Oxford University
Press, 1979), p. 255.

hopelessness of relief' (*BL* III 173). That loathing was intensified by a real fear of solitude which emerges in her letters and is further explored in her fiction. There was, for example, the fear that isolation would poison her character, that 'dreary solitude' would make her ' "a stern, harsh, selfish woman" '—'this fear struck home—again and again I have felt it for myself' (*BL* III. 319). In addition, at times Brontë seems to have worried that the absence of companionship, far from promoting concentration and productivity, was actually disabling: 'Thoughts—under such circumstances—cannot grow to words, impulses fail to ripen into action' (*BL* III. 5). Most threatening of all, though, was the fear of madness. Brontë entertained the suggestion rather playfully in a letter to her publisher in 1851:

I secretly think on the contrary, I ought to be put in prison, and kept on bread and water in solitary confinement—without even a letter from Cornhill—till I have written a book. One of two things would certainly result from such a mode of treatment pursued for twelve months; either I should come out at the end of that time with a 3 vol. MS. in my hand, or else with a condition of intellect that would exempt me ever after from literary efforts and expectations. (*BL* III. 207)

However, its echo is much more grimly picked up in *Villette*—the very book she was struggling to write: 'The world can understand well enough the process of perishing for want of food: perhaps few persons can enter into or follow out that of going mad from solitary confinement.'[5]

Yet in spite of this Brontë remained harsh with such vulnerability, characterizing as 'weakness' the impulse to cling 'dependently to the society of friends' (*BL* III 261), and measuring herself unfavourably against Harriet Martineau, about whom she believed, 'neither solitude nor loss of friends would break her down' (*BL* III. 193). Perhaps the most curious aspect of her attitude is that even given the isolation of Haworth and the loss of her sisters, there remains something wilful about Brontë's conviction that she was 'a *lonely* woman and likely to be *lonely*. But it cannot be helped and therefore *imperatively must be borne*' (*BL* IV. 6). In truth, Brontë had many more opportunities for social contact than she chose to avail herself of. Instead, she eked out those 'treat[s]' in a self-denying, almost punitive, scheme of deprivation and reward:

I thought I would persist in denying myself till I had done my work, but I find it won't do, the matter refuses to progress, and this excessive solitude presses

[5] Charlotte Brontë, *Villette*, (London: Smith, Elder & Co., 1853), II. 221.

too heavily, so let me see your dear face, Nell, just for one reviving week. (*BL* IV. 10).

II

The combination of the isolation of Haworth and Brontë's own divided feelings with the literary world led her into associations with other women writers which were essentially, or at least initially, non-personal—safely engaged on the more neutral ground of the written word (and foreshadowing the detached relationships that Lucy Snowe maintains through the controlling medium of the letter in *Villette*). For example, her friendship with the novelist and biographer Julia Kavanagh began with an 'introduction' through an account of Kavanagh offered by W. S. Williams. Declaring that the character Williams sketched 'belongs to a class I peculiarly esteem' (*BL* II. 182), Brontë was moved to send Kavanagh an inscribed copy of *Jane Eyre*. The two women were hardly fellow-thinkers, and Kavanagh's theories of a distinctively feminine prose with 'three great redeeming qualities . . . Delicacy, Tenderness and Sympathy', for example, would have been anathema to Brontë, who steadfastly resisted all notions of separate standards for male and female writers.[6] However, Brontë continued to take an interest in Kavanagh, frequently enquiring after her and declaring to Williams that she 'would rather know her than many far more brilliant personages' (*BL* II. 287).

Characteristically, though, when the connection seemed likely to become more direct, Brontë retreated with prickly reserve: 'I by no means ask Miss Kavanagh to write to me—Why should she trouble herself to do it? What claims have I on her? She does not know me—she cannot care for me except vaguely and on hearsay' (*BL* II. 349). When a year later in 1850 they did meet, on Kavanagh's insistence, it seems that Brontë saw something of herself in the other woman, describing Kavanagh in terms she was inclined to apply to herself: 'a little almost dwarfish figure . . . this poor little feeble, intelligent, cordial thing wastes her brain to gain a living' (*BL* III. 118). Subsequently Brontë's interest took the form of more tangible support when she suggested to George Smith that 'one half of whatever you realize [in pursuing Emily Brontë's publisher Newby for outstanding debts] must be retained in your possession to add to any sum

6 Julia Kavanagh, *English Women of Letters* (London: Hurst & Blackett, 1863), p. 188.

you may decide on giving Miss Kavanagh for her next work' (*BL* III. 159).

Despite Brontë's interest and generosity, and suggestions of influence between the two authors, her relationship with Julia Kavanagh never really advanced beyond acquaintance.[7] However, two women writers, Elizabeth Gaskell and Harriet Martineau, did penetrate Brontë's reserve in important ways. Yet even in the initial stages of these friendships the same remote, almost theoretical, attitude was apparent. So attachment pre-dated acquaintance, with Brontë speculating that she could look up to the two women 'if [she] knew them' (*BL* III. 40).

The attraction to Martineau was first and foremost to the writer, a distinction made clear in her comparison of Martineau with Gaskell: 'She can never be so charming a woman as Mrs. Gaskell, but she is a greater writer' (*BL* III. 266). Perhaps it is not surprising, then, that the friendship begun in response to works of literature, should have become strained and have finally terminated on the same grounds. Initially Brontë sent an inscribed copy of *Shirley* to Martineau, 'in acknowledgement of the pleasure and profit she [*sic*] he has derived from her works. . . . In his mind *Deerbrook* ranks with the writings that have really done him good, added to his stock of ideas and rectified his views of life' (*BL* III. 56). Brontë's account of her subsequent visit to Martineau at Ambleside is telling in its somewhat over-stated enthusiasm, for what emerges most of all is not their compatibility, but the keenness with which, in spite of its absence, Brontë held on to the friendship: 'She is a great and a good woman. . . . She is both hard and warm-hearted, abrupt and affectionate—liberal and despotic. I believe she is not at all conscious of her own absolutism' (*BL* III. 189). The publication of *Letters on the Law of Man's Social Nature and Development*, jointly written by Martineau and H. G. Atkinson, shocked Brontë and caused the first reaction away from Martineau: 'I deeply regret its publication for the lady's sake; it gives a death blow to her future usefulness. Who can trust the word, or rely on the judgment of an avowed atheist?' (*BL* III. 214). However, Brontë seems to have been less than candid about her reactions. Martineau claimed that Brontë had ex-

---

[7] Robert Colby suggests that Kavanagh's *Nathalie* (1850) may be seen as a forerunner to *Villette* with its continental school setting, its rebellious heroine, and its principal romance, and conversely Mrs Oliphant insisted that Kavanagh's books were 'all so many reflections of *Jane Eyre*'. Robert Colby, *Fiction with a Purpose: Major and Minor Nineteenth-Century Novels* (Bloomington: Indiana University Press, 1967), p. 196; Margaret Oliphant, 'Modern Novelists—Great and Small', *Blackwood's*, May 1855, p. 558.

pressed her enthusiasm for the work, and when Brontë wrote to Gaskell only four days after expressing her 'regret', she commended Gaskell's tolerant sympathy toward Martineau's book:

Your remarks on Miss Martineau and her book pleased me greatly from their tone and spirit: I have even taken the liberty of transcribing for her benefit one or two of the phrases because I know they will cheer her . . . most fully do I agree with you in the dislike you express of that hard contemptuous tone in which her work is spoken of by many critics. (*BL* III. 215)[8]

In fairness, perhaps Brontë was initially overwhelmed by the general outcry against the book. Certainly her opinion seemed to mellow, for she later defended Martineau to Margaret Wooler: 'I believe if you were in my place, and knew Miss Martineau as I do . . . you would separate the sinner from the sin' (*BL* IV. 39). And in August 1851 Brontë was acting as an intermediary between George Smith and Martineau in arrangements to publish a new novel by Martineau.[9]

Brontë's judgement of Martineau's writing was astute. Warning Smith not to be '*too* sanguine', she observed: 'perhaps the nature and bent of her genius hardly warrant the expectation of first-rate excellence in fiction' (*BL* III. 270). The work that resulted, *Oliver Weld*, was in fact a disappointment. It satisfied neither Smith nor Brontë, who considered 'the artistic defects . . . many and great' (*BL* III. 301). The manuscript was returned to Martineau, and with the frankness in exchange of critical opinion which was to lead in the end to estrangement Brontë wrote:

You think perhaps it will do good? Not so much good as 'Deerbrook' did. Better the highest part of what is in your own self than all the political and religious controversy in the world. Rest a little while; consider the matter over, and see whether you have not another 'Deerbrook' in your heart to give England. (*BL* III. 303)

Martineau burnt the manuscript, and later called it 'a foolish prank', but Brontë noted to Ellen Nussey, 'it is obvious she is much chagrined' (*BL* III. 320).

Just as it had been a literary friendship, the final break was very much the result of a literary quarrel. On the publication of *Villette*,

[8] Vera Wheatley, *The Life and Work of Harriet Martineau* (London: Secker & Warburg, 1957), p. 330.

[9] There may have been a degree of self-interest in Brontë's eagerness on this matter. She herself was having difficulty writing *Villette*, and while insisting that it could be written '*not one whit faster*', this was a way of placating her increasingly impatient publisher.

Brontë wrote to Martineau, urging her to express her candid opinion of the novel: 'I know you will give me your thoughts upon my book, as frankly as if you spoke to some near relative whose good you preferred to her gratification' (BL IV. 38). Martineau was highly critical of the novel, and the pain given by her private opinion was intensified by the criticism she made as reviewer for the Daily News:

> . . . so incessant is the writer's tendency to describe the need of being loved. . . . There are substantial, heartfelt interests for women of all ages, and, under ordinary circumstances, quite apart from love: there is an absence of introspection, an unconsciousness, a repose of women's lives—unless under peculiarly unfortunate circumstances—of which we find no admission in this book. (BL IV. 44)

Martineau's own Autobiography throws a revealing light on the quarrel, for it makes clear how essentially incompatible the two women were temperamentally and how virtually inevitable their conflict was:

> It seemed to me, from the earliest time when I could think on the subject of Women's Rights and condition, that the first requisite to advancement is the self-reliance which results from self-discipline. Women who would improve the condition and chances of their sex must, I am certain, be not only affectionate and devoted, but rational and dispassionate, with the devotedness of benevolence, and not merely of personal love. . . . Nobody can be further than I am from being satisfied with the condition of my own sex, under the law and custom of my own country; but I decline all fellowship and co-operation with women of genius or otherwise favourable position, who injure the cause by their personal tendencies. . . . The best friends of the cause are the happy wives and the busy, cheerful, satisfied single women, who have no injuries of their own to avenge, and no painful vacuity of mortification to relieve.[10]

Brontë's response to Martineau's criticisms was predictably, and perhaps understandably, absolute:

> The differences of feeling between Miss M and myself are very strong and marked; very wide and irreconcilable. Besides, I fear language does not convey to her apprehension the same meaning as to mine. In short, she has hurt me a good deal, and at present it appears very plain to me that she and I had better not try to be close friends; my wish, indeed, is that she should quietly forget me. (BL IV. 55)

---

[10] Harriet Martineau, Harriet Martineau's Autobiography, with Memorials ed. Maria Weston Chapman (London: Smith, Elder & Co., 1877), I. 399.

Brontë saw it as a personal attack carried into a public forum in a spirit 'strangely and unexpectedly acrimonious' (*BL* IV. 58). This 'literary quarrel' was given a further dimension by Elizabeth Gaskell's commentary on it. Gaskell was sharply aware of the implications of personal judgement which existed beyond any artistic ramifications in Martineau's review: '[there were] expressions of censure which she believed to be unfounded but which, if correct and true, went deeper than any merely artistic fault.'[11] It was both as a friend and as a fellow-author that Gaskell could offer a sympathetic understanding of vulnerability to particular opinions:

An author may bring himself to believe that he can bear blame with equanimity, from whatever quarter it comes; but its force is derived altogether from the character of this. To the public, one reviewer may be the same impersonal being as another; but an author has frequently a far deeper significance to attach to opinions. They are the verdicts of those whom he respects and admires, or the mere words of those for whose judgment he cares not a jot.[12]

Whether accurately or not, Brontë saw in Gaskell a kindred spirit: 'For the sake of variety I could almost wish that the concord of opinion were less' (*BL* III. 268). Gaskell's frank admiration was a source of pleasure and consolation for Brontë: her approbation of *Jane Eyre* and *Shirley* took the sting 'from the strictures of another class of critics' (*BL* III. 45). As writers who achieved success at approximately the same time, Brontë and Gaskell compared notes on the 'lionizing' process and their impressions of London and its literary life, and in the way of friends they exchanged books and discussed matters of interest such as Harriet Taylor Mill's *Westminster Review* article on the emancipation of women and the visit of Harriet Beecher Stowe to England.

Despite Brontë's claim for Gaskell's superiority 'in attainment and experience' (*BL* III. 40), it was Brontë who offered most of the professional advice in the relationship. Although she did ask Gaskell if she were ever tempted to make her characters 'more amiable than Life, by the inclination to assimilate your thoughts to the thoughts of those who always *feel* kindly, but sometimes fail to *see* justly' (*BL* IV. 76), Brontë was not seeking advice—'Don't answer the question; it is not intended to be answered'—and was never amenable to interference with her writing. In contrast, she frequently gave Gaskell

[11] Elizabeth Gaskell, *The Life of Charlotte Brontë*, II. 279.
[12] Gaskell, *Life*, II. 279.

authorial direction. Like Anna Jameson, Brontë suggested to Gaskell that periodical 'piecemeal' publication of *North and South* was not desirable, but she tried to console Gaskell in her vexation at what she had ' "gone and done" ' by pointing to the positive side: ' "North and South" will thus be seen by many into whose hands it would not otherwise fall' (*BL* IV. 153). Similarly, she approved of Gaskell's outline for *Ruth*: 'its purpose may be as useful in practical result as it is high and just in theoretical tendency', but queried the projected ending: 'Why should she die?' (*BL* III. 332). She predicted that a certain class of critic would 'fix upon the mistake of the good Mr. Benson and his sister . . . [and] stick like flies caught in treacle', and she offered Gaskell sympathetic encouragement in the face of the impending furore: 'These, however, let us hope will be few in number and clearer-sighted commentators will not be wanting to do justice' (*BL* III. 332).

Brontë followed the progress of Gaskell's tale 'The Moorland Cottage' and finally expressed her approval: 'That small volume has beauty for commencement, gathers power in progress, and closes in pathos' (*BL* III. 204). She singled out for praise the treatment of 'Mrs. Brown's persistent, irrational, but most touching partiality for her son' (*BL* III. 204), which in many ways echoed her own treatment of Mrs. Reed in *Jane Eyre*, another mother blindly partial to her delinquent son and impervious to the emotional needs of the heroine. Indeed, if 'The Moorland Cottage' owes something to *Jane Eyre*, so too does Gaskell's later novel, *Sylvia's Lovers* (originally *Philip's Idol*), where Philip's confession, ' "I ha' made thee my idol; and, if I could live my life o'er again, I would love my God more, and thee less" ', clearly recalls Jane Eyre's admission: 'I could not, in those days, see God in His creature: of whom I had made an idol.'[13]

III

Brontë was not simply or completely isolated, then, from the literary world. None the less she had nothing like the range of acquaintance within the wider literary subculture that Gaskell maintained, and for the most part she repelled the overtures of would-be patrons such as the Kay-Shuttleworths, just as she declined most invitations from George Smith to visit London (and when there she was happier to see

[13] Gaskell, *Sylvia's Lovers*, Knutsford edn. (1863; rpt. London: Smith, Elder & Co., 1906), p. 523; Brontë, *Jane Eyre*, Clarendon edn. (1847; rpt. Oxford: Oxford University Press, 1969), p. 346.

'things not people'). Her two most important and long-standing friendships, with Ellen Nussey and Mary Taylor, existed largely apart from the literary world. Nevertheless each has a particular interest for this study.

Ellen Nussey was no intellectual companion for Brontë, but rather, as Brontë admitted, 'no more than a conscientious, observant, calm, well-bred Yorkshire girl' (*BL* III. 63). However, Brontë's relationship with Nussey is significant in two ways. First, for all the solace Brontë derived from Ellen Nussey's continued affection, there was an element of excess in Brontë's responses, a projection of feeling onto the relationship which apparently had little to do with Nussey:

I am at this moment trembling all over with excitement after reading your note; it is what I never received before—it is the unrestrained outpouring of a warm, gentle, generous heart; it contains sentiments unrestrained by human motives, prompted by the pure God himself; it expresses a noble sympathy which I *do* not, *cannot* deserve. (*BL* I. 139)

In a sense, then, Nussey provided an outlet for Brontë's romanticizing, and thus it was to her that Brontë made the declaration, 'Why are we to be divided? Surely, Ellen, it must be because we are in danger of loving each other too well—of losing sight of the *Creator* in idolatry of the *creature*' (*BL* I. 151), which is echoed in Jane Eyre's words about Rochester.[14]

Related to this, Brontë's correspondence with Nussey has the freedom and ease of expression that, as already discussed, was frequently a feature of homosocial relationships, and which finds its reflection in her fiction in the freedom of representation of the intensities of Shirley's and Caroline's relationship in *Shirley*. In fact, like many other literary women—and like her own female characters in *Shirley*—Brontë entertained the fantasy of living in self-sufficient isolation with Ellen:

Ellen I wish I could live with you always, I begin to cling to you more fondly than ever I did. If we had but a cottage and a competency of our own I do think we might live and love on till Death without being dependent on any third person for happiness. (*BL* I. 146)

It is revealing, however, for the later consideration of Brontë's fictional treatment of single women and 'old maids' that the life she envisaged with Ellen Nussey is marked by self-denial, even repression:

[14] Brontë, *Jane Eyre*, p. 346.

If I could always live with you . . . I might one day become better, far better, than my evil wandering thoughts, my corrupt heart, cold to the spirit, and warm to the flesh will now permit me to be. I often plan the pleasant life which we might lead together, strengthening each other in that power of self-denial, that hallowed and glowing devotion which the past saints of God often attained to. (*BL* I. 147)

Mary Taylor provided a much more radical influence in Charlotte Brontë's life. With her, Brontë felt a freedom and openness beyond that which she felt toward any other friend: 'I sat down and wrote to you such a note as I ought to have written to none but M. Taylor who is nearly as mad as myself' (*BL* I. 146). In contrast to the expressions of self-laceration and self-denial which Ellen Nussey seemed to inspire in Brontë, Mary Taylor's effect was consistently challenging. In fact the difference is strikingly underscored in a single letter written to Ellen Nussey in August 1841:

Mary's letter spoke of the pictures and cathedrals she had seen—pictures the most exquisite—and cathedrals the most venerable—I hardly know what swelled to my throat as I read her letter—such a vehement impatience of restraint and steady work. Such a strong wish for wings—wings such as wealth can furnish—such an urgent thirst to see—to know—to learn—something internal seemed to expand boldly for a minute—I was tantalized with the consciousness of faculties unexercised—then all collapsed and I despaired.

My dear Nell—I would hardly make that confession to any one but yourself—and to you rather in a letter than 'viva voce'—these rebellious and absurd emotions were only momentary I quelled them in five minutes—I hope they will not revive—for they are acutely painful. (*BL* I. 240)

Rose Yorke's taunt to Caroline Helstone, ' "I am resolved that my life shall be a life . . . not a long slow death like yours in Briarfield Rectory" ', might almost have been Mary Taylor's to Brontë, and certainly Taylor, already resident in Brussells, played an important role in Brontë's decision to leave Haworth for Belgium: 'Mary Taylor cast oil on the flames—encouraged me and in her own strong energetic language heartened me on' (*BL* I. 245).[15]

The deep respect Brontë felt for Mary Taylor was equalled only by that she felt for her sister, Emily. In both women she was drawn to a

---

[15] Brontë, *Shirley*, p. 451. In fact the character of Rose Yorke was based on Mary Taylor, and Taylor herself was struck by the accuracy of the representation: 'There is a strange feeling in reading it of hearing us all talking' (*BL* III. 135). The connection will be discussed further in Chapter 5.

fierce independence, strength and integrity of character. Taylor, she claimed, had 'more energy and power in her nature than any ten men you can pick out in the united parishes of Birstall and Gomersal. It is vain to limit a character like hers within ordinary boundaries— she will overstep them. I am morally certain Mary will establish her own landmarks' (*BL* I. 223). And on learning of Taylor's decision to emigrate to New Zealand she wrote: 'it is as if a great planet fell out of the sky' (*BL* II. 17).

Taylor's feminist politics were uncompromisingly clear in action and thought even from her school days. Although her articles on women's work for the *Victoria Magazine* did not begin to appear until well after Brontë's death, they had been long in composition, and Taylor wrote of them to Brontë as early as 1849 as her 'other book':

I write at my novel a little and think of my other book. What this will turn out God only knows. It is not and never can be forgotten. It is my child, my baby and I assure you such a wonder never was. I intend him when full grown to revolutionize society and faire époque in history. (*BL* II. 324)[16]

The 'novel' in question was *Miss Miles or a Tale of Yorkshire Life 60 Years Ago*, a polemical work stressing the importance of work for women. In some respects it was reminiscent of Gaskell—in, for example, its concern for women bonded together 'through many changes and many sorrows', united against their suffering at the hands of men. Recognizing that 'knowledge is power', the rebellious heroine, Maria, alleges that women are kept deliberately ignorant of business matters. Similarly, the more docile heroine, Dora, feels a fresh bond with her mother after the mother has been cheated by Dora's stepfather:

'She is on my side now. . . . I will tell her not to be submissive any more. I will not have the money if she gets it. She shall, at least, not endure all the scolding and do all the work that she does, and lead such a miserable life. We will keep together and defy him.'[17]

There are similarities with Gaskell, too, in the novel's final resolution with women finding solace in living together. In a sense Taylor lived out that fantasy, and provided Brontë with an example in reality of

[16] The first article appeared in 1865. In 1870 they were collected into one volume, *The First Duty of Women: a Series of Articles Reprinted from the Victoria Magazine 1865 to 1870* (London: Emily Faithfull, 1870).
[17] Mary Taylor, *Miss Miles or a Tale of Yorkshire Life 60 Years Ago* (London: Remington & Co., 1890), p. 50.

the female self-sufficiency she had toyed with in her letters to Ellen Nussey. So Mary's cousin, Ellen Taylor, wrote to Brontë from New Zealand in 1850: 'Mary and I are settled together now: I can't do without Mary and she couldn't get on by herself. I built the house we live in, and we made the plan ourselves, so it suits us. We take it in turns to serve in the shop, and keep the acounts, and do the house-work' (*BL* III. 134).

Beyond its own modest merit and the insight it offers into Taylor's feminist politics, *Miss Miles* is particularly interesting for the way in which the relationship between the two principal characters is so sug-gestive of the friendship between Taylor and Brontë. Taylor's characters share the kind of closeness that Brontë claimed for herself and Taylor: 'No one understood them as they understood each other. Their joint affairs were to themselves the most interesting things in the world, and their comments on them could have been uttered to no one else.'[18] Their fictional lives too show significant parallels. Maria is from childhood, like Taylor, 'blessed with a healthy instinct that set authority at defiance', and she strikes out on her own to earn a living away from the place of her birth, leaving her friend Dora in desperate isolation.[19] As in Taylor's and Brontë's relationship, the fictional friendship continues through correspondence:

Through all this time Maria's letters were all that held her mind fast to the ac-tual world, and soothed her feelings so as to enable her to bear her lot. True the closely written sheets could only pass between them at intervals of a month at least . . . [but they] continued to know each other thoroughly, and each to have a friend.[20]

In fact, although with characteristic integrity Taylor destroyed all Brontë's letters, which were probably the most revealing she wrote, it is tantalizing to speculate that this novel, written at a time when Taylor was receiving letters from Brontë, may reflect something of the nature of Brontë's correspondence. One of the novel's letters in particular seems stamped with Brontë's temperament and style:

But when the real parting was accomplished, and the solitude came, her for-titude broke down. She longed so for a word from her friend that she became almost hysterical when day after day the post brought no letter from her.
My Dear Miss Bell,
    I suppose our childish friendship is at an end. I ought to have known that it would be, when you got out into the actual world; everybody told us it

would. . . . As this is a farewell letter, I will tell you what my prospects are, for you to think of when you have time. I sit by myself till I know myself on the verge of idiocy. I know, too, what I have long dreaded, that this is an ordinary fate. Women die off so sometimes. The first step is, of course, that they will sink out of sight—no one knows what becomes of them. . . . Do not write to me any more, for I feel less when I am not stirred.[21]

The hysteria is comparable to Brontë's obsessive dependence on mail: 'I cannot help feeling something of the excitement of expectation till the post hour comes, and when, day after day, it brings nothing, I get low' (*BL* III. 77). The 'sink[ing] out of sight' recalls Lucy Snowe's reaction to Dr. John's neglect in writing: 'Those who live in retirement . . . are liable to be suddenly and for a long while dropped out of the memory of their friends', and the concluding gesture of defensively renouncing all contact rather than risk disappointment is characteristic of Brontë's reactions: 'It is painful to be dependent on the small stimulus letters give—I sometimes think I will renounce it altogether, close all correspondence on some quiet pretext, and cease to look forward at post-time for any letters but yours' (*BL* III. 125).[22] In any case, given the threat of madness felt by Brontë in the face of isolation, Taylor's expression of the importance of friendship in *Miss Miles* might have stood as an epigraph for Brontë: 'One approving friend will sometimes keep the mind steady, when on the borders of insanity, from the sheer darkness surrounding it.'[23]

Mary Taylor's forthrightness was evident in all her correspondence. She complained, for example, that it was impossible to squeeze a moral out of *Jane Eyre*: 'Has the world gone so well with you that you have no protest to make against its absurdities? Did you never sneer or declaim in your first sketches? I will scold you when I see you' (*BL* II. 235). And in response to *Shirley* she wrote:

You are a coward and a traitor. A woman who works is by that alone better than one who does not and a woman who does not happen to be rich and who *still* earns no money and does not wish to do so, is guilty of a great fault. . . . It is very wrong of you to *plead* for toleration for workers on the ground of their being in peculiar circumstances and few in number or singular in disposition. Work or degradation is the lot of all except the very small number born to wealth. (*BL* III. 104)

Yet Taylor's praise and enthusiasm were as generous as her criticism was frank: 'After I had read [*Jane Eyre*] I went to the top of Mount

---

[21] Ibid., p. 105.   [22] Brontë, *Villette*, p. 205.   [23] Taylor, *Miss Miles*, p. 53.

Victoria and looked for a ship to carry a letter to you' (*BL* II. 235). From their school days Taylor, unlike Nussey, encouraged Brontë's imaginative genius: 'when she said there was no more, I said, "But go on! *Make it out*! I know you can"' (*BL* I. 91), and after Brontë's career had begun, Taylor exhorted: 'Look out then for success in writing. You ought to care as much for that as you do for going to Heaven.'[24] It is an indication of the gratitude Brontë felt for Taylor's serious acceptance of her professional life that the long and detailed account Brontë wrote of her first visit to London as the author of *Jane Eyre* was addressed to Taylor (*BL* II. 250–4).

Mary Taylor demonstrated a loyalty to the memory of her friend, which was comparable to Gaskell's 'fervent desire' to create a 'right understanding' of Brontë as woman and writer:

I wish I could set the world right on many points, but above all respecting Charlotte. It would do the world good to know her and be forced to revere her in spite of their contempt for poverty and helplessness. No one ever gave up more than she did and with full consciousness of what she sacrificed. (*BL* IV. 198)

Consequently, despite her fierce respect for Brontë's privacy, Taylor co-operated fully with Gaskell in writing the *Life* in an effort to ensure that Brontë's story was dealt with justly. Taylor had a sense of a grim truth in need of telling—'I can never think without gloomy anger of Charlotte's sacrifices to the selfish old man' (*BL* IV. 198)— which made her response to the revised edition of the *Life* predictably hostile and uncompromising:

As to the mutilated edition that is to come, I am sorry for it. Libellous or not, the first edition was all true, and except the declamation all, in my opinion, useful to be published. Of course I don't know how far necessity may make Mrs. Gaskell give them up. You know one dare not always say the world moves.[25]

IV

In Chapter 2 we saw that Gaskell, as a mother of four daughters and resident in an industrial city, was brought into contact with the problems of the 'superabundant' woman, women's employment, emi-

---

[24] Mary Taylor, as quoted in Joan Stevens, *Mary Taylor Friend of Charlotte Brontë: Letters from New Zealand and Elsewhere* (New Zealand: Auckland University Press, 1972), p. 82.

[25] Joan Stevens, *Mary Taylor*, p. 134.

gration, and the like. Similarly, despite the limited horizons of Charlotte Brontë's world, she too was in touch with the issues and preoccupations surrounding the Woman Question. For Brontë these were not simply questions of passing concern, but rather the problems of everday living. As a single woman, 'doomed to be an old maid' (*BL* I. 184), she told Margaret Wooler: 'I speculate much on the existence of the unmarried and never-to-be-married women nowadays' (*BL* II. 77). Brontë, much more than Gaskell, saw the prospect as grim, liable to embitter its victims: 'she has not been disappointed, and consequently soured. In a word, she is a married instead of a maiden lady' (*BL* I. 260). Furthermore, her 'speculation' on singleness was not simply a rational response to the demographic odds, as it was for a writer like Frances Cobbe. In Brontë's case it was complicated by her obsessive sense of her 'personal ugliness', and hence the sternness with which she dismissed false hopes:

. . . it is an imbecility which I reject with contempt—for women who have neither fortune nor beauty—to make marriage the principal object of their wishes and hopes and the aim of all their actions—not to be able to convince themselves that they are unattractive—and that they had better be quiet and think of other things than wedlock. (*BL* I. 296)

Yet in spite of her apprehensiveness and distaste for single life—or, perhaps, because of it—Brontë remained a defiant apologist for single women: 'there is no more respectable character on this earth than an unmarried woman who makes her own way through life quietly perseveringly' (*BL* II. 77), and she upheld a woman's right to refuse marriage as staunchly as more strident champions of the cause. She saw those women 'reared on speculation with a view to their making mercenary marriages' as 'piteously degraded' (*BL* II. 221), and she argued that married women who 'indiscriminately urge their acquaintances to marry' were gravely irresponsible: 'it is a solemn and strange and perilous thing for a woman to become a wife. Man's lot is far—far different' (*BL* IV. 145). As we shall see in the following chapter, Brontë's general ambivalence to the single life for women is betrayed in her unresolved attitudes towards her fictional spinsters.

The example of Brontë's own life had contributed a good deal to Gaskell's understanding and sympathy on the question of women's employment. Brontë saw dependency as the 'one great curse of a single female life' (*BL* III. 5), and much of her adult life was spent dealing with the exigencies of earning a living. She was all too familiar with the trials of governessing and with the difficulties and limitations of other options for employment. None the less, even with that knowledge Brontë retreated from radical solutions:

It is true enough that the present market for female labour is quite overstocked, but where or how could another be opened? Many say that the professions now filled only by men should be open to women also; but are not their present occupants and candidates more than numerous enough to answer every demand? Is there any room for female lawyers, female doctors, female engravers, for more female artists, more authoresses? One can see where the evil lies, but who can point out the remedy? (*BL* II. 213)

In a similar way her thinking on the Woman Question more generally, while not uninformed, was marked by a kind of quietism. For example, she wrote to Gaskell of the 'evils—deep-rooted in the foundations of the social system', but she concluded that they were problems 'which no efforts of ours can touch; of which we cannot complain; of which it is advisable not too often to think' (*BL* III. 150).

In general, Brontë's letters reveal a fairly conventional view of female friendships, although her fiction, like Gaskell's, suggests a more far-reaching conception. In a letter to W. S. Williams, for example, she suggested, like many other female writers, that whereas the issue of women friends was of little relevance to married women, it was possible that single women might be a source of comfort to each other:

You allude to the subject of female friendship and express wonder at the infrequency of sincere attachments amongst women—As to married women, I can well understand that they should be absorbed in their husbands and children—but single women often like each other much and derive great solace from their mutual regard. (*BL* III. 63)

She was hesitant, however, to see that comfort in friendship extended to the possibility of support in communities. Generally, she mistrusted communities, wary of the dynamics of any collection of individuals:

. . . all coteries, whether they be literary, scientific, political or religious, must, it seems to me, have a tendency to change truth into affectation. When people belong to a clique, they must, I suppose, in some measure, write, talk, think and live for that clique; a harassing and narrowing necessity. (*BL* II. 207)

And that mistrust was exacerbated by the fact that her thinking on sisterhoods, one of the principal options for communal activity for women, was so coloured by sectarian antipathy.   .

V

It was perhaps with Mary Taylor's criticism of *Jane Eyre* in mind that Brontë wrote rather defensively to George Smith on the completion of *Villette*:

You will see that 'Villette' touches on no matter of public interest. I cannot write books handling the topics of the day; it is of no use trying. Nor can I write a book for its moral. Nor can I take up a philanthropic scheme, though I honour philanthropy. (*BL* IV. 14)

Although she respected Gaskell's endeavour in writing *Ruth*, and Harriet Beecher Stowe's in writing *Uncle Tom's Cabin*, she forswore such an enterprise as beyond her capacity: 'To manage these great matters rightly they must be long and practically studied—their bearing known intimately, and their evils felt genuinely; they must not be taken up as a business matter and a trading speculation' (*BL* IV. 14).

However, the one topical area where intimate knowledge and sincerity were not problems for Brontë was that of the position of governesses. Undoubtedly, it was out of a sense of truth to life rather than of social purpose that she dealt with the subject, but nevertheless Brontë's work did highlight the plight of the governess, caught in the vexed position of sharing neither the advantage of an employee's detachment nor the involvement of a family member. For example, Mrs. Pryor is warned she must 'never transgress the invisible but rigid line which established the difference between [her] and [her] employers', and Lucy Snowe feels the paradox of professionalism in personal relationships when she declines Mr. Home's offer of a trebled salary to 'accept the office of companion to his daughter. . . . Rather than be a companion, [she] would have made shirts and starved.'[26] Harriet Martineau's objection to Brontë's handling of the subject is ironic both because the character of Lucy Snowe, as Robert Colby suggests, seems influenced by Martineau's literary governess, Maria Young in *Deerbrook*, and because Martineau's objection in itself suggests something of a tribute to the penetration and verity of Brontë's treatment: 'governesses especially have reason to remonstrate, and do remonstrate that their share of the human conflict is laid open somewhat rudely and inconsiderately and sweepingly to social observation.'[27]

[26] Brontë, *Shirley*, p. 423; *Villette* II. 271.
[27] Colby, *Fiction with a Purpose*, p. 195; Harriet Martineau, 'Death of Currer Bell', *Daily News*, Apr. 1855, quoted in *BL* IV. 180.

Just as Gaskell's treatment of the bond between mistress and servant reinforced calls for mutual and class responsibility between women, Brontë's fiction demonstrated that she too shared that sense of responsibility. So, for example, in *Jane Eyre* Blanche Ingram's disdain for servants and governesses is as sure an index of the bankruptcy of her character, as the kind, almost familial, relationship of the Rivers sisters to their servant, Hannah, is of the goodness of theirs. Similarly in *Shirley* Caroline's virtue is evidenced by her thoughtfulness toward the parsonage servant, Fanny: 'If she lingered much later, dusk would draw on, and Fanny would be put to the trouble of coming to fetch her: it was both baking and ironing day at the Rectory, she remembered—Fanny would be busy.'[28]

In contrast to Gaskell Brontë did nothing to challenge the contemporary estimation of nursing as a profession, or to suggest a rightful place for women in the medical world. Whereas Gaskell tended to see healing as the natural domain of women, all Brontë's medical practitioners are male, and no broader realm of female folk medicine exists beyond the official medical establishment. Furthermore, unlike Gaskell's saintly Ruth, Brontë's nurses tend to confirm a low general opinion of nurses, particularly in their 'addict[ion] to habits of intemperance'. It is, for example, Grace Poole's drunkenness that allows Bertha to start the fire which destroys Thornfield, and in *Shirley* Martin Yorke succeeds in clearing a path for Caroline to visit Robert by luring the nurse away with the promise of alcohol. When Robert complains to MacTurk of his attendant's intemperance, the doctor is neither sympathetic, nor surprised:

If she had not smoked—if she had not taken gin, it would have been better, he thought; but she did both. Once—in her absence—he intimated to MacTurk, that 'that woman was a dram-drinker.'

'Pooh! my dear sir; they are all so,' was the reply he got, for his pains. 'But Horsfall has this virtue,' added the surgeon,—'drunk or sober, she always remembers to obey *me*.'[29]

Brontë's hostility to conventual life is evident in her creation of the unfeeling and self-absorbed Eliza Reed, who is seen as eminently suited to her vocation and deserving of her chosen fate, 'walled up alive in a French convent'.[30] Similarly, in *The Professor* Crimsworth's pupil Sylvie is destined for the cloister:

[28] Brontë, *Shirley*, p. 461.
[29] Brontë, *Shirley*, p. 644.
[30] Brontë, *Jane Eyre*, p. 303.

. . . her whole soul was warped to a conventual bias, and in the tamed, trained subjection of her manner, one read that she had already prepared herself for the future course of life, by giving up her independence of thought and action into the hands of some despotic confessor.[31]

Certainly, Brontë's attitude is more directly revealing of her sectarianism than of her thinking on women's communities, but nevertheless, as we shall see, it extends to inform her treatment of the school communities in *The Professor* and *Villette*.

More broadly, in the following chapter we shall consider the ways in which the ambivalence we have discussed in Brontë's life toward solitude and society is reflected in the depiction of women's relationships in her fiction, and how the 'need of being loved' is balanced against a more stoical and solitary determination to obtain self-sufficiency.

[31] Charlotte Brontë, *The Professor* (London: Smith, Elder & Co., 1857), I. 202.

5

Charlotte Brontë's Fiction

A School of One's Own

I

In discussing the work of Elizabeth Gaskell I argued that despite her claim of 'taking to men so much more than to women', the truth of her fiction revealed a more complex and primary allegiance to women based on fundamental bonds of motherhood and a shared lot as victims. In Charlotte Brontë's work the priorities are different, the allegiances more divided. On the one hand Brontë makes broad claims, in *Shirley* particularly, for the possibilities of friendship between women, and all her novels are haunted by that 'mother-want', which is so pervasive in Gaskell, and which suggests the vital importance of an essentially female bond. On the other, in direct contrast with Gaskell, at crucial moments of choice in Brontë's fiction it is the conjugal relationship that is validated ahead of the maternal, or sororal. Furthermore, in her final novel, *Villette*, a more radical and more threatened move is evident away from mutuality of any kind and toward self-containment and preservation.

The strongest impression we receive from the opening chapters of *Jane Eyre* is of the emotional bleakness of Gateshead for Jane, of her desperate isolation as an orphan faced with the vicious exclusiveness of the Reed family. Within that household the servant Bessie offers the only source of affection or support for the child and becomes the first in a series of mother figures for Jane—the initial example of the recurring image which has been characterized as 'a nurturing or principled or spirited woman on whom [Jane] can model herself, or to whom she can look for support.'[1] So, after her terror in the Red Room Jane reaches for Bessie's hand for comfort and Bessie attempts to act as Jane's advocate. Bessie's occasional acts of kindness continue to sustain Jane, and their bond is cemented by the sympathetic

---

[1] See Adrienne Rich, 'Jane Eyre: The Temptations of a Motherless Woman', *On Lies, Secrets, and Silence: Selected Prose 1966–1978* (New York: Norton, 1979), p. 91.

insight of Bessie's own mother: ' "My mother said, when she came to see me last week, that she would not like a little one of her own to be in your place." '[2] As the rest of the house sleeps, it is Bessie who prepares Jane for her departure to Lowood, just as she appears in Jane's life eight years later when Jane, alone once more, is about to embark on a new chapter in her life at Thornfield. In their final encounter when Jane returns to Gateshead before Mrs. Reed's death, Bessie is shown as mistress and mother in the lodge, having fulfilled the potential she showed in her youthful relationship with Jane: 'the floor was spotless; the grate and fire-irons were burnished bright, and the fire burnt clear. Bessie sat on the hearth, nursing her last-born, and Robert and his sister played quietly in a corner' (*JE* 283).

At Lowood school Jane enjoys a constancy of support and affection such as she has not known before. Whereas Bessie's kindness had been subject to the vagaries of her temper, Helen Burns 'at all times and under all circumstances, evinced for [Jane] a quiet and faithful friendship' (*JE* 91). Their relationship is marked, too, by a physical intimacy, which underscores Jane's craving for nurture. After Helen's death Miss Temple fills the emotional void. She acts as Jane's protector against the patriarchal figure of Lowood, Mr. Brocklehurst, and Jane confesses that she 'derived a child's pleasure from the contemplation of her face' (*JE* 83). Reviewing their relationship on Miss Temple's departure from Lowood, Jane makes explicit the role the teacher has played: 'her friendship and society had been my continual solace; she had stood me in the stead of mother, governess, and, latterly, companion' (*JE* 99).

In the next episode of her life Jane is welcomed to Thornfield by Mrs. Fairfax with a kindness 'offered . . . before it was earned' (*JE* 118). Greeted by the old lady as an 'equal', welcomed as a 'companion', Jane feels 'a thankfulness for her kindness, and a pleasure in her society' (*JE* 131). Later, Jane's exodus from Thornfield gives an external, physical reality to her inner emotional desperation. Without moral support, she has left her few belongings on the waggon that transported her; without sustaining affection, she is literally starving; and without human warmth, she is in danger of freezing to death. It is from this fate that Jane is saved by the two sisters at Moor-House, Diana and Mary Rivers, whose very names are indicative of the role

[2] Charlotte Brontë, *Jane Eyre*, Clarendon edn. (1847; rpt. Oxford: Oxford University Press, 1969), p. 16. All further references to this work appear in the text, abbreviated as *JE*.

they fulfil for Jane—Diana, the chaste, moon-identified goddess who presides over childbirth, and Mary, the Christian archetype of the virgin mother.[3] The sisters' warmth, 'their spontaneous, genuine, genial compassion', is continually contrasted with their brother's chilling 'evangelical charity' (*JE* 444). Jane feels an instinctive trust with Diana particularly and in time Diana assumes the role of teacher, an exalted position in Brontë's fiction:

I was fain to sit on a stool at Diana's feet, to rest my head on her knee. . . . I liked to learn of her: I saw the part of instructress pleased and suited her; that of scholar pleased and suited me no less. Our natures dovetailed: mutual affection—of the strongest kind—was the result (*JE* 447).

Whereas the sisters simply accept Jane, St. John interrogates her while she is still too weak to give account of herself. More significantly, while Diana comments on Jane's thinness and anticipates her hunger by bringing her cake, St. John regulates and restricts her food when she first arrives, and again when she comes downstairs after her three days of unconsciousness: ' "Now you may eat; though still not immoderately" ' (*JE* 441). This withholding of nourishment, so contrary to a fundamental tenet of mothering, is most immediately reminiscent of Brocklehurst's near-criminal niggardliness in feeding the children of Lowood school, which Miss Temple ameliorates to the best of her ability. But Mrs. Reed is also guilty of the same behaviour, banishing Jane without her supper. There too Bessie rebels against the prohibition and frequently smuggles 'a bun or a cheese-cake' from the kitchen to feed Jane. Even in Rochester's fantasy of monopolizing Jane by taking her to a cave on the moon ' "with me there, and only me" ', Adèle observes: ' "She will have nothing to eat: you will starve her" ' (*JE* 336).

Just as Miss Temple has offered crucial support to Jane in opposition to Brocklehurst by exposing his charges as unjust, so Diana strengthens Jane in her movement away from St. John by her reaction against his plans to take Jane to India: ' "Madness!. . . . You would not live three months there, I am certain. You shall never go: you have not consented, have you, Jane?" ' (*JE* 530).

All these women in Jane's life, then, suggest the need for, and importance of, a nurturing, supportive female presence. It is significant, especially in the light of Gaskell's perception of women united as victims, that regardless of their personal strength, these women are all in

[3] See Adrienne Rich, *On Lies, Secrets and Silences*, p. 103.

positions of relative powerlessness—Bessie as a servant in the Reed household; Helen as a child in the world of adults, and a pupil in a world of teachers; Miss Temple as Brocklehurst's employee and Mrs. Fairfax as Rochester's; Diana and Mary as dutiful sisters to their brother, the ruling male of the Rivers family—and in that powerlessness they are all united 'on terms of equality', not 'the mere result of condescension' (*JE* 121).

Beyond the individual women in Jane's life, there is a powerful and pervasive maternal force embodied in the natural world, which becomes at times as much an actual presence as a symbolic force. Its central focus is the moon, and Brontë suggests a spiritual link between it and her heroine. When Jane first encounters Rochester, for example, her serenity is associated with the presence of the moon: ' "I am not at all afraid of being out late when it is moonlight" ' (*JE* 138). Without the guidance of an earthly mother, Jane seems to be watched over by the moon throughout her relationship with Rochester. For example, as Jane awaits Rochester's return for their wedding, she senses a message of foreboding in the moon's fleeting appearance: 'her disk was blood-red and half-overcast: she seemed to throw on me one bewildered, dreary glance, and buried herself again instantly in the deep drift of cloud' (*JE* 349). As Rochester overshadows all else in Jane's concern, the moon seems to withdraw: 'the moon shut herself wholly within her chamber, and drew close her curtain of dense cloud' (*JE* 350). It is not until Jane fully understands and rejects the future Rochester offers her that the moon intervenes, and it does so then with a gesture as direct and crucial as any mediation offered by her earthly surrogates:

I watched her come—watched with the strangest anticipation; as though some word of doom were to be written on her disk. She broke forth as never moon yet burst from cloud: a hand first penetrated the sable folds and waved them away; then, not a moon, but a white human form shone in azure, inclining a glorious brow earthward. It gazed and gazed on me. It spoke, to my spirit: immeasurably distant was the tone, yet so near, it whispered in my heart—

'My daughter, flee temptation!'

'Mother, I will.' (*JE* 407)

Having been encouraged to flight, Jane is aided and nourished by the natural world:

Nature seemed to me benign and good: I thought she loved me, outcast as I was; and I, who from man could anticipate only mistrust, rejection, insult, clung to her with filial fondness. To-night, at least, I would be her guest—as I was her child: my mother would lodge me without money and without price. . . . I saw ripe bilberries gleaming here and there, like jet beads in the heath: I gathered a handful, and eat them with the bread. My hunger, sharp before, was, if not satisfied, appeased by this hermit's meal. (*JE* 413)

The culmination of the natural world's maternal supervision of Jane's relationship with Rochester comes with the strange and timely answer to her entreaty: ' "Shew me—shew me the path!" ' (*JE* 535). The voice heard as an 'inward sensation', calling Jane back to Rochester, is characterized as ' "the work of nature. She was roused, and did—no miracle—but her best" ' (*JE* 536).

In important ways, then, *Jane Eyre* explores a craving within the heroine which is met by a nourishing, supportive maternal capacity in a series of female figures who populate her pilgrimage and, more broadly, in a prevailing female presence in the natural world. However, there is much in the female world of the novel to complicate and qualify the claims one might make about Brontë's attitude to women's relationships.

To begin with, balanced against that protective, maternal capacity Brontë recognizes a capacity for violence, both actual and imaginative, in women. Jane, for example, first experiences the relief of fighting back when she punches John Reed in the nose with 'as hard a blow as [her] knuckles could inflict' (*JE* 27). Later, while observing Blanche Ingram direct miscalculated barbs at Rochester, Jane imagines the harm she might do: 'I knew, if shot by a surer hand, [the arrows might] have quivered keen in his proud heart' (*JE* 233). Before her wedding she resists Rochester's sultan-like efforts to possess her as a slave by crushing his hand, 'which was ever hunting [hers], vigorously, and thrust[ing] it back to him red with passionate pressure' (*JE* 339), and she keeps him at bay by using her tongue as 'a weapon of defence', 'a needle of repartee' (*JE* 343). In all this the heroine has a certain justice on her side, that of the victim against the oppressor. The same might even be said of Bertha Mason's acts of violence which, significantly, are directed at Rochester, and later against her brother, but never against Rochester's agent, her gaoler Grace Poole, whose alcohol-induced sleep would make her an easy victim. Even in her visitation to Jane's room Bertha makes no attempt to harm Jane, and her action in tearing the wedding veil, for all its indication of personal rage, is paradoxically akin to the mediation of the natural, maternal force in warning against the impending marriage.

Indeed, such combativeness in women might seem justifiable, even appropriate, in the face of the threat of male violence that pervades the novel, whether in the form of John Reed's simple physical tyranny or Rochester's temperamental fierceness. However, it is important to recognize that the response of Brontë's female characters to that threat is different from the corresponding response in Gaskell's women. For Gaskell it is more simply a victim's response of self-preservation, often sought through retreat—a bonding together of women away from the source of violence. In Brontë it goes beyond self-preservation and acquires a combative edge which implicates the heroine in a mutual contest, rather than dissociates her from it. For example, of the confrontation with Rochester already mentioned, Brontë notes: 'The crisis was perilous; but not without its charm: such as the Indian, perhaps, feels when he slips over the rapid in his canoe' (*JE* 386). The continuing tussle between Rochester and Jane, one of 'fierce favours' and assertions of power, is depicted by Brontë as essentially a playing out of sexual energy and attraction.

As further qualification to the overall view of women's relationships, despite the importance of maternal surrogates, in some ways the novel challenges any simple trust in a sacred notion of motherhood. Most simply, like Gaskell, Brontë depicts failed mothers who dispel any naïve adherence to an ideal and indicate that motherhood as a biological fact is no guarantee of maternal capacity. For example, Celine Varens has abandoned Adèle to the 'slime and mud of Paris', and Jane's guardian Mrs. Reed consistently refuses to offer Jane the least affection or regard. The depth of Jane's need for love is evidenced by her willingness, indeed her 'yearning', to forgive her aunt on her death-bed. Yet such is Mrs. Reed's emotional sterility that she remains unmoved, 'unchanged, and unchangeable' (*JE* 289). The only difference is that now Jane is no longer powerless, and with the battle lines once again drawn up, she feels 'a determination to subdue her—to be her mistress in spite both of her nature and her will. [Jane's] tears had risen, just as in childhood: [she] ordered them back to their source' (*JE* 289). Mrs. Reed's failure is in quite specific ways a failure to mother. When Jane first arrives at Gateshead, Mrs. Reed reacts instinctively against the newborn child: ' "I hated it the first time I set my eyes on it—a sickly, whining, pining thing" ', in contrast to her husband's softness: ' "Reed pitied it; and he used to nurse it and notice it as if it had been his own" ' (*JE* 290). After Reed's death Mrs. Reed assumes the most negative patriarchal role, ruling

Gateshead as a tyrant, favouring her own children with proprietorial regard and indulging her male child shamelessly. Her fierce exclusiveness exposes a negative aspect to the strength of maternal love, a contraction of feeling in maternity.

Perhaps more telling still, there are indications in the novel of the heroine's unconscious rejection of motherhood, despite her girlhood attachment to her doll and the later solicitude toward Adèle. Her vague disturbance at the repeated dream of an infant—'this strange recurrence of one image' (*JE* 277)—becomes more focused in two dreams just before her wedding is due to take place. In the first Jane is 'burdened with the charge of a little child', her movements 'fettered'. Her primary concern is not the shivering, wailing infant, 'too young and feeble to walk', but the attempt to reach Rochester on the road ahead: ' "I strained every nerve to overtake you, and made effort on effort to utter your name and entreat you to stop" ' (*JE* 355). In the second dream Jane is once again forced to carry the child: ' "I might not lay it down anywhere, however tired were my arms—however much its weight impeded my progress" ' and hampered in her efforts to reach Rochester by its presence: ' "the child clung round my neck in terror, and almost strangled me." ' This time in bending forward to ' "take a last look" ', the child becomes a victim of her longing: ' "the wall crumbled; I was shaken; the child rolled from my knee" ' (*JE* 357). The dream may be seen partly as a rejection of her young 'charge', and hence of her social status as a governess, but it also represents a refusal to give priority to claims of dependence associated with maternal protectiveness. And the choice Jane makes for her lover in the dream is repeated in reality only shortly after when she takes leave of Adèle:

I remember Adèle clung to me as I left her: I remember I kissed her as I loosened her little hands from my neck; and I cried over her with strange emotion, and quitted her because I feared my sobs would break her still sound repose. She seemed the emblem of my past life; and he, I was now to array myself to meet, the dread, but adored, type of my unknown future day. (*JE* 361)

It also provides a parallel to the choice Miss Temple makes at Jane's expense when leaving her alone at Lowood:

But destiny, in the shape of the Rev. Mr. Nasmyth, came between me and Miss Temple: I saw her in her travelling dress step into a post-chaise, shortly after the marriage ceremony, I watched the chaise mount the hill and disappear beyond its brow; and then retired to my own room; and there spent in solitude the greatest part of the half-holiday granted in honour of the occasion. (*JE* 100)

All this stands in marked contrast to Gaskell who, as we have seen, gives precedence to the claims of the child before the lover, the maternal ahead of the conjugal.

In fact the difference goes deeper still, for unlike Gaskell whose images of motherhood suggest tenderness and well-being, the images to which Brontë returns are startling at times in their violation of a maternal norm or ideal. For example, when Jane suppresses the thought of being soon parted from Rochester, she speaks of 'strangl[ing] a newborn agony—a deformed thing which I could not persuade myself to own and rear' (*JE* 305). And similarly in refusing to affix labels bearing her married name to her trunks, she claims: 'Mrs. Rochester! She did not exist: she would not be born till tomorrow, some time after eight o'clock a.m.; and I would wait to be assured she had come into the world alive, before I assigned to her all that property' (*JE* 347).

In the end the need for love that plagues Jane—'if others don't love me, I would rather die than live' (*JE* 80)—is satisfied, not by the mother figures in her life, but by Rochester. As foreshadowed in Jane's dreams, it is a choice for the male—that is, for specifically masculine qualities of strength and potency. Before Rochester appears at Thornfield, when Jane has only Mrs. Fairfax and Adèle for company, she feels restless with its stagnation and confinement: 'I did not like re-entering Thornfield . . . to slip again over my faculties the viewless fetters of an uniform and too still existence' (*JE* 141). With Rochester's advent comes an enlivening force: 'Thornfield Hall was a changed place. . . . It had a master; for my part I liked it better' (*JE* 144). Even though she rejoices in the company of Adèle and Mrs. Fairfax in the 'sense of mutual affection [that] seemed to surround us with a ring of golden peace' (*JE* 309), Jane looks beyond that ring, attributing its preservation to Rochester: 'I half ventured to hope that he would, even after his marriage, keep us together somewhere under the shelter of his protection, and not quite exiled from the sunshine of his presence' (*JE* 309).

Jane's quest is essentially to find a place to which she can belong. She has sought it in returning to Gateshead before Mrs. Reed's death, just as later she attempts to create it with her newly inherited wealth at Moor-House. But it is only with Rochester that she finds what she seeks, as she declares to him: '"wherever you are is my home,—my only home"' (*JE* 308). Well before Rochester has chosen her, Jane declares her kinship with him: 'I feel akin to him. . . . I have something in my brain and heart, in my blood and nerves, that assimilates me mentally to him. . . . I am of his kind' (*JE* 219).

In her acts of choice, then, Jane's primary allegiance is toward the male, and her final home in the isolation of Ferndean excludes all but passing engagement with her 'sisters', Mary and Diana. In a way Ferndean is reminiscent of precisely the monopoly Rochester fantasized in his plans to take her to caves on the moon. The importance of the female figures in Jane's pilgrimage is not devalued by the novel's ending, but Brontë's priorities are made clear. With Rochester Jane finds a totality in relationship hitherto lacking, even in the closest female friendships. Indeed, in a sense her relationship with Rochester incorporates all that has gone before—not simply the sexual attraction and energy of lovers, but the tenderness of a mother toward the victim of the Thornfield fire and the dependence of a child on the strength of her 'master'.

II

In *Shirley* Brontë created portraits of two of the women she most cherished—Emily Brontë as Shirley, and Mary Taylor as Rose Yorke.[4] Perhaps it is not surprising, then, that this novel, an act of friendship in its very composition, should stand as Brontë's most positive statement about the possibilities for friendship between women. In its exploration of the central relationship between Shirley and Caroline and of the tension between male and female spheres, and in its preoccupation with the problems confronting single women, this work represents Brontë's closest approach to an explicitly feminist novel. However, as we shall see, in the end the novel neither endorses the prospect of women living without men nor accepts the antagonism between genders as inevitable.

---

[4] Although Brontë wrote to Ellen Nussey disclaiming any close correspondence between her fictional characters in *Shirley* and persons in her life (*BL* III. 37), she also told Gaskell that 'the character of Shirley was meant for her sister Emily' (*GL* 249), and Mary Taylor acknowledged the accuracy of the representation of her character in the figure of Rose Yorke (*BL* III. 135). Furthermore, within the novel itself there are moments when the narrator intrudes with details that serve little purpose other than to verify the directness of the representation to reality, almost as a personal, coded offering to Mary Taylor. See, e.g., the 'magic mirror's' predictions for Rose's and Jessie's futures in Vol. I, Ch. IX, or the account of Jessie's burial in a 'heretic cemetery'—like Martha Taylor's in Belgium—in Vol. II, Ch. XII.

Such antagonism is nevertheless considered in some detail in the novel. Its opening scenes, for example, with the curates Malone, Sweeting, and Donne participating in a 'triangle of visits, which they keep up all the year through', set up lines of opposition between the sexes which are gradually explored and expanded.[5] Their company-keeping—'not friendship; for whenever they meet they quarrel' (*S* 10)—is an exclusively male affair, where women exist only on the periphery to attend to rude commands: ' "Cut it, woman," said [Malone]; and the "woman" cut it accordingly. Had she followed her inclinations, she would have cut the parson also' (*S* 11). More than a failure of manners, such behaviour is symptomatic of a more funda-mental disregard. So when Malone leaves his dinner and walks to Robert Moore's mill, he remains oblivious to his natural surround-ings which embody a female force or principle in this novel, as in *Jane Eyre*: '[He] was not a man given to close observation of Nature; her changes passed, for the most part, unnoticed by him' (*S* 24).

When Malone reaches the mill, he and Moore encourage each other in a display of self-congratulatory misogyny. Denying any plans for marriage, Moore exclaims, ' "On what grounds this gossip rests, God knows. I visit nowhere—I seek female society about as assiduously as you do, Mr. Malone" ' (*S* 29). Anticipating the character of Thornton in Gaskell's *North and South*, Moore 'love[s] his machinery' (*S* 39) and accords it first priority in his life. Thus Shirley later accuses him: ' "You would immolate me to that mill—your Moloch!" ' (*S* 608). So intent is Moore on avoiding 'female society' that he frequently cooks his meals alone at the mill and spends the night there with his foreman Joe Scott rather than return to the home he shares with his sister: ' "It is my fancy . . . to have every con-venience within myself, and not to be dependent on the feminity in the cottage for every mouthful I eat or every drop I drink" ' (*S* 32). Malone sees this separatism as 'proper order', a guarantee against being 'ruled by women' (*S* 32).

Moore's mill is not simply physically off limits to the women in his life. It is a place that is devoid of, and alien to, feminine principle. He and Malone meet—as others are soon to congregate—on a man's mission, the defence of the mill against possible attack from riotous mill-workers, and they take a male pleasure in the prospect of

---

[5] Charlotte Brontë, *Shirley*, Clarendon edn. (1849; rpt. Oxford: Oxford University Press, 1979), p. 9. All further references to this work appear in the text, abbreviated as *S*.

violence. While Malone 'never felt more in tune for a shindy in his life' (*S* 23), Moore awaits the arrival of the waggons bearing his new frames 'with a sense of warlike excitement' (*S* 38). That pleasure is contrasted with the women's reaction against violence, and the opposition is played out in a continuing conflict between Moore and the central female figures, Caroline and Shirley. For example, Caroline interrupts Moore's reading of *Coriolanus* with the objection: ' "you sympathize with that proud patrician who does not sympathize with his famished fellow-men, and insults them" ' (*S* 103), and she challenges Moore's harshness toward his workers with a protest which again foreshadows Margaret Hale's towards Thornton in *North and South*: ' "I cannot help thinking it unjust to include all poor working people under the general and insulting name of 'the mob,' and continually to think of them and treat them haughtily" ' (*S* 105). Similarly, once the riot has occurred Shirley's enquiry after 'the wounded' is mistakenly interpreted by Moore as applying to 'our side'. However, Shirley makes her sympathies and her disapproval overt in her clarification: ' "it was of your victims I was thinking when I inquired after the wounded" ' (*S* 406).

The men Shirley sees as 'victims', though, are not simply that. The frame-breakers also derive satisfaction from their violence: 'they would have had great pleasure in shooting either of the leaders [Moore and Helstone] from behind a wall: and the leaders knew this, and, the fact is, being both men of steely nerves and steady-beating hearts, were elate with the knowledge' (*S* 43). In light contrast to the masculine eagerness for violence, the march of the children on the day of the school-feast is a 'priest-led and woman-officered company', neither 'on combat bent, nor of foemen in search' (*S* 339). More seriously, although Shirley and Caroline are actually secretly present at the riot, they remain, significantly, on the outskirts of the violence, associated more with the peaceful natural world: ' "we stand alone with the friendly night, its mute stars, and these whispering trees, whose report our friends [the men fighting] will not come to gather" ' (*S* 585).

Brontë makes it clear that Caroline's and Shirley's dissociation from the action is the result of choice, not of incapacity or faint-heartedness. They have risked danger in coming to the mill to carry warning of the impending attack, and Caroline feels a strong impulse to intervene to protect Robert Moore. As the conflict commences and the 'fighting animal' is roused in the men involved, 'quite paramount above the rational being', Caroline and Shirley are themselves affected: 'Both the girls felt their faces glow and their pulses throb' (*S* 388). However, unlike the male participants, their excitement is tempered by the fact that 'they desired neither to deal or to receive blows' (*S* 388). Indeed, Shirley's earlier plan to distribute financial relief has been aimed at defusing class tension and hence avoiding confrontation: ' "it is not yet come to fighting. What I want to do is to *prevent* mischief" ' (*S* 301), and in 'the aftertaste of battle' she can genuinely lament, ' "This is what I wished to prevent" ' (*S* 389), as Moore and his company cannot. Similarly, when Shirley is presented with a gun on the night of the riot, her strength and courage are shown as judiciously balanced by her sense of the consequences of violence: ' "I should hate to [use] it . . . but I think I could do it, if goaded by certain exigencies which I can imagine" ' (*S* 376).

In comparison with the exclusively masculine world of the mill, the friendship between Caroline and Shirley is in its own way similarly exclusive, offering to each of the women what they cannot find elsewhere. A 'safe sense of equality' (*S* 250) exists between them and a degree of 'harmony' that surprises Shirley herself: ' "I have never in my whole life been able to talk to a young lady as I have talked to you this morning" ' (*S* 246). While Shirley is delighted to find 'her own way of thinking and talking . . . understood and responded to by this new acquaintance' (*S* 250), the friendship meets an even more important need for Caroline, offering relief from a world circumscribed by prohibitions. As a dutiful 'daughter' she has been condemned to a lonely and purposeless existence by her uncle's veto on visits to the cottage of Robert and Hortense Moore, imposed as a result of a political feud between the two men. As a 'lover feminine' she is helplessly passive in her relationship with Robert Moore: 'A lover masculine so disappointed can speak and urge explanation; a lover feminine can say nothing: if she did the result would be shame and anguish, inward remorse for self-treachery' (*S* 117). It is, then, at the point when Caroline feels that 'she must seek and find a change somehow, or her heart and head would fail under the pressure which strained them' (*S* 208) that Shirley enters her life and provides sisterly solace.

In the confidence of their friendship the two women entertain ideas of self-sufficiency. When, for example, Shirley proposes that they go on a picnic to Nunnwood forest (the name itself echoing the exclusiveness of their plans), she specifically proposes that she and Caroline go alone for, she protests, the 'presence of gentlemen' necessarily alters the occasion and dispels 'quietude' (*S* 239). Together they discuss the shortcomings of the males of their acquaintance and toy with the notion of remaining single: ' "if I were convinced that they are necessarily and universally different from us—fickle, soon petrifying, unsympathizing—I would never marry" ' (*S* 242). In fact their speculations on living without men are somewhat undercut by the fact that neither Caroline nor Shirley reveal to each other their secret love for Robert and Louis respectively. None the less their relationship is not presented simply as a negative retreat from heterosexual relationships, but as having a value unique to its especially female qualities:

'Shirley, I never had a sister—you never had a sister; but it flashes on me at this moment how sisters feel towards each other. Affection twined with their life, which no shocks of feeling can uproot, which little quarrels only trample an instant that it may spring more freshly when the pressure is removed; affection that no passion can ultimately outrival, with which even love itself cannot do more than compete in force and truth. Love hurts us so, Shirley: it is so tormenting . . . in affection is no pain and no fire, only sustenance and balm. I am supported and soothed when you—that is, *you only*—are near, Shirley.' (*S* 296)

Another important female bond is explored in the relationship between Caroline and her mother. Like Shirley, Mrs. Pryor enters Caroline's life at a crucial time and meets Caroline's need for love, which the males in her life have specifically failed to satisfy. Mr. Helstone is not suited 'either by nature or habits, to have the charge of a young girl' (*S* 87), and Robert Moore is equally oblivious to Caroline's needs, as he himself comes to realize: ' "[Mrs. Pryor] was faithful when I was false—was she not? I never came near your sick-bed, and she watched it ceaselessly" ' (*S* 734). Indeed, Mrs. Pryor's revelation that she is Caroline's mother proves the turning-point in the younger woman's illness, giving Caroline the will to live. She has long felt the 'mother-want' common to so many of the female characters of women writers, including, as we have seen, Jane Eyre: 'the deep, secret, anxious yearning to discover and know her mother strengthened daily' (*S* 208). Well before the reunion takes place, Caroline feels a bond toward her unknown mother based on a sense of shared injustice and ill-treatment at the hands of her father: ' "If my mother suffered what I suffered when I was with papa, she must have had a dreadful life" ' (*S* 115). Accordingly, with more than the speculative enthusiasm of Shirley, and with more cause, Mrs. Pryor acts as something of an apologist for single life, warning Caroline:

'Two people can never literally be as one: there is, perhaps, a possibility of content under peculiar circumstances, such as are seldom combined; but it is well not to run the risk: you may make fatal mistakes. Be satisfied, my dear: let all the single be satisfied with their freedom.' (*S* 427)

In keeping with Mrs. Pryor's wariness of heterosexual relationships, she offers Caroline an alternative, suggesting that they live together on her 'small independency' in 'a house of my own' (*S* 429). Although Mrs. Pryor's plan actually corresponds to the recurring wish of Caroline's childhood that her mother might appear and say, ' "Caroline, my child, I have a home for you; you shall live with me" ' (*S* 362), she does not, of course, avail herself of Mrs. Pryor's offer. Yet even at the end of the novel when she is united with Robert Moore, Caroline demonstrates a primary fidelity to her mother, declaring to Robert: ' "Tell me what you wish—what you would like—and I will consider if it is possible to consent; but I cannot desert her, even for you: I cannot break her heart, even for your sake" ' (*S* 734).

Thus, to a certain extent *Shirley* seems to point to an exclusiveness of male and of female relationships and to an antipathy between an industry-centred male world and a nature-centred female world. However, the novel does not rest with a simple diagnosis of opposition between the sexes. Rather it suggests that there is something lacking in any world—female no less than male—that deliberately excludes the otherness that might complement it. Furthermore, it challenges conventional, dichotomized sex roles, extending in the character of Shirley the sense of possibilities for the feminine, and questioning in a number of male characters the adequacy of the masculine, while seeking in all the ideal of an integrated whole.

Robert Moore, for example, is shown to develop from his early arrogance and disregard to a more compassionate, more identifiably 'feminine' understanding. By the end of the novel, after he has been humiliated by Shirley and in a sense exorcised of his male pride, Brontë suggests that Moore is a changed man: ' "Unless I am more considerate to ignorance, more forbearing to suffering than I have hitherto been, I shall scorn myself as grossly unjust" ' (*S* 616), and it is this change that enables him to trust the softer side of his character, the side which draws him to Caroline and which he has hitherto scorned as weakness.

Moore's conversion is, all the same, perhaps too contrived a device to weigh heavily in any argument for the novel's integration of male and female worlds. More tellingly, although the novel's central relationship, the friendship between Shirley and Caroline, may in its specialness and self-sufficiency be represented in some ways as a repudiation of heterosexual relationship, it is in some respects actually an imitation of it, like that 'rehearsal for the real' so approvingly described by Eliza Lynn Linton and Dinah Mulock.[6]

This is evident at the simplest level in the role-playing involved in the relationship, recalling the stronger/weaker dichotomy suggested in Mulock's *A Woman's Thoughts* or, indeed, in Gaskell's fictional pairs of sisters. From the outset Shirley is associated with masculine strength, as she says of herself: ' "They gave me a man's name; I hold a man's position: it is enough to inspire me with a touch of manhood" ' (*S* 224). She habitually refers to herself as 'Captain Keeldar',—for example on the occasion when she entreats Caroline to come away with her to the Scottish Highlands, thereby giving the proposal an apparently heterosexual context: ' "However, when Captain Keeldar is made comfortable, accommodated with all he wants, including a sensible genial comrade, it gives him a thorough pleasure to devote his spare efforts to making that comrade happy. And should we not be happy, Caroline, in the Highlands?" ' (*S* 274). On the night of the attack on the mill the protection of Caroline falls to Shirley, a role assigned to her by Caroline's uncle, Mr. Helstone. It is very much as an honorary male that Shirley is enlisted to help and Helstone bestows upon her the 'great compliment' of lending her his guns. Shirley is perfectly aware of the nature of the transaction, and insists on making explicit what Helstone is inclined to obscure: ' "Now . . . you want me as a gentleman—the first gentleman in Briarfield, in short, to supply your place, be master of the Rectory, and guardian of your niece and maids while you are away" ' (*S* 374), just as she is quite clear about the precariousness of her honorary status: ' "They won't trust me . . . that is always the way when it comes to the point" ' (*S* 352).

As the evening of the attack progresses, Shirley continues to play out a male role, bearing arms, leading the run to the mill, offering to carry Caroline across the treacherous plank over the river, and finally

---

[6] See Chapter 1, p. 16.

'authoritatively' restraining Caroline from rushing down to the mill. Caroline for her part is characteristically 'more timid', deriving confidence from Shirley's strength on the night of the riot, for example, or again in fulfilment of her duties at the school feast: 'this year Shirley was to be with her, and that changed the aspect of the trial singularly . . . it would be enough to give one courage only to look at her' (*S* 329).

Beyond the role-playing within the relationship, the dynamics and intensity of Caroline's and Shirley's interaction owe something to a heterosexual norm. There is an air of courtship about their early exchanges, as when Shirley lays a bouquet in Caroline's lap and stands regarding her 'with something of the aspect of a grave but gallant little cavalier', a 'temporary expression of face . . . aided by the style in which she wore her hair' (*S* 223). Again, Shirley takes on the aspect of a lover when she stands apart observing Caroline at the school-feast festivities: ' "I like to watch those I love in a crowd, and to compare them with others: I have thus compared you. You resemble none of the rest, Lina" ' (*S* 351).

It is logical, therefore, that Shirley sees Robert Moore as her rival, albeit half-comically: ' "I feel disposed to call him out, if I could only get a trustworthy second: I feel desperately irritated" ' (*S* 294). Much of the energy of Shirley's banter with Caroline stems from her teasing about Caroline's attachment to Moore. Even so, there is a certain earnestness in the contest for a place in Caroline's affections and an edge of truth in her accusations: ' "He keeps intruding between you and me: without him we should be good friends. . . . If we were but left unmolested, I have that regard for you that I could bear you in my presence for ever. . . . You cannot say as much respecting me" ' (*S* 295).

At the same time, Shirley is paradoxically as much Moore's agent as his rival. Not only does she facilitate various meetings of Caroline and Robert, and keep the possibility of a relationship with Moore before Caroline's imagination, she actually substitutes for Moore in a way that gives fundamental significance to the notion of 'rehearsal for the real'. Shirley is the figure through whom Caroline's love is in time transferred to Robert, in a way reminiscent of *Twelfth Night* where Olivia learns to love in Viola qualities that she will love in Sebastian with the resolution of the fifth act. Just as Olivia has the freedom to express and develop that love in the artificial or preliminary interaction of the earlier acts with Viola, similar dynamics are evident between Shirley and Caroline,—for example, when they discuss Shirley's plan to quieten the unrest by relieving the hardships of the working class:

'If once the poor gather and rise in the form of the mob, I shall turn against them as an aristocrat: if they bully me, I must defy; if they attack, I must resist,—and I will.'

'You talk like Robert.'

'I feel like Robert, only more fierily. Let them meddle with Robert, or Robert's mill, or Robert's interests, and I shall hate them. At present I am no patrician, nor do I regard the poor round me as plebeians; but if once they violently wrong me or mine, and then presume to dictate to us, I shall quite forget pity for their wretchedness and respect for their poverty, in scorn of their ignorance and wrath at their insolence.'

'Shirley—how your eyes flash!'

'Because my soul burns. Would you, any more than me, let Robert be borne down by numbers?'

'If I had your power to aid Robert, I would use it as you mean to use it. If I could be such a friend to him as you can be, I would stand by him as you mean to stand by him—till death.'

'And now, Lina, though your eyes don't flash, they glow. You drop your lids; but I saw a kindled spark.' (*S* 300)

With time Shirley overtly aids the transference of Caroline's affection to Robert, challenging her to acknowledge the strength of her feelings: ' "Cary, let me give your fidelity a motive: we are going for Moore's sake. . . . You would die blindly and meekly for me, but you would intelligently and gladly die for Moore" ' (*S* 381).

Any effort to see Shirley's and Caroline's relationship as broadly representative of an alternative for women without men is further challenged by the simple fact that Shirley does not generally like women. In this sense the very uniqueness of her relationship with Caroline cuts two ways: it is at once an indication of its value and a barrier to extrapolating from it to make generalizations about female capacities for friendship. It is not that Shirley dissociates herself from the world of women. If anything, she has a dutiful sense of herself as representative of her sex. Part of her anger at Robert Moore's proposal of marriage, for example, is derived from Shirley's sense of the contempt it implies: ' "you have the worst opinion of me . . . that I am a traitor to all my sisters: that I have acted as no woman can act, without degrading herself and her sex" ' (*S* 609). And Shirley's sense of responsibility finds practical expression in the will she makes favouring the Sympson sisters at their brother Henry's expense: ' "your sisters will have nothing, so I have left them some money: though I do not love them, both together, half so much as I love one lock of your fair hair" ' (*S* 568). None the less it remains true that

Shirley 'liked the society of few ladies: indeed she had a cordial pleasure in that of none except Mrs. Pryor and Caroline Helstone' (*S* 562).

As we have seen, both Mrs. Pryor and Shirley sound cautionary notes on the sober realities of the married state, which are reinforced by the various histories of mismatched couples—the Yorkes, the Helstones, and the Pryors. Brontë's own sense of a woman's right to refuse marriage finds focus in Shirley who declines no less than six proposals of marriage before accepting Louis Moore's, and her bitterest fight with her uncle arises from her denial of his assumed right to dispose of her, as one more piece of property, in marriage: ' "What, in the name of common law and common sense, would you, or could you do, if my pleasure led me to a choice you disapproved?" ' (*S* 533). Mr. Sympson entirely misunderstands the nature of that 'choice', for to him the alternatives lie in simple opposition: ' "Is it your intention ever to marry, or do you prefer celibacy?" ' (*S* 532). However, the novel demonstrates that a decision to remain single may be at once a most principled and painful choice—' "I *can* live alone, if need be" ' (*S* 580)—one which Caroline and Shirley face with grim resolve, and which has nothing to do with a positive preference for celibacy.

Indeed, Brontë's whole treatment of the unmarried women in *Shirley* further qualifies any apparent repudiation of heterosexual relationships in favour of Shirley's retreat with Caroline to Nunnwood forest or the Highlands, or Mrs. Pryor's plan to set up house with Caroline. The combination of willed, self-conscious sympathy and instinctive distaste evident in Brontë's letters on the subject of single women is present too in the novel. On the one hand, through Caroline's acquaintance with the old maids of the district, Miss Mann and Miss Ainley, Brontë exposes the injustice of the neglect and scorn these women suffer. In this Robert Moore is the chief offender, making Miss Mann a figure of fun: 'he had amused himself with comparing fair youth—delicate and attractive—with shrivelled eld, livid and loveless, and in jestingly repeating to a smiling girl the vinegar discourse of a cankered old maid' (*S* 197). But it is more generally a masculine failing: 'all the neighbourhood—at least all the female neighbourhood—knew something [of Miss Ainley's kindness]: no one spoke against Miss Ainley except lively young gentlemen, and inconsiderate old ones, who declared her hideous' (*S* 203), and Fanny succinctly diagnoses its cause: ' "gentlemen think only of ladies' looks" ' (*S* 196). Caroline, predictably, sees beyond the surface of appearances: 'Miss Mann's goblin-grimness scarcely went deeper than the angel-sweetness of hundreds of beauties' (*S* 199) and is sympathetically struck by the 'loneliness of her condition' (*S* 200).

On the other hand, in marked contrast with Gaskell, Brontë in her prose reveals an attitude which is less scrupulously fair than that of her heroine, less staunchly able to conceive of women living without men, and yet remaining unscarred by their singleness. To begin with, Brontë falls into the trap of her own definitions. When Caroline protests: ' "How wrong it is to neglect people because they are not pretty, and young, and merry" ' (*S* 196), the description of unmarried women is by implication established—those who are not pretty, not young, and not merry. And for all that fault is found with Robert Moore for 'hat[ing] ugliness', the novel gives the overwhelming impression that singleness is the price the old maids pay for their ugliness, and that the obsession with appearance is the author's:

In her first youth she must have been ugly; now, at the age of fifty, she was *very* ugly. At first sight, all but peculiarly well-disciplined minds were apt to turn from her with annoyance; to conceive against her a prejudice, simply on the ground of her unattractive look. Then she was prim in dress and manner: she looked, and spoke, and moved the complete old maid. (*S* 202)

When Caroline compares Miss Ainley to nuns 'with their close cell, their iron lamp, their robe strait as a shroud, their bed narrow as a coffin' (*S* 440), celibacy becomes merged with sterility. Indeed, there is something life-denying about *Shirley's* old maids. Miss Mann makes it an aim in life 'to avoid excitement' (*S* 198), and is antagonized by Caroline's 'white dress and lively look . . . the everyday garb of brown stuff or gray gingham, and the everyday air of melancholy, suited the solitary spinster better' (*S* 350). And although Caroline rejects the notion that the spinster's virtue lies in the 'abnegation of self' in a life of service to others, and Brontë makes a passionate plea for 'better chances of interesting and profitable occupation' for single women (*S* 441), the result of Caroline's association with Miss Ainley and Miss Mann is, in effect, to undertake an apprenticeship in the very self-denial she has rejected:

To do her justice she executed her plans conscientiously, perseveringly. It was very hard work at first—it was even hard work to the end, but it helped her to stem and keep down anguish: it forced her to be employed; it forbade her to brood; and gleams of satisfaction chequered her gray life here and there when she found she had done good, imparted pleasure, or allayed suffering.(*S* 205)

However, between the extremes of confirmed bachelor and old maids Brontë investigates a further alternative—a more integrated, less dichotomized conception of sex roles. As we have seen, Shirley embodies strengths usually identified as masculine. Conversely, certain male characters in the novel demonstrate a capacity for motherly gentleness. For example, Shirley's and Caroline's fantasizing about their mothers—Shirley's 'Titan visions' of a 'mighty and mystical parent' and Caroline's 'filial hopes' of a 'gentle human form'—is interrupted, and in some sense challenged, by the appearance of William Farren, bearing a crying infant in his arms: 'the man sat down with him, dandling him on his knee as tenderly as any woman; the two little girls took their places one on each side' (S 363). Similarly the portrait of Louis Moore further demonstrates that nurturing tenderness is not the exclusive domain of women: ' "I have long since earned her undying mother's gratitude by my devotion to her boy: in some of Henry's ailments I have nursed him—better, she said, than any woman could nurse: she will never forget that" ' (S 718).

Indeed Farren and Louis Moore show more capacity for tenderness than the women who tend Caroline. Hortense Moore, Caroline's cousin and teacher, fails to provide the love Caroline craves, disclaiming feelings of fondness toward her pupil: ' "I am not one who is prone to take violent fancies" ' (S 77). Even Mrs. Pryor, Caroline's natural mother, is reserved: 'Nothing could be less demonstrative than the friendship of the elder lady' (S 249) and only gradually relaxes under Caroline's influence from her 'shy, freezing, ungenial' manner (S 503), suggesting the learned, rather than innate, nature of her role toward her daughter.

Caroline's claim that mothers love their children ' "almost better than they love themselves" ' (S 454) is effectively dismissed by Mrs. Yorke as sentimental nonsense, and in a sense there is no one more qualified than Mrs. Yorke to dispel the mystique of motherhood—qualified, that is, by virtue of her own resounding failure as a mother. Within the Yorke household the children hold their mother in mutinous contempt, and for her part Mrs. Yorke loves only the baby of her six children because of its total dependence upon her and sees her children as her emotional rivals: 'it was not in their mother's nature to bear to see any living thing caressed but herself' (S 678). In a way reminiscent of the negative maternal imagery of *Jane Eyre* Brontë underscores Mrs. Yorke's attack on the mystique of motherhood by describing her as 'as much disposed to gore as any vicious "mother of the herd" ' (*S* 456).

The ending of the novel with the pairing of Caroline and Robert, and Shirley and Louis, confirms the general movement towards a more androgynous sense of sex-roles. The sudden and unlikely appearance of Robert's double in the figure of his brother Louis allows for a comedy-like resolution, again reminiscent of *Twelfth Night*, in which the partners complement each other in a balance of strength and gentleness, enthusiasm and composure. This desired wholeness is highlighted by Brontë's continual play on the duality of roles for each partner, which provides in some ways a more complex integration of facets of equality than the starker, more symbolic blinding of Rochester at the end of *Jane Eyre*. So in this novel Shirley acknowledges Louis as her 'master', while he identifies her as his 'sovereign'. His ostensibly subservient position as an employee in Shirley's house is modified by the reversal of power relations in their teacher–student interaction, and when Louis finally becomes the master of Fieldhead, he ' "would never have learned to rule, if she had not ceased to govern" ' (*S* 592). Similarly, Robert's characteristic authority is tempered by his financial ruin, once more like Gaskell's Mr. Thornton, and by his time of illness during which Caroline is forced to take the initiative with unaccustomed daring in order to arrange their meetings. In all, Brontë suggests the completeness of the bond where feminine and masculine are integrated rather than opposed, and she does so through a narrative voice which, in a departure from *The Professor* and *Jane Eyre*, is not identified as belonging to either gender and thus embodies in a sense the integration it relates.

III

Brontë's last novel, *Villette*, offers her most specific consideration of a community of women. In Chapter 3, when discussing Gaskell's community of women in *Cranford*, I considered the short story, 'Mr. Harrison's Confession', which anticipated the novel, noting that one of the most important changes in the development from the story to the novel was the change in gender of the narrator from male to female. The effect, I argued, was to forsake the simple comic opportunities offered by the presentation of Mr. Harrison as an alien in Duncombe, besieged by pursuing women, in favour of a gentler irony and deeper understanding offered by *Cranford*'s narrator, Mary Smith, who as a woman is safely accepted into Cranford's 'Eleusinian circle'. Brontë's fiction offers a similar opportunity for a comparison of the two female communities of Mdlle. Reuter's and Madame Beck's schools in the reworking of her male-narrated *The Professor* as Lucy Snowe's tale in *Villette*. In Brontë's case, of course, the comparison is significantly different because the first work is the product of a young artist, while *Villette* is written with the maturity of a career's end, and so the contrast involves a good deal more than the more clear-cut case of rewriting in Gaskell.[7] None the less much can still be learned from the altered perspective of *Villette* to enlighten a consideration of Brontë's depiction of women's friendship and community.

As in 'Mr. Harrison's Confessions', the simplest result of the male perspective in *The Professor* is that every observation and interaction with the female community is in some way coloured by the sexual potential of heterosexual relations. So, for example, there is a marked tendency not merely to observe but to analyse and assess the physical appearance of the female inhabitants of Mdlle. Reuter's school, as when M. Pelet encourages Crimsworth to anatomize Zoraïde Reuter's looks:

'In what does she not suit you, William? She is personally agreeable, is she not?'

'Very; her hair and complexion are just what I admire, and her turn of form, though quite Belgian, is full of grace.'

'Bravo! and her face? her features? How do you like them?'

'A little harsh, especially her mouth.'

'Ah, yes! her mouth,' said M. Pelet, and he chuckled inwardly. 'There is character about her mouth—firmness—but she has a very pleasant smile; don't you think so?'

'Rather crafty.'

'True, but that expression of craft is owing to her eyebrows; have you remarked her eyebrows?'[8]

---

[7] It would be a mistake, all the same, to discount *The Professor* as mere *juvenilia*. Brontë herself remained convinced of the merits of the novel. Although she wrote comically of it as her 'idiot child' after its nine rejections by publishers (*BL* III. 206) and regarded the beginning as 'very feeble', she considered the 'middle and later portion of the work, all that related to Brussels, the Belgian school etc. . . . as good as I can write: it contains more pith, more substance, more reality, in my judgement than much of "Jane Eyre"' (*BL* II. 161).

[8] Charlotte Brontë, *The Professor* (London: Smith, Elder & Co., 1857), I. 182. All further references to this work appear in the text, abbreviated as *P.*

In further questioning Crimsworth on the appearance of his new female pupils Pelet plays upon the sexual component latent in the classroom confrontation: 'my principal was endeavouring . . . to excite ideas and wishes in my mind alien to what was right and honourable' (*P* I. 188). Crimsworth perceives a 'precocious impurity' in his pupils, and the sketches he offers are charged with a peculiarly physical distaste: '[Aurelia's] outward dress, as I have said, is well attended to, but in passing behind her bench, I have remarked that her neck is gray for want of washing, and her hair, so glossy with gum and grease, is not such as one feels tempted to pass the hand over, much less to run the fingers through' (*P* I. 195).

However, in contrast with Gaskell's style, the change to a female narrator in *Villette* does not result in a more sympathetic, less clinical view. The distaste is scarcely tempered in *Villette* where Lucy Snowe's reaction to the 'swinish multitude' is very much akin to Crimsworth's. One marked difference, though, is that in *Villette* the 'objective' analyses swapped by Crimsworth and Pelet are turned by Lucy against herself in her fixation with her own reflection in mirrors. For example, in the glass at Miss Marchmont's Lucy sees 'a faded, hollow-eyed vision', suffering from a 'blight' which was 'chiefly external'.[9] Later she allows Ginevra to gratify herself by comparing their reflections in the dressing-room looking-glass, and in the great mirror at the opera she sees herself 'as others see me. No need to dwell on the result. It brought a jar of discord, a pang of regret; it was not flattering, yet, after all, I ought to be thankful: it might have been worse' (*V* II. 91). Yet, allowing for the difference of Lucy's self-scrutiny, the general feeling in both novels is of Brontë's obsession with physical appearances, mentioned earlier in relation to *Shirley*, fuelled by a characteristic xenophobia which leads her in *The Professor*, for example, to speculate on 'that deformity of person, and imbecility of intellect, whose frequency in the Low Countries would seem to furnish proof that the climate is such as to induce degeneracy of the human mind and body' (*P* I. 199).

In both novels too there is a strong feeling of that 'contagion' in communities, considered in Chapter 1, which was seen as a consequence of close female association.[10] Deceit and self-interest are the ruling passions in both schools, 'back-biting and tale-bearing . . .

---

[9] Charlotte Brontë, *Villette* (London: Smith, Elder & Co., 1853), I. 65. All further references to this work appear in the text, abbreviated as *V*.

[10] See Chapter 1 above, pp. 20–1.

universal' (*P* I. 192), and in each novel communality seems to generate a pack-mentality. Both classes seek to defy the authority of their teachers and to humiliate them. Yet they are so fickle that when Lucy Snowe quashes the 'growing revolt of sixty against one' by pushing the trouble-maker, Dolores, into a closet, the girls readily take pleasure from 'the act of summary justice' (*V* I. 154).

Although Crimsworth is an outsider to the 'sanctum sanctorum' (*P* I. 160) simply by virtue of his sex, Lucy is also an outsider in crucial ways, divided from the members of the school community by her religion, nationality, and language. Indeed, in many ways Lucy is more desperately lonely in the female community of Villette than in the confinement of two rooms shared with Miss Marchmont.

The change of gender in the narrator, then, might not seem to have brought about an immediately more sympathetic view of women and of female communities. However, it does result in a more funda-mental change and development between the two works. Gaskell had complained of the Brontës' aspirations toward male 'objectivity': 'They did everything they knew how to do in order to throw the colour of masculinity into their writing. They were spiritually sincere, but on account of this desire to appear male, technically false. It makes their writing squint',[11] and perhaps Brontë recognized something of that herself when she described the beginning of *The Professor*—the elaborate attempt to establish Crimsworth's origins, the most purely fictional and furthest removed from the autobiographical intensity of the Belgium section—as 'very feeble' (*BL* II. 161) or when she con-fessed:

In delineating male characters I labour under disadvantages: intuition and theory will not always adequately supply the place of observation and experi-ence. When I write about women I am sure of my ground—in the other case, I am not so sure. (*BL* II. 312).

In any case, by dropping the artifice of a male narrator in *Villette* Brontë tapped far deeper recesses of her imagination, offering a pro-found understanding of the powerlessness that pertains specifically to the female sex. This understanding in the second novel emerges in a sense of threat so far-reaching that the heroine's primary energy is directed not toward communality, or even mutuality, but toward self-preservation and self-containment.

[11] Elizabeth Gaskell quoted in Lynn Sukenick, 'On Women and Fiction', *The Authority of Experience: Essays in Feminist Criticism*, eds. A. Diamond and L. R. Edwards (Amherst: University of Massachussetts Press, 1977), p. 31.

Despite similarities between the narrators—their passive personalities, their status as orphans, alone and in need of employment—Crimsworth is never as vulnerable in *The Professor* as Lucy Snowe is in *Villette*. In the opening chapters of *The Professor* Crimsworth is, in some minimal sense at least, the master of his fate. He takes a stand against his uncles' plan for him to join the Church and is therefore compelled to find employment, unlike Lucy who takes a position only when 'there remained no possibility of dependence on others' (*V* I. 63). Crimsworth is safeguarded from any emotional dependence superadded to the humiliation of his servile position as the employee of his brother by his feelings of natural antipathy towards Edward. Lucy, in contrast, is pathetically grateful for her 'little morsel of human affection' and sees Miss Marchmont as 'rather like an irascible mother' (*V* I. 66). Crimsworth's detachment allows him a degree of freedom. Since confinement so often corresponds in Brontë's work to oppression, it is significant that Crimsworth takes frequent long walks in the country, whereas Lucy's world shrinks to the two rooms she occupies with the crippled Miss Marchmont: 'All within me became narrowed to my lot. Tame and still by habit, disciplined by destiny, I demanded no walks in the fresh air; my appetite needed no more than the tiny messes served for the invalid' (*V* I. 67).

In the journey to Belgium the difference of gender is strongly registered. At every point the female narrator stresses the cost of various undertakings, scrupulously accounting for all expenditure. Her extreme anxiety makes it clear how uneasy is her relation to the power and confidence that money bestows, and that lack of power is evident to those who attend to her:

How could inn-servants and ship-stewardesses everywhere tell at a glance that I, for instance, was an individual of no social significance and little burdened by cash? They *did* know it, evidently: I saw quite well that they all, in a moment's calculation, estimated me at about the same fractional value. (*V* I. 110)

Lucy is cheated by the boatman because as a woman she is easily taken advantage of, and similarly as a woman she is helpless in the matter of her lost trunk and dogged by fear as she walks alone through the dark streets of Villette. While Lucy chances upon Madame Beck's doorstep as a hapless victim of fate, Crimsworth is spared such vagaries by his letter of introduction from Hunsden to a distinguished Belgian resident, confident of the formalities of his male world. The contrast is clearly illustrated by the spirit in which each

takes breakfast on the morning after arriving on the Continent.
Crimsworth is exhilarated by the grandeur of the 'public room' in
which he takes his morning meal and 'lingered over my breakfast as
long as I could; while it was there on the table, and while the stranger
continued talking to me, I was a free, independent traveller' (*P* I.
110). Lucy, in contrast, feels uncomfortable because 'all present were
men' and because she is not familiar with the codes of this world:

> It cannot be denied that on entering this room I trembled somewhat; felt
> uncertain, solitary, wretched; wished to Heaven I knew whether I was doing
> right or wrong; felt convinced that it was the last, but could not help myself.
> Acting in the spirit and with the calm of a fatalist, I sat down at a small table,
> to which a waiter presently brought me some breakfast; and I partook of that
> meal in a frame of mind not greatly calculated to favour digestion. (*V* I. 111)

In one simple way Crimsworth's ordeal is more easily faced because,
unlike Lucy, he speaks French. However, this fact has a figurative
import as well, for in the reworking of the novel Brontë's female
narrator is truly an alien without purchase on her new world—unable
to speak its language.

Up to this point in each novel the contrast is marked enough. However the most important differences are explored in the contrast of the
roles each assumes within the school community. In the broadest
terms, it emerges that Crimsworth acts as an agent and Lucy is acted
upon as a victim, and this fundamental distinction shapes the widely
diverging course of each novel.

Ostensibly the earlier roles are now reversed, with Crimsworth, as
a male, becoming the outsider. Certainly, he is shut out in some
ways, as exemplified by the boarded window of his bedroom, which
forbids a view of the garden of Mdlle. Reuter's school. But the
voyeurism this inspires—'the first thing I did was . . . to find some
chink or crevice which I might enlarge, and so get a peep at the consecrated ground' (*P* I. 125)—identifies him with the powerful figures
in the school, with those who place themselves in a position to
manipulate and anticipate events by a systematic surveillance and
invasion of privacy. It is only a short while in any case until he is
admitted into the 'sanctum sanctorum' and has triumphed over his
token exclusion: 'as I glanced at the boarded window [I thought], "I
shall now at least see the mysterious garden: I shall gaze both on the
angels and their Eden" ' (*P* I. 146).

Within Mdlle. Reuter's school Crimsworth enjoys the power of the
male in sexual interactions. After the initial playfulness in the first

interview with Mdlle. Reuter, relations between the directress and the narrator become 'a regular drawn battle' with Mdlle. Reuter 'hoping in the end to find some chink, some niche, where she could put in her little firm foot and stand upon my neck—mistress of my nature' (*P* I. 174). However, Crimsworth has the power to rebuff the advances Mdlle. Reuter dare not make explicit, and by his 'hardness and indifference' elicits a 'slavish homage' from the directress, his employer. Similarly, the initiative is entirely his in his relationship with Frances Henri. He enjoys a double power over his lover, that of male and teacher—just as Lucy's is to be a double dependence, as female and pupil. Crimsworth flaunts his power in their first encounter, when he perceives that Frances is unable to keep pace with the class in dictation:

I would not help her, I went on relentless. She looked at me; her eye said most plainly, 'I cannot follow you.' I disregarded the appeal, and, carelessly leaning back in my chair, glancing from time to time with a *nonchalant* air out of the window, I dictated a little faster. (*P* I. 246)

The initiative continues to be his as he favours Frances with special attention, seeking her out for confidential interviews. While Mdlle. Reuter may wish to terminate the relationship, the means open to her are less threatening than those employed by Madame Beck against Lucy. Mdlle. Reuter withholds Frances's address from Crimsworth, but he never suffers infringements against his person as Lucy does when she is locked in on several occasions and drugged on the night of the fête.

In contrast, the very terms on which Lucy undertakes employment with Madame Beck are distinctly less advantageous than Crimsworth's corresponding position. Not by being invited, but by pleading for shelter, Lucy is taken on in the menial position of nursery governess to Madame Beck's children. From the very first night she is spied upon by the directress or by Madame Beck's 'staff of spies' (*V* I. 139). Her workbox is habitually searched, her conversations listened to, and her letters read. Even M. Paul maintains a surveillance from his room hired specifically as 'a post of observation': '"I watch you and the others pretty closely, pretty constantly, nearer and oftener than you or they think"' (*V* III. 82).

In the struggle with Madame Beck and her system Lucy's vulnerability within the community of Rue Fossette is further emphasized. While Crimsworth recognizes the nature of Mdlle. Reuter's game

from the outset, Lucy only gradually perceives the extent of Madame
Beck's duplicity, imagining at first that there 'never was a mistress
whose rule was milder' (*V* I. 136). And whereas Crimsworth's
masculinity counterbalances his position as an employee of Mdlle.
Reuter, Lucy is in a position of almost total subjection. Revealing her
own deeply internalized terms of reference, Lucy characterizes the
power of Madame Beck's position and personality as masculine:

At that instant, she did not wear a woman's aspect, but rather a man's.
Power of a particular kind strongly limned itself in all her traits, and that
power was not *my* kind of power: neither sympathy, nor congeniality, nor
submission, were emotions it awakened. I stood—not soothed, nor won, nor
overwhelmed. It seemed as if a challenge of strength between opposing gifts
was given, and I suddenly felt all the dishonour of my diffidence—all the
pusillanimity of my slackness to aspire. (*V* I. 148)

Madame Beck's domination even takes the form at times of physical
threat, as when she first locks Lucy in her chamber and then intervenes bodily to bar her way to M. Paul:

But Madame was before me; she had stepped out suddenly; she seemed to
magnify her proportions and amplify her drapery; she eclipsed me; I was hid.
She knew my weakness and deficiency, she could calculate the degree of
moral paralysis—the total defaults of self-assertion—with which, in a crisis, I
could be struck. (*V* III. 247)

Lucy is equally a victim of M. Paul. He, like Madame Beck, spies
on Lucy, and keeps her locked in—first in the attic, and then in the
school room as his 'half-worried prey' (*V* III. 72), where she becomes
faint with hunger and heat. Paul also holds emotional sway over Lucy
as she is susceptible to his veering moods, 'blindly reliant upon his indulgence' (*V* III. 50) and vulnerable to his 'most irritable nature',
which opposition 'might quickly render violent and implacable' (*V* I.
261).

In *The Professor* Crimsworth holds the initiative in his love relationship and can venture out to search the city for Frances. Indeed, the
sexually suggestive imagery describing their reunion underlines his
active masculine role. In a location reminiscent of Mdlle. Reuter's
garden, Crimsworth forges forward to take possession of his lover:

I approached, wondering to what house this well-protected garden apper-
tained; I turned the angle of the wall, thinking to see some stately residence; I
was close upon great iron gates; there was a hut serving for a lodge near, but I
had no occasion to apply for the key—the gates were open; I pushed one leaf

back, rain had rusted its hinges, for it groaned dolefully as they revolved. Thick planting embowered the entrance. (*P* II. 43)

In contrast, Lucy can only wait passively in the hope that Paul will not leave Belgium without finding a way to see her. One scene in particular forms a striking contrast to Crimsworth's reunion with Frances for the equally suggestive imagery encapsulates the reversal of sexual roles. As Lucy sits in the refectory attempting to compose herself, she discovers that she is not safe from M. Paul's interference: 'no corner was sacred from intrusion' (*V* II. 136). The window through which Paul first sees her is described as 'piercing . . . the wall' of her sanctuary, and he approaches despite the fact that 'No other professor would have dared to cross the carré, before the class-bell rang' (*V* II. 136). Lucy's response to his unwelcome entrance is pointedly characterized by Paul as that ' "of a she wild creature, new caught, untamed, viewing with a mixture of fire and fear the first entrance of the breaker-in" ' (*V* II. 137).

This reversal of the narrator's role from the aggressor in *The Professor* to the victim in *Villette* involves much more than a reworking or reorganization of the narrative structure. The vulnerability and powerlessness of Lucy Snowe affects the whole vision of *Villette* which becomes permeated by a sense of threat. The later novel explores an imagination besieged—full of the threat of violation and the vulnerability of an inner space, and as such the male 'squint' of *The Professor* gives way to a fundamentally female view in *Villette*.

The image of the garden is common to both novels, and as central to each work as the garden itself is to the schools. In each it is an inner, exclusively feminine region, mysterious and apparently sacred, like the 'garden inclosed' in the Song of Solomon. Mdlle. Reuter, for example, will not change her premises because she is unwilling to forsake the garden, to which she carefully regulates access. Similarly, only the 'privileged'—or the stealthy—are admitted to the garden of Rue Fossette. In both novels, too, the garden is vulnerable to invasion. In *The Professor* this may be only the sanctioned intrusion of Crimsworth, but in *Villette* the trespass is more dramatic, again reminiscent of the biblical image where notions of entrance and seduction are merged. Dr. John, for example, forces his way into the garden: 'It was sacrilege—the intrusion of a man into that spot, at that hour. . . . He wandered down the alleys, looking on this side and on that—he was lost in the shrubs, trampling flowers and breaking branches in his search—he penetrated at last the "forbidden walk" '

(*V* I. 219), and M. de Hamal, in his pursuit of Ginevra Fanshawe has frequently 'mount[ed] . . . the high wall' around the garden (*V* III. 308) and 'invaded the sanctity of this place' (*V* I. 242).

Common to both novels, this notion of a sacred inner space is, however, expanded beyond the single image of the garden in *Villette*, in ways that it is not in *The Professor*. So, for example, Lucy retreats to the school-room only to have Paul intrude: 'The closed door of the first classe—my sanctuary—offered no obstacle; it burst open' (*V* I. 259), as he does again later as the 'breaker-in'. Similarly Madame Beck stage-manages a tantalizingly incomplete entrance of young male spectators into the ballroom on the fête day. While the only men admitted into the ballroom itself are the fathers, Madame Beck keeps the young males at bay by 'a sort of cordon stretched before them', which she patrols like 'a dragon'. In this case the threat is not merely recognized, but manipulated for effect: 'the admission of these rattle-snakes, so fascinating and so dangerous, served to draw out madame precisely in her strongest character—that of a first-rate *surveillante* . . . their presence furnished a most piquant ingredient to the entertainment' (*V* I. 282). Again, invasion—and, implicitly, violation—is the 'mortal dread' of Lucy, when she is locked in the attic by M. Paul: 'here it began to grow dusk: the beetles were fading from my sight; I trembled lest they should steal on me a march, mount my throne unseen, and, unsuspected, invade my skirts' (*V* I. 266). Indeed, that sense of violation even extends to Paul's frequent, stealthy interference with Lucy's desk, imaged in strikingly physical, almost erotic, terms:

Now I knew, and had long known, that that hand of M. Emanuel's was on the most intimate terms with my desk; that it raised and lowered the lid, ransacked and arranged the contents, almost as familiarly as my own. . . . Now, as he sat bending over the desk, he was stirring up its contents; but with gentle and careful hand: disarranging indeed, but not harming. (*V* III. 41)

This repeated motif of a suggestively sexual threat is underscored throughout the novel by a pervasive usage of language suggesting violation. So Lucy is engrossed by Vashti's dramatic resistance to 'the rape of every faculty' (*V* II. 195), and she physically resists being attired as a man, insisting that 'things must not be forced upon [her]' (*V* I. 273). The idea of penetration is raised again and again. At times it is represented in a fairly simple, traditionally figurative way. Lucy seeks to 'penetrate the real truth' (*V* III. 290); M. Paul urges each young actress 'to penetrate herself well with a sense of her personal insignificance' (*V* I. 274); Paulina hides her letter until she can 'penetrate the seal' in private (*V* III. 104). But frequently such language, used both literally and figuratively, is more disturbing and threatening. So Dr. John 'penetrate[s] at last "the forbidden walk"' (*V* I. 219); M. Paul 'knock[s]' the script into the 'smooth round pates' of his students (*V* I. 253); in the storm which rouses Lucy's desire to escape her current existence the sky is 'pierced by white and blinding bolts', and Lucy quells her longings 'by driving a nail through their temples' (*V* I. 212); she suppresses her hostility to the 'lecture pieuse' by stabbing the desk with scissors, and fends Ginevra off by sticking her with a pin; and in the final confrontation with Madame Beck, Lucy feels 'her eye grazing me with its hard ray like a steel stylet' and cries out when 'pierce[d] deeper than I could endure' (*V* III. 321). In all, violence and violation remain a pervasive imaginative possibility.

Within this world women are not only made victims, but also make themselves so. The violence which was seen as combative in *Jane Eyre* becomes much more inwardly directed and masochistic in *Villette*. For example, in her slavish desire to serve Graham, the young Paulina lies at his feet: 'Once I saw Graham—wholly unconscious of her proximity—push her with his restless foot. She receded an inch or two. A minute after one little hand stole out from beneath her face, to which it had been pressed, and softly caressed the heedless foot' (*V* I. 54). In the service of her father, the other male in her life, Paulina hems a handkerchief:

> . . . at which she bored perseveringly with a needle, that in her fingers seemed almost a skewer, pricking herself ever and anon, marking the cambric with a track of minute red dots; occasionally starting when the perverse weapon— swerving from her control—inflicted a deeper stab than usual; but still silent, diligent, absorbed, *womanly*. (*V* I. 23, my italics)

Similarly the violence Lucy figuratively inflicts on herself with the nail driven into the temples of her desires is lingeringly and graphically described: 'they did not die: they were but transiently stunned, and at intervals would turn on the nail with a rebellious wrench; then did the temples bleed, and the brain thrill to its core' (*V* I. 212). The impulse finds actual expression later, when in sharpening her pens in front of M. Paul, Lucy deliberately cuts herself: 'I wanted to restore him to his natural state, to set him at his ease, to get him to chide' (*V* III. 191).

In Brontë the response to threat is not a bonding together of women, as one might expect to find in Gaskell, but a self-protective acquisition of power, which sees Lucy insulate herself against others in the progress from nursery governess, to teacher and finally to directress of her own school. Paradoxically, Lucy's masochism is essential to her developing assertion of power. It may seem a perverse imitation of those external factors that make Lucy a victim, but it is, too, *self*-inflicted and *self*-controlling. It is, above all, control that Lucy admires in Madame Beck, just as she recognizes that the lack of such control makes one vulnerable as Paulina is when she openly demonstrates affection for Graham: 'She ran the risk of incurring such a careless, impatient repulse' (*V* I. 49). And control over the self is the one forum for power that cannot be taken away, as Brontë recognizes earlier in *Jane Eyre*, where the young Jane, subject to the insuperable cruelty and oppression of the Reed household can plot, none the less, to starve herself.

Self-evidently, though, such power is dangerously partial. A more complete acquisition of power involves learning to play the game and then using the rules against others—males and females—in a way that at once protects and isolates the self. Lucy's initiation is a gradual process. Through much of the novel a natural passivity ensures that she is reliant upon others for the impetus to act. So Madame Beck goads her into teaching: ' "Will you . . . go backward or forward?" ' (*V* I. 148); M. Paul bullies her into acting in the play; Mrs. Bretton buys her the pink dress and coerces her into wearing it. However, once each of these steps is taken Lucy asserts possession of her new ground. As a teacher she exerts her control over the class, humiliating three of the trouble-makers and pushing a fourth into the closet, locking her in as others, more powerful than Lucy, are to keep her confined. As an actress Lucy experiences, albeit temporarily, a rush of 'right power' (*V* I. 275). In an assertion of her own ego, 'the crowd were nothing to [her]', and having 'accepted the part to please another: ere long, warming, becoming interested, taking courage, [she] acted to please [her]self' (*V* I. 277). That self-assertion has begun before the performance with her refusal to wear male costume, agreeing only to a token vest and collar: ' "but it must be arranged in my own way" ' (*V* I. 273), and it continues in the tormenting of Graham with her stage courtship of Ginevra.

Thus Lucy proves to be a dangerous protégée for Madame Beck, for once initiated into the ways of Rue Fossette, she learns to use them for her own ends. She does her own spying, observing Dr. John from behind an 'open door [which] served . . . as a screen' (*V* I. 198), and in much the same spirit of conspiracy and deceit which pervades the pensionnat, she disguises the tracks that Dr. John has left in his visit to the garden: 'I found a moment's leisure to efface [them] very early in the morning, ere common eyes had discovered them' (*V* I. 226). Likewise Lucy learns to lie, gratifying herself with an entirely false account of Dr. John's behaviour told to an unsuspecting Ginevra: 'There was pleasure in thinking of the contrast between the reality and my description' (*V* II. 148). The final rite of initiation comes with the confrontation with Madame Beck, 'the sole flash-eliciting, truth-extorting rencontre which ever occurred between me and Madame Beck' (*V* III. 254), a contest for which all that has gone before prepares her:

> Two minutes I stood over Madame, feeling that the whole woman was in my power, because in some moods, such as the present—in some stimulated states of perception, like that of this instant—her habitual disguise, her mask and her domino, were to me a mere network reticulated with holes; and I saw underneath a being heartless, self-indulgent, and ignoble. She quietly retreated from me; meek and self-possessed, though very uneasy, she said, 'If I would not be persuaded to take rest she must reluctantly leave me.' Which she did incontinent, perhaps even more glad to get away, than I was to see her vanish. (*V* III. 435)

It is a vital test for Lucy and one in which Madame Beck is unable to exert either her will or her rules, for Lucy has seen through, and hence mastered, the woman and her system.

In Lucy's progression toward her own dominion at Faubourg Clotilde the one figure who stands out as 'a marvellous sight: a mighty revelation' is the actress, Vashti:

> I had seen acting before, but never anything like this: never anything which astonished Hope and hushed Desire; which outstripped Impulse and paled Conception; which, instead of merely irritating imagination with the thought of what *might* be done, at the same time fevering the nerves because it was *not* done, disclosed power like a deep, swollen, winter river thundering in cataract, and bearing the soul, like a leaf, on the steep and steely sweep of its descent. (*V* II 192)

The interest of the figure is not simply that Vashti's rage is a projection of the release of Lucy's own repressed emotions, functioning as the 'maddened double' found in much nineteenth-century women's writing.[12] Beyond that, in the analysis Lucy offers of Vashti's emotional processes, she recognizes and identifies with an essential feature of her own habits of mind—the capacity to distance the contact and claims of the world outside herself by objectifying them (a talent reminiscent of Brontë's own 'second-hand' friendships discussed in Chapter 4):

I have said that she does not *resent* her grief. No; the weakness of that word would make it a lie. To her, what hurts becomes immediately embodied: she looks on it as a thing that can be attacked, carried down, torn in shreds. Scarcely a substance herself, she grapples to conflict with abstractions. Before calamity she is a tigress; she rends her woes, shivers them in convulsed abhorrence. Pain, for her, has no result in good; tears water no harvest of wisdom; on sickness, on death itself, she looks with the eye of a rebel. Wicked, perhaps, she is, but also she is strong. (*V* II. 190)[13]

The most revealing example of this capacity in Lucy, and its consequences in her life, is provided by Brontë's treatment of letters in the novel. When Lucy receives mail, it is the letter itself which is all important. Her response is to the physical object, 'firm, substantial, satisfying . . . a morsel of real solid joy' (*V* II. 151). She describes the 'post-hour' as 'her hour of torment' and longs for a letter as animals 'always on the verge of famine, await their food' (*V* II. 209). Later too she finds M. Paul's letters 'real food that nourished, living water that refreshed' (*V* III. 347). The true nature of Lucy's preoccupation, her obsession with the letter and not what it represents, is made explicit when she loses a letter, and refuses to be consoled either by the fact that she has already read it, or, more importantly, by the presence of Graham, its author, offering her the actual kindness and attention, of which the letter is only a token.

The explanation for Lucy's behaviour centres on the control that can be gained once the flux of experience has been rendered static in the object of the letter. In Lucy's mind the latter can stand for the former: '[there] came for me seven weeks as bare as seven sheets of blank paper: no word was written on one of them' (*V* II. 207). In the fixity of the letter the opposing impulses of Reason and Feeling can coexist, separated in the two replies she writes to Graham, without the inner turmoil of an urge to resolution. The actual process of writing is satisfyingly self-contained, for as has been pointed out

[12] Noted by Gilbert and Gubar, *The Madwoman in the Attic*, pp. 76–9.

[13] In a way parallel to her perception of Vashti as 'Scarcely a substance herself', Lucy repeatedly represents herself as a mere shadow.

about letter-writing generally 'it is possible to write oneself in and out of [a] passion, for which words are both a catalyst and a record.'[14] And in exactly the same kind of process that she admires in Vashti—looking on 'what hurts . . . as a thing'—Lucy seals her letters hermetically and buries them: 'I was not only going to hide a treasure—I meant also to bury a grief. That grief over which I had lately been weeping, as I wrapped it in its winding sheet, must be interred' (V II. 268).

Lucy's letters also give her control because they keep others at a distance—the letter's very existence is founded on the notion of distance, communication with those absent. In this way Lucy is not vulnerable to the vagaries of temper of M. Paul, or the fluctuations in attentiveness of Graham. She becomes mistress of her emotions—gratification is hers simply by reading her letters over, as she does many times. So too she can savour her pleasure without the pressure of another's response:

I opened a drawer, unlocked a box, and took out a case, and—having feasted my eyes with one more look, and approached the seal, with a mixture of awe and shame and delight, to my lips—I folded the untasted treasure, yet all fair and inviolate, in silver paper, committed it to a case, shut up box and drawer, reclosed, relocked the dormitory, and returned to class, feeling as if fairy tales were true and fairy gifts no dream. Strange, sweet insanity! And this letter, the source of my joy, I had not yet read: did not yet know the number of its lines. (V II. 153)

The letters offer Lucy an alternative reality—an improvement in the artifice which allows the possibility of 'making written language the medium of better utterance than faltering lips can achieve' (V II. 131). Through them she can continue relationships in her imagination, 'away from tarnishing actuality'.[15] This imaginative life with the distance and control it allows is, of course, part of an intensely private, almost solipsistic world. It is not surprising, then, that just as Graham's letter is more important than his presence, so too Lucy can live with equanimity with Paul's absence, given the 'real food' of his letters.

At a certain level it is difficult to separate this 'objectifying' capacity in the heroine from a similar tendency in Brontë's own imaginative process. Beyond the parallels one might draw between Brontë's per-

[14] See Ruth Perry, *Women, Letters and the Novel* (New York: AMS Press, 1980), p. 110.
[15] Ibid., p. 114.

sonal obsession with mail considered in Chapter 4 and Lucy Snowe's, this objectifying is most obvious in Brontë's writing in the characteristic habit of personification: 'That hag disappointment was greeting her with a grisly "All-hail" ' (*V* I. 201). It is also manifest in the creation of an insistently physical—frequently specifically spatial—conception of the psyche: the 'closet' marked 'Lucy's room' in Paul's heart, for example, or the repeated 'inner spaces'. The effect of such a conception is to give peculiar reality and power to psychological states, for when the descriptive terms of an external reality are equally applied to an internal state areas of correspondence and direct relation are made startlingly clear—confinement is readily understood as repression, intrusion is difficult to separate from notions of violation. When Madame Beck takes away Lucy's letters it is not simply an offence against her property, but more fundamentally against her self. In the terms which Brontë has created Madame Beck is stealing part of Lucy's self; or when Lucy seals her letters in a jar she is in a very real sense making herself emotionally and psychologically untouchable, as she has been physically untouchable throughout much of the novel.

In a sense that symbolic gesture is actually realized in Faubourg Clotilde. In *Villette* self-sufficiency for the heroine, which was passingly entertained in the idea of the Moor-House as a refuge for Jane Eyre and the Rivers sisters, and in the various plans of Mrs. Pryor and Shirley for retreat with Caroline, has become a reality. It is true that in many ways M. Paul is characteristic of the kind of appropriate male partner we might expect from Brontë, and that he is banished only at the end of the novel. We might be inclined to question, therefore, how seriously Lucy Snowe's lone status at the end of the novel is to be regarded. However, it is revealing that whereas the ending of *The Professor* has established an ideal of mutuality, in which Crimsworth and Frances run their separate schools and finally retire to familial bliss in the English countryside, that ideal is deliberately abandoned in *Villette*. In the context of Lucy Snowe's development throughout the novel this change is no mere perversity of Brontë's part. Lucy's acquisition of an isolating, insulating power and her preoccupation with self-preservation make the self-sufficiency of her world at Faubourg Clotilde, and the satisfaction she derives from it as 'the three happiest years of [her] life' (*V* III. 344), the logical culmination of her story. It does not represent a separatist triumph any more than a repudiation of the male, who is punitively condemned ·

to drown. Women have no more place in Lucy Snowe's world than men. In this final work of an essentially solitary artist the heroine's choice is for an 'empire over self', fundamentally antipathetic to mutuality and communality alike.[16]

[16] George Eliot, *The George Eliot Letters*, ed. Gordon S. Haight (London: Oxford University Press, 1954), II. 135.

6

George Eliot Surpassing her Sex

The Most Churlish of Celebrities

I

In many ways George Eliot was ideally placed to enjoy the fruits of participation in a literary community. Her move from the '*walled-in* world' of Coventry to London in January 1851, when at the age of thirty-one her career was still before her, opened up opportunities far exceeding any available to Brontë in her isolation at Haworth or even to Gaskell in the more sophisticated world of Manchester.[1] Furthermore, her residence in London at the home of the publisher John Chapman, a focus for a wide circle of 'liberals of all stripes . . . and a steady stream of literary people of every description', and her occupation as editor of the *Westminster Review* both contributed to the diversity and depth of her circle of acquaintances.[2] Thus, before she had begun to write fiction or attained personal celebrity, Eliot was exposed to a community to which Gaskell and Brontë only comparatively later earned access by their literary accomplishments.

Although Eliot's life was never lived in quite the 'mental greenhouse' that Mrs Oliphant jealously envisaged, Eliot was a freer agent than either Gaskell or Brontë since she was not bound in the same ways by family concerns.[3] Unlike Gaskell, Eliot had no children and when her father Robert Evans died in May 1849, she escaped the bondage of the dutiful daughter, under which Brontë laboured until her death. Increasingly, too, Eliot was liberated by literary earnings far in excess of those of her sister authors.

---

[1] George Eliot, *The George Eliot Letters*, ed. Gordon S. Haight (London: Oxford University Press, 1954), I. 71. All further references to this work appear in the text, abbreviated as *EL*.

[2] Gordon Haight, Introduction, *George Eliot Letters*, I. xliv.

[3] Margaret Oliphant, *Autobiography and Letters of Mrs. Oliphant*, ed. Mrs Harry Coghill (Edinburgh: Blackwood & Sons, 1899), p. 4.

II

In some respects, then, one might have expected that Eliot would provide the supreme example of a woman writer functioning within a literary community. With her passport to literary circles provided by proximity, acquaintance and, later, celebrity the opportunities for professional interaction with other women writers might seem limitless. Ironically, for the major part of her literary career Eliot dwelt in an isolation as extreme in some ways as Brontë's, living 'apart from the world, with no opportunity of observing the effect of books except through newspapers' (*EL* III. 23).

Eliot's isolation was due partly to social disapproval of her union with Lewes, which meant that women especially were unlikely visitors to her circle, as Charles Norton observed in January 1869:

She is not received in general society, and the women who visit her are either so émancipée as not to mind what the world says about them, or have no social position to maintain. Lewes dines out a good deal, and some of the men with whom he dines go without their wives to his house on Sundays. (*EL* V. 7)

Norton did not exaggerate the effect of Eliot's illicit union with Lewes, and disapproval of the woman was frequently inseparable from disapproval of the author. Her publishers William and John Blackwood worried about the disclosure of the true identity of the author of *Adam Bede*: 'The dropping of the incognito is the most serious part of the business and will, I feel satisfied, affect the circulation in families of any future work' (*EL* III. 221). Their anxiety seems justified for even in published 'critical' estimates the grounds for judgement were blurred. In 'George Eliot and Her Critics', for example, Charlotte Yonge refused to see Eliot's 'sin' as 'covered by the glory of her genius': 'George Eliot's practical disregard of moral obligations in her own case, *when they involved a sacrifice*, incapacitates her, in a very considerable degree from dogmatizing on "duty"—nay, more—reduces all talk of duty to a mockery.'[4] Similarly Eliza Lynn Linton wrote: 'though she did no other woman personal injustice, she did set an example of disobedience to public law which wrought more mischief than was counteracted by even the noblest exhortations to submit to the restraints of righteousness, however irksome they might be.'[5]

[4] Charlotte Yonge, 'George Eliot and Her Critics', *Monthly Packet*, Sept. 1885, p. 494.
[5] Eliza Lynn Linton, 'George Eliot', *Women Novelists of Queen Victoria's Reign*, p. 88.

In a sense George Lewes was not only a cause of Eliot's isolation, but the manager of it as well. So, for example, overnight visits from friends were forbidden as 'incompatible with the quiet prosecution of his work' (*EL* III. 31), and Lewes objected to Eliot's attendance at 'any public manifestation without him' on grounds which she considered just, 'since his absence could not be divined by outsiders' (*EL* IV. 413). He also censored Eliot's mail as he explained to her Coventry friend Sara Hennell: '[I] will tell you why I "mislaid" and suppressed that portion of your letter. I have always held that it is very injurious to an author to occupy himself with what others say about his works, for good or evil. . . . No one speaks about her books to her, but me; she sees no criticisms' (*EL* IV. 58).

Yet Eliot should not be seen simply as a victim in all this. She was well aware of Lewes's protectiveness, referring, for example, to the suppression of Sara Hennell's letter as one instance of 'magical disappearances . . . effected now and then by the sleight of hand of some spirit that doesn't rap' (*EL* IV. 60), and she was happy to depend upon his intervention as a buffer between herself and the world. She supported a conscious policy of keeping distant, finding it 'more necessary than ever to keep rigidly to my rule of paying no visits in or near London' (*EL* IV. 477). To Barbara Bodichon, who had assured Eliot that she was 'right to get rid of the world' (*EL* III. 107), Eliot explained: 'for myself I prefer excommunication. I have no earthly thing that I care for, to gain by being brought within the pale of people's personal attention, and I have many things to care for that I should lose—my freedom from petty worldly torments, commonly called pleasures' (*EL* III. 367).

This preference for 'excommunication' was more than a concern for industriousness and personal freedom. Temperamentally Eliot was akin to Charlotte Brontë in finding social obligations a torment: 'If the severest sense of fulfilling a duty could make one's parties pleasant, who so deserving as I? I turn my inward shudder into outward smiles, and talk fast with a sense of lead on my tongue' (*EL* IV. 178). Similarly she compared a crowd of women admirers in Berlin in 1870 to 'a flock of birds waiting each to have a peck' (*EL* V. 84), explaining that she was not ungrateful for their admiration: 'But the sick animal longs for quiet and darkness' (*EL* V. 86).

Ironically, rather than counteracting her social ostracism, George Eliot's success as a novelist isolated her still further. Whereas for Gaskell and Brontë celebrity brought new, important friendships—

not least with each other—the same was not generally true for Eliot. By the time celebrity began to outweigh social disapproval, Eliot's lot was already cast, and, as Virginia Woolf suggested, 'she lost the power to move on equal terms unnoted among her kind, and the loss for a novelist was serious.'[6]

Rather than too little too late, Eliot's eventual celebrity was daunting in its magnitude. Consequently other women writers could not approach Eliot on 'a level of sisterly equality', but inevitably found themselves pressed into 'passive and subordinate postures, listening and looking upwards'.[7] Eliza Lynn Linton, for example, acknowledged that Eliot stood 'head and shoulders above the best of the rest' and yet maintained that Eliot was 'almost oppressively great—almost too colossal in her supremacy'.[8] And Barbara Bodichon, a much more sympathetic observer, noted to Eliot after the extraordinary success of *Adam Bede*: 'Almost all women are jealous of you' (*EL* III. 103).

There was a certain inevitability about this, for Eliot's genius, no less than her success, was bound to inspire awe, especially among aspiring authors. In addition, though, Eliot's aloof disposition served to isolate her further, as Eliza Lynn Linton waspishly suggested:

But never for one instant did she forget her self-created Self—never did she throw aside the trappings or airs of the benign Sibyl. . . . She was so consciously 'George Eliot'—so interpenetrated head and heel, inside and out with the sense of her importance as the great novelist and profound thinker of her generation.[9]

Even allowing for Lynn Linton's personal antipathy toward Eliot, it is true that Eliot demonstrated that psychology of the exceptional individual which recognizes its own excellence and is therefore severe on others who fail to meet the highest standards, and this attitude directly affected the ways in which Eliot, as the foremost woman writer of the day, related to the female literary community.

Most immediately, such thinking made Eliot particularly exacting in her requirements of other women writers. She herself had a strong sense of vocation and saw one of the greatest deficiencies of 'feminine literature' as the failure to appreciate 'the sacredness of the writer's art'. In the face of the 'silliness' of many incompetent female novel-

---

[6] Virginia Woolf, 'George Eliot', *Times Literary Supplement*, 20 Nov. 1919, p. 657.

[7] Elaine Showalter, 'The Greening of Sister George', *Nineteenth Century Fiction*, Vol. 35, No. 3, p. 294.

[8] Linton, 'George Eliot', pp. 112 and 63.

[9] Eliza Lynn Linton, *My Literary Life* (London: Hodder & Stoughton, 1899), p. 99.

ists, Eliot felt that critical severity was a 'chivalrous duty': '. . . in depriving the mere fact of feminine authorship of any false prestige which may give it a delusive attraction, and in recommending women of mediocre faculties—as at least a negative service they can render their sex—to abstain from writing.'[10] Her general estimation of women's writing was witheringly low. With a few remarkable exceptions, she believed, the 'feminine literature' of England was 'made up of books which could have been better written by men', and the 'few women who write well are very far above the ordinary level of their sex.'[11] Similarly in her reviewing Eliot continually referred to a norm of inferiority. For example, Geraldine Jewsbury's *Constance Herbert*, 'if measured by the standard of ordinary feminine novelists . . . would perhaps seem excellent', whereas, if measured against Jewsbury's earlier works, it was evidently 'deficient'.[12] And Holme Lee's *Kathie Brand* was distinguished from 'the generality of women's novels by its absence of affectation, maudlin sentimentality, and dogmatic assertions on philosophical, political, and religious points.'[13] For Eliot the literary endeavour was too important to permit suffering fools gladly, for 'bad literature', she wrote in *Leaves from a Note-Book*, 'is spiritual gin.'[14]

Perhaps Eliot was justified in her assessment. However, it is more relevant for this study to question not so much the validity of her judgements as the effect her attitudes were likely to have on her interaction with other women writers. In this respect such sternness was inevitably forbidding and was further exacerbated by a certain scornfulness evident both in her correspondence and in her periodical writing. In the *Westminster Review* of April 1856, for example, Eliot contemplated the 'compensating advantages to the world' that would come from 'thin[ning] the ranks of the authoresses'.[15] Again, in her more famous and forthright statement, 'Silly Novels by Lady Novelists', Eliot characterized and dismissed with devastating satire the majority of women's writing: 'There seems to be a notion abroad among women, rather akin to the superstition that the speech and

[10] George Eliot, 'Silly Novels by Lady Novelists', *Westminster Review*, Oct. 1856, pp. 316–24.

[11] George Eliot, 'Woman in France: Madame de Sablé', *Westminster Review*, Oct. 1854, p. 448; Eliot, 'Silly Novels', p. 323.

[12] George Eliot, 'Belles Lettres', *Westminster Review*, July 1855, p. 294.

[13] George Eliot, 'Belles Lettres', *Westminster Review*, Jan. 1857, p. 320.

[14] George Eliot, 'Authorship', *Essays and Leaves from a Note-Book: The Works of George Eliot* (London: Vii :re & Co., n.d.), XXI. 291.

[15] George Eliot, 'Art and Belles Lettres', *Westminster Review*, Apr. 1856, p. 643.

actions of idiots are inspired, and that the human being most exhausted of common sense is the fittest vehicle of revelation.'[16] The brilliant humour of the essay works, of course, at the expense of lesser women writers, and when Eliot describes her previous misguided sympathy for struggling authoresses, for example, she does so with characteristic scorn:

We had imagined that destitute women turned novelists as they turned governesses, because they had no other 'lady-like' means of getting their bread. On this supposition, vacillating syntax and improbable incident had a certain pathos for us, like the extremely supererogatory pincushions and ill-devised nightcaps, that are offered for sale by a blind man. . . . This theory of ours, like many other pretty theories, has had to give way before observation.[17]

In 'Woman in France' Eliot demonstrates a similar distaste for the taint of worldly pressures on literary production, admiring in French writers the fact that they were 'unstrained by mistaken effort . . . [and] not trying to make a career for themselves.'[18] It is little wonder, then, that women such as Mrs Oliphant, who did actually write out of financial necessity, should have felt resentful of Eliot's purist attitudes and, in her later career, the luxury to maintain them. If one compares Eliot's confident—albeit justified—sense of superiority and detachment to Charlotte Brontë's concern and tactful aid in the affairs of Julia Kavanagh, or Elizabeth Gaskell's intervention to obtain a literary fund pension for 'a poor authoress' in Knutsford, it is not difficult to accept the contention that other women felt betrayed by Eliot: 'Victorian women writers . . . thought she had rejected them because she avoided intimacy; they thought she had despised them because she had held them to a rigorous standard.'[19]

Admittedly, Eliot was never less rigorous with herself than with others, as the 'paralyzing despondency' she frequently felt at the prospect of attempting to equal the standard of her previous work suggests (*EL* V. 29). All the same, her critical severity and air of superiority were barriers to any easy interaction between Eliot and other women writers, especially since these were combined with a personal reserve, amounting at times to a general antipathy, towards other women. Even before her predominantly male-centred life in London, Eliot wrote to her former teacher Maria Lewis that young ladies held for

---

[16] Eliot, 'Silly Novels', p. 310.
[17] Ibid., p. 303.
[18] Eliot, 'Woman in France', p. 449.
[19] See Elaine Showalter, *A Literature of Their Own*, p. 111.

her 'the minimum of attraction . . . in a menagerie of the varieties of the human race' (*EL* I. 102), and she confided to Sara Hennell that 'somehow my male friends always eclipse the female' (*EL* II. 38). She made her reservations most explicit in an exchange recorded by her devoted follower Edith Simcox:

She said—expressly what she has often implied to my distress—that the love of men and women for each other must always be more and better than any other . . . she had never all her life cared very much for women. . . . She went on to say, what I knew also, that she cared for the womanly ideal, sympathized with women and liked for them to come to her in their troubles, but while feeling near to them in one way, she felt far off in another; the friendship and intimacy of men was more to her.[20]

In fact Eliot's pronouncements to Simcox should be regarded with some reservation, since Simcox's attachment to Eliot was clearly obsessional and their encounters suggest conscious effort on Eliot's part to establish some distance between them. None the less the masculine focus of her life—the successive importance of Dr. Brabant, Charles Bray, George Combe, John Chapman, George Lewes and John Blackwood, and John Cross—did enable the novelist Pearl Craigie, for example, to appeal to Eliot as proof that the 'really distinguished women have been trained and influenced by men', and it justifies Elaine Showalter in her claim that 'Eliot was reserved, inaccessible and opaque. In her maturity she violated the values of sisterly communion in the female sub-culture by avoiding close friendships with other women writers.'[21] In a sense it seems ironic that Eliot should have been so pleased by Gaskell's *Cranford* (*EL* III. 198), since as she made clear in 'Woman in France', and, as we shall see, in the priorities in her fiction, the prospect of a community of women without men held little charm for her:

Women become superior in France by being admitted to a common fund of ideas, to common objects of interest with men; and this must ever be the essential condition at once of the true womanly culture and of true social well-being. We have no faith in feminine conversazioni.[22]

---

[20] Edith Simcox, 'Autobiography of a Shirt-Maker', handwritten MS, Bodleian Library, entry for 9 Mar. 1880, fo. 8.

[21] Pearl Craigie, quoted in Showalter, *A Literature of Their Own*, p. 226; Showalter, op. cit., p. 107.

[22] Eliot, 'Woman in France', p. 472.

III

In her early adulthood at Coventry Eliot repeatedly described herself as 'a solitary' (*EL* I. 121), '*alone* in the world' (*EL* I. 102) and 'not rich in friends' (*EL* I. 70). Among her few female friends the sisters Sara Hennell and Cara Bray provide the most interest for this study. Eliot thought it 'impossible that [she] should ever love two women better' (*EL* II. 19) and declared to Sara: 'while I retain your friendship I retain the best that life has given me next to that which is the deepest gravest joy of all human experience' (*EL* II. 182)—although revealingly, even in this declaration of friendship, Eliot makes explicit the precedence she accords heterosexual attachments. From Sara Hennell in particular Eliot derived her earliest intellectual companionship, discussing tasks of translation, their current reading and, later, Eliot's new acquaintances in London. Before the more powerful influences of London gained the ascendancy in Eliot's life and before the strain of unequal talent told on the friendship, Eliot valued the judgement of her 'best plainspoken friend' as generally better than her own (*EL* I. 225) and regarded Hennell as 'the *only* friend I possess who has an animating influence over me' (*EL* I. 217).

Eliot's friendship with Sara Hennell offers some parallel with Charlotte Brontë's relationship with Ellen Nussey, for in each case the youthful friend provided emotional release as a surrogate partner. We have seen that Brontë wrote to Nussey as her lover, and likewise Eliot addressed Hennell as her 'Dearly beloved spouse' (*EL* I. 223), signed herself 'Your loving wife, Mary Ann' (*EL* I. 187) and wrote: 'I have thought of you . . . almost as often as a lover of his Geliebte. . . . How I wish I could kiss you and talk to you' (*EL* I. 146). Both friendships provide examples of those homosocial relationships, discussed in Chapter 3, which offered 'one very real behavioural and emotional option socially available to nineteenth century women'.[23]

Within a year of moving to London Eliot had made the acquaintance of Bessie Parkes, 'a dear, ardent, honest creature' (*EL* II. 9), the daughter of the radical reformer Joseph Parkes who had subsidized Eliot's translation of Strauss. Bessie Parkes was, as we have seen, a good friend of Elizabeth Gaskell and the founding editor of the *English Woman's Journal*. Through Parkes Eliot became acquainted—either personally or by report—with Parkes's fellow workers, Barbara Bodichon, Anna Jameson, Matilda Hays, Adelaide Procter, and Isa Craig, all of

---

[23] Smith-Rosenberg, 'The Female World of Love and Ritual', p. 8.

whom were writers with a particular interest in the Woman Question. Eliot was thus kept in touch with the contemporary issues concerning women and followed the developments of Parkes's publishing ventures, offering editorial advice and subscribing to the *Journal*. She expressed herself glad to help with the women's press in any way '*except by writing*' (*EL* V. 428), a refusal which she claimed bore 'no special relation to the "Englishwoman's Journal," but includes that and all other Reviews' (*EL* II. 431). This was, strictly speaking, true since by 1858 Eliot had given up writing for periodicals and was preoccupied with writing fiction. However, it was also diplomatic since she would never have published in Parkes's *Journal* in any case. She acknowledged some 'talent and real ardour for goodness' in Parkes (*EL* II. 438) and admired and recommended to friends certain articles on women's employment and education, but she was characteristically offended by the mediocrity of the *Journal* and wished that Parkes could be aided in its production by 'a hypercritical friend at her elbow' (*EL* III. 15).[24]

In the end, though, Eliot's friendship with Parkes was marked by an inequality which was a feature of so many of her relationships with women. Although Parkes did open up important areas for Eliot and was one of the few friends for whom Eliot felt 'peculiar regard' because of their loyalty after the disclosure of her union with Lewes (*EL* IV. 396), the friendship never really developed beyond a teacher–student relationship, with Parkes as the 'dear child' whom Eliot exhorted not to 'be playing pranks and shocking people, because I am told they lay it all to me and my bad influence' (*EL* II. 44).

In contrast, Eliot's friendship with Barbara Bodichon was much more challenging. The two women met through Parkes in 1852 and somewhat uncharacteristically Eliot was attracted to Bodichon from the first, drawn to her 'strong noble nature' (*EL* II. 211) and admiring of her activist zeal: 'Her activity for great objects is admirable, and contact with her is fresh inspiration to work while it is day.'[25] Their friendship was reminiscent in some ways of that between Charlotte Brontë and Mary Taylor, not only in the radicalizing stimulus Bodichon, like Taylor, provided for her more conservative friend,

---

[24] Like Gaskell, Eliot was approached to contribute to *Victoria Regia*, the anthology that was to be produced as a show-piece by the all-women's Victoria Press, founded by Emily Faithfull with Parkes's aid. Although neither woman made a contribution in the end, Gaskell's failure seems to have been due to an inability to fulfil a commitment made to Faithfull and not, like Eliot's, a refusal to be associated with the venture (*EL* IV. 77).

[25] George Eliot, Journal, quoted in Gordon S. Haight, *George Eliot: A Biography* (New York: Oxford University Press, 1968), p. 205.

but also in the attraction her daring, energetic nature exercised over the virtually antithetical cautious, passive temperament of the writer. As Bodichon's biographer, Hester Burton, observed: 'The one was full of noble intentions: the other of noble deeds.'[26]

Despite their temperamental differences Bodichon was the woman to whom Eliot felt closest, 'the first friend who has given any symptom of knowing me' (*EL* III. 63). Their intimacy was possible partly because Bodichon, as the illegitimate daughter of a Radical politician and self-described as 'one of the cracked people of the world . . . never happy in an English genteel family life', was capable of defying the social taboos surrounding Eliot.[27] So, for example, she went on holiday with Lewes and Eliot at Tenley in July 1856, shortly after their return from the 'elopement' to Germany and she was one of the most regular visitors to their house when she was in London. However, more than her liberated unconcern, it was Bodichon's warmth and generosity that explained the actual degree of intimacy she maintained with Eliot. She was absorbed in Eliot's domestic concerns, offering advice on servants and the careers of Lewes's sons, lending her paintings for decorations and her country cottage for holidays and helping to nurse Thornton Lewes in the months before his death. Eliot consulted Bodichon about living with Lewes as early as the summer of 1854 and was assured that whatever her decision or its consequences, Bodichon 'would stand by her so long as [she] lived.'[28] Accordingly, Bodichon was the first person to whom Eliot wrote after Lewes's death and one of the few in whom Eliot confided about her impending marriage to Cross.

Although their friendship pre-dated Eliot's novel-writing career, Bodichon's interest in, and encouragement of, Eliot's fiction writing was intense. It was Bodichon in distant Algiers who, on the basis of one long extract of *Adam Bede*, declared categorically: 'I can't tell you how I triumphed in the triumph you have made. It is so great a one. . . . I *know* that it is you . . . [it] instantly made me internally exclaim that it is written by Marian Evans, there is her great big head and heart and her wise wide views' (*EL* III. 56). Her enthusiasm gave Eliot 'more joy—more heart glow, than all the letters or reviews or other testimonies of success' (*EL* III. 64). The trust Bodichon enjoyed

---

[26] Hester Burton, *Barbara Bodichon 1827–1891* (Edinburgh: T. A. Constable, 1949), p. 185.

[27] Ibid., p. 92.

[28] Ibid., p. 188.

enabled her to say things to Eliot that others neither would nor could. So, for example, she joked about Eliot's domestic situation: 'I think I shall say I am not married to Dr. Bodichon just to titter the people! they torment me so' (*EL* III. 107) and, more significantly, she ignored Lewes's prohibition on Eliot's friends discussing her fiction. She frankly discussed the problems relating to the disclosure of Eliot's true identity as the author of *Adam Bede*:

From their way of talking it is evident they thought you would do the book more harm than the book do you good in public opinion.

I tried to make Mrs. O. J[ones] say she would like to know you (not that you would like to know her) but she seemed to feel fear! I do not think she would call even if she knew you were George Eliot. . . . Oh Marian, Marian, what cowards people are. (*EL* III. 103)

And with equal forthrightness she wrote on the publication of *Middle-march*:

I think it *is* your best work. . . . I am sure it is the most interesting only I dread the unfolding and feel quite certain it is a horrible tragedy coming. . . . I do not know if you meant to produce this sort of terrible foreshadowing of inevitable misery and I see some of 'em have read it and only see wit character and liveliness, and call it light reading now I find it heavy reading to my heart though I think it a most noble book and thank you for it. (*EL* IX. 33)

As well as holding a privileged position as a commentator on Eliot's work, Bodichon was also the most likely figure to enlist Eliot's sympathy on women's issues. A tireless worker for the cause, Bodichon devoted much energy and substantial sums of money to enable the setting up of the *English Woman's Journal* and the foundation of Girton College and she published two works relating to the Woman Question, *Women and Work* in 1857 and *A Brief Summary in Plain Language of the Most Important Laws Concerning Women* in 1854. Not surprisingly, it was Bodichon who obtained Eliot's signature for the petition to accompany the Married Women's Property Bill in 1856, and she later introduced Eliot to Elizabeth Blackwell, the pioneer woman doctor, and Emily Davies, the founder of Girton College.

The third important female friendship of Eliot's early years in London was with Harriet Martineau. The two women had in fact met in 1845 at the house of a Coventry magistrate, Charles Bracebridge, when Eliot found the distinguished visitor 'quite one of those great people whom one does not venerate the less for having seen' (*EL* I. 189). It was not until they met again at John Chapman's in 1852, however, that they became friends, and in that year Eliot visited Martineau at Ambleside, just as Charlotte Brontë had two years before. Like Brontë, Eliot was determined to 'think highly' of Martineau whose 'powers and industry' she respected (*EL* II. 4), and she was enthusiastic about the visit (*EL* II. 62). Yet, again like Brontë, her initial impressions of Martineau betrayed some ambivalence, as though, if she succeeded in her determination to think well of Martineau, it was not because the task was entirely easy: 'There are so many in the world who have more than all her foibles, without her bright and good qualities, and yet people give her much harder measure than they are willing to grant to those said do-nothings' (*EL* VIII. 64). At the same time Eliot felt no hesitation in her professional appreciation of Martineau, claiming she was 'the only English woman that possesses thoroughly the art of writing' (*EL* II. 31). However, the friendship came to an abrupt end with the eruption of Martineau's disapproval at Eliot's decision to live with George Lewes. Gordon Haight describes Martineau in his biography of Eliot, 'spreading [malicious gossip] among her numerous correspondents with a virulence that makes one consider pathological theories of sexual jealousy.'[29] Although hurt, Eliot seems not entirely surprised by Martineau's behaviour: 'Amongst her good qualities we certainly cannot reckon zeal for other people's reputation. She is sure to caricature any information for the amusement of the next person to whom she turns her ear-trumpet' (*EL* II. 180). And Eliot later deplored the same capacity for malice in Martineau's *Autobiography*:

One regrets continually that she felt it necessary not only to tell of her intercourse with many more or less distinguished persons . . . but also to pronounce upon their entire merits and demerits, especially when, if she had died as soon [as] she expected, these persons would nearly all have been living to read her gratuitous rudenesses. (*EL* VI. 353)

In a curious way there is a certain parallel in Martineau's termination of her friendships with Brontë and Eliot. It exists not just in her sudden outbursts of vitriolic disapproval—each made public in its way—but also in the substance of that disapproval. The weakness of Brontë's heroines in their 'need of being loved' and the choices they make in their search for a strong male partner seem not unrelated to the real choices that Eliot was making in her life: each was a kind of betrayal of the 'self-reliance' Martineau valued so highly and of the

---

[29] Haight, *George Eliot*, p. 167.

'universal, eternal, filial relation' she extolled as 'the only universal and eternal refuge'.[30]

IV

The foundation of these friendships belonged to that earlier period of Eliot's life before her emergence as a successful novelist when she was freer in her relations with other women. Her more specifically literary relationships with women were more distant and problematic. Eliot did have a sense of the potential, at least, for an artistic community to support and encourage its members. So, for example, she lamented Barbara Bodichon's isolation in Algiers, when writing to her in 1863: 'I am sorry to think of you without any artistic society to help you and feed your faith' (*EL* IV. 119). At the same time Eliot's isolation gave her cause enough to recognize how far the truth fell short of the ideal. Thus she wrote on receipt of Gaskell's 'sweet encouraging words' regarding *Scenes of Clerical Life* and *Adam Bede*:

Only yesterday I was wondering that artists, knowing each other's pains so well, did not help each other more, and, as usual, when I have been talking complainingly or suspiciously, something has come which serves me as a reproof.

The 'something' is your letter, which has brought me the only sort of help I care to have—an assurance of fellow-feeling, of thorough truthful recognition from one of the minds which are capable of judging as well as of being moved. (*EL* III. 198)

In a similar vein, and perhaps with some thought of her own experience, she wrote to Sara Hennell of the Scottish poet Robert Buchanan, who had come to London 'in the faith that he should find the greatest and most generous minds there' and had met instead with 'the usual trials of disappointment in that faith' (*EL* IV. 129).

Nevertheless, like many nineteenth-century women writers, George Eliot 'studied with a special closeness the works written by their own sex', despite her general protestations that she rarely read fiction for the effect was usually 'paralyzing, and certainly justifies me in that abstinence from novel reading which, I fear, makes me seem supercilious or churlish' (*EL* VI. 76).[31] Admittedly Eliot's interest was due partly to her role as a reviewer which placed her, unlike Gaskell or

---

[30] Martineau, *Autobiography*, I. 399; Harriet Martineau, *Deerbrook* (London: Edward Moxon, 1839), III. 6.

[31] Moers, *Literary Women*, p. 43.

Brontë, in a specifically academic or professional relation to the literary community. So in the light of 'Silly Novels by Lady Novelists', for example, that interest could be seen simply as a grim determination to know the worst. There was, however, more to it than this. Eliot derived a sense of communion from reading, which she preferred in many ways to more direct contact: 'contrary to the general, I like reading what my friends write and finding out a great deal more about them than one can ever know in any other way' (*EL* II. 263). Indeed, it was reading primarily that provided links for Eliot with those women writers whom she respected. Significantly, the works to which she turned between February and June 1857, as she embarked on her novelist's career, were predominantly written by women and included *Cranford, The Life of Charlotte Brontë, The Professor, Aurora Leigh, Sense and Sensibility, Emma, Northanger Abbey*, and *Persuasion* (*EL* II. 310–69).[32] And rather like Charlotte Brontë, Eliot felt drawn to the creators of the works she respected, theorizing about acquaintances whom she avoided in practice. For example, in her admiration for *Aurora Leigh*, which she had reviewed glowingly for the *Westminster Review* in January 1857, she wrote to Sara Hennell: 'I wish I had seen Mrs. Browning as you have, for I love to have a distinct human being in my mind, as the medium of great and beautiful things' (*EL* II. 278). She claimed that no other book gave her 'a deeper sense of communion with a large as well as beautiful mind' (*EL* II. 341). She read it for the third time during the composition of *Scenes*, and once more as she wrote *The Mill on the Floss* (*EL* III. 150).

Eliot regarded Charlotte Brontë as 'perhaps the best' contemporary novelist (*EL* II. 355), equal to George Sand in 'passion' and 'fire' (*EL* II. 91) and worthy to be ranked with Scott, Balzac, and Dickens as one of the 'real "makers"' amid the 'great mass' of imitators.[33] However, there was, of course, no possibility—let alone likelihood—of fellowship between the two, since Brontë died in 1855 before Eliot's novel-writing career had begun, and Eliot had to be content with tales that Lewes told of 'a little, plain, provincial, sickly-looking old maid' (*EL* II. 91).

Ironically, although it was in response to Gaskell's letters of frank admiration that Eliot wrote regretting the lack of communality between

---

[32] This focus on women writers was marked, but not entirely exclusive. Eliot also mentions having read Hawthorne's *The Scarlet Letter* (*EL* II. 311) and Sophocles (*EL* II. 319) during this period.

[33] George Eliot, 'Art and Belles Lettres', *Westminster Review*, Apr. 1856, p. 638.

artists, the two women never met. The opportunities for meeting must have existed, for Gaskell was a regular visitor to London and, unlike Brontë, willingly took advantage of the social privileges accorded to celebrity in making acquaintances. Presumably the social taboo on the Lewes household was too great for Gaskell. However genuine Gaskell's admiration for Eliot was, her reticence was not surprising in the wife of a Unitarian minister, who found herself unable to 'help liking [Eliot]—*because* she wrote those books. Yes I do! I have tried to be moral, and dislike her and dislike her books—but it won't do' (*GL* 594). Eliot in return felt genuine, if more qualified, respect for Gaskell as an artist. She admired *Ruth*, although not as 'enduring or classical fiction' (*EL* II. 86), appreciated the 'high quality' of *Sylvia's Lovers* (*EL* IV. 79) and while regretting the treatment of Branwell, considered *The Life of Charlotte Brontë* 'deeply affecting throughout' and admirably done in 'industry . . . care . . . [and] feeling' (*EL* II. 319). In 'Silly Novels by Lady Novelists' Eliot ranked Gaskell with Charlotte Brontë and Harriet Martineau as women of 'genius or effective talent',[34] probably in truth having the latter in mind for Gaskell. As in her 'contact' with other women writers, she felt unable 'to help loving her as one reads her books' (*EL* II. 86), and when she replied to Gaskell's letters she stressed a feeling of connectedness:

> I had indulged the idea that if my books turned out to be worth much, you would be among the willing readers. . . . I had the pleasure of reading Cranford for the first time in 1857, when I was writing the 'Scenes of Clerical Life,' and going up the Rhine one dim wet day in the spring of the next year, when I was writing 'Adam Bede,' I satisfied myself for the lack of prospect by reading over again those earlier chapters of 'Mary Barton.' (*EL* III. 198)

Like Gaskell, Harriet Beecher Stowe was inspired by her admiration of Eliot's works to write to their creator, which she did in May 1869. The correspondence with Beecher Stowe differed, however, in that it continued intermittently until Eliot's death. Eliot's estimation of Beecher Stowe's talent was high—probably inflatedly so.[35] But it was not simply her respect for the author that inspired Eliot to write to Beecher Stowe as a 'dear friend and fellow labourer', and with such uncharacteristic confidentiality: '[I] almost wish that you could have a momentary vision of the discouragement, nay, paralyzing

---

[34] Eliot, 'Silly Novels', p. 322.
[35] See, e.g., Eliot's review of Beecher Stowe's novel *Dred*, in the *Westminster Review*, Oct. 1856, p. 326.

despondency in which many days of my writing life have been past' (*EL* V. 29). Rather, Eliot was drawn to the fact that Beecher Stowe seemed to offer 'a model of womanly authorship', for she was particularly concerned that gifted women should not be 'unsexed' by their talent: 'Nothing offended her more than the idea that because a woman had exceptional intellectual powers, therefore it was right that she should absolve herself, or be absolved, from her ordinary household duties.'[36] Accordingly, Eliot deferred to Beecher Stowe: 'you have had longer experience than I as a writer, and fuller experience as a woman, since you have borne children and known the mother's history from the beginning. I trust your quick and long-taught mind as an interpreter little liable to mistake me' (*EL* V. 29).

After the initial enthusiasm a certain coolness appeared in Eliot's letters to Beecher Stowe. Eliot's reservations about Beecher Stowe's spiritualist professions were compounded by her disapproval of Beecher Stowe's defence of Lady Byron in 'The True Story of Lady Byron's Life'. Far from seeing it as a gesture of sisterly solidarity, Eliot was 'sorry that it seemed necessary to publish what is only worthy to die and rot' (*EL* V. 54).

Rather than close literary friendships, the most marked legacy of Eliot's celebrity was the host of admiring disciples such as Edith Simcox, Elma Stuart, and Maria Congreve, who gathered around her in later life. They did not, however, offer Eliot any real opportunity for communality in the sense of the mutual exchange of 'the greatest and most generous minds' (*EL* IV. 129). To begin with, most of these women were not writers.[37] They were also most often substantially younger than their idol and offered a kind of worship, which was frequently obsessive in its intensity. Elma Stuart, for example, requested and received a lock of Eliot's hair; the young American, Harriet Peirce, wrote: 'I *love* to love you, you are so love-worthy. And once in a long time I *love* to say so to you. But I would not have it burden you with the weight of a rose leaf . . .' (*EL* VIII. 461); and Edith Simcox's Autobiography provided an extraordinary record of passionate attachment: 'I kissed her again and again and wondered meditatively how it was that one should be glad just because somebody else was what she was.'[38]

[36] Gilbert and Gubar, *The Madwoman in the Attic*, p. 533; John Cross, ed., *George Eliot's Life as Related in Her Letters and Journals* (Leipzig: Tauchnitz, 1885), IV. 282.

[37] Elaine Showalter suggests that 'Women writers, who felt some stirrings of female power in themselves . . . were much more resistant to kneeling at the shrine' (*A Literature of Their Own*, p. 293).

[38] Simcox, Autobiography, entry for 16 Jan. 1878, fo. 69.

Perhaps the most surprising thing is not that Eliot inspired this coterie of devotees, but that a personality in many ways so severe as hers tolerated such mindless adulation, for tolerate, and even encourage, it she did. It may be that since they required very little of Eliot and had the advantage over literary women of not offending Eliot's strict standards for her craft, they could be easily and benevolently tolerated: 'As to my hands, dear pagan, they are ugly—but you have a vision of your own, oh why should I undo it? It is good for you to worship as long as you believe that what you worship is good' (*EL* VI. 26). Also their toleration was due in some respects to Lewes, who with intimate knowledge of Eliot's vacillating confidence and a sense that 'women . . . owe her a peculiar gratitude' (*EL* V. 225) orchestrated Eliot's exposure to encouraging admiration.

This legacy of devotion rather than friendship provided some consolation to Eliot in later years for the absence of a family of her own. Although that absence was the result of a conscious choice, and Eliot 'profoundly rejoice[d]' that she had never 'brought a child into this world' (*EL* V. 52), she counted 'the growth of a maternal feeling towards both men and women who are much younger' as one of the satisfactions of growing older (*EL* V. 5) and felt 'conscious of having an unused stock of motherly tenderness' (*EL* V. 52). Accordingly, she frequently purported to take a 'motherly interest' in letters to these women and designated herself their 'spiritual mother' (*EL* VI. 167).

As her deference to Harriet Beecher Stowe indicates, and elements of her fiction betray, Eliot's attitude to the non-fulfilment of maternal capacity was at very least ambivalent. However much she 'rejoiced', the absence of children was felt as a lack, and Eliot regarded her works as surrogate children. For example, in 1860 she referred to *The Mill on the Floss* as her 'youngest child' (*EL* III. 335) and to her fictional characters as 'spiritual children' (*EL* VI. 245). Lewes explained to Blackwood that she regarded 'the idea of the M.S. being taken away from her as if it were her baby' (*EL* VI. 136).

V

Although Eliot's disparagement of women such as Dinah Mulock, Margaret Oliphant, and Mary Braddon may demonstrate that 'the cultured woman, while never engaged in overt competition with men, was very much in competition with other women', what is most striking is the degree to which Eliot saw herself as above such rivalry.[39] She was,

[39] See Elaine Showalter, *A Literature of Their Own*, p. 104.

for example, clearly insulted by comparisons of her work with that of other women writers. So, when compared to Dinah Mulock, Eliot wrote sternly to her old friend in Geneva Francois D'Albert-Durade to set the record straight: 'the most ignorant journalist in England would hardly think of calling me a rival of Miss Mulock—a writer who is read only by novel readers, pure and simple, never by people of high culture. A very excellent woman she is, I believe—but we belong to an entirely different order of writers' (*EL* III. 302).[40]

The comparison which incensed Eliot perhaps more than any other was that between herself and Elizabeth Gaskell made by Swinburne in 1877 in his *Note on Charlotte Brontë*. The entire work was vicious in its treatment of Eliot, but the most galling feature for Eliot, who regarded 'imitators' with such contempt, was the suggestion of debt, amounting almost to plagiarism, owed by Eliot in writing *The Mill on the Floss* to Gaskell's *The Moorland Cottage*:

And the fuller and deeper tone of colour combined with the greater sharpness and precision of outline may be allowed to excuse the apparent amount of obligation—though we may hardly see how this can be admitted to explain the remarkable reticence which reserves all acknowledgment and dissembles all consciousness of that sufficiently palpable and weighty and direct obligation—to Mrs. Gaskell's beautiful story of 'The Moorland Cottage.'[41]

Gordon Haight describes Eliot's reaction to Swinburne's remarks: '"He suggested," she exclaimed, and angrily doubled the fist that rested on her knee, "that I'd taken some things in *The Mill on the Floss* from a story by Mrs. Gaskell called *The Children of the Moor*"', and Haight concludes matter-of-factly: 'that is, *The Moorland Cottage*, which George Eliot had never seen.'[42] However, Yvonne Ffrench declares with equal confidence that Eliot 'made no attempt to disguise the fact of her debt to Mrs. Gaskell.'[43] It is in fact impossible to establish conclusively whether Eliot owed anything directly to Gaskell's work. On the one hand, significant parallels exist between the two works and it is plausible that Eliot might have encountered the tale

---

[40] Given Eliot's reaction to the comparison, it is ironic that Robert Colby suggests in 'Miss Evans, Miss Mulock, and Hetty Sorrell' that Eliot's creation of Hetty Sorrell owes a significant debt to the ninth chapter of Mulock's *A Woman's Thoughts about Women* (*English Language Notes*, 2 Mar. 1965, pp. 206–11).

[41] Algernon Swinburne, *A Note on Charlotte Brontë* (London: Chatto & Windus, 1877), p. 30.   [42] Haight, *George Eliot*, p. 525.

[43] Yvonne Ffrench, 'Elizabeth Cleghorn Gaskell', *From Jane Austen to Joseph Conrad*, eds. R. Rathburn and Martin Steinmann, Jr. (Minneapolis: University of Minnesota Press, 1958), p. 136.

since it was widely reviewed when it appeared in 1850 illustrated by the popular contemporary artist Birket Foster. On the other hand, since we know that Eliot read Gaskell's much more successful work *Cranford* for the first time in 1857, four years after its original publication, it is equally plausible that she would not have read the essentially 'popular' Christmas volume of an author in whom she was not especially interested at the time of the book's appearance. Whatever the truth, it is revealing none the less that Eliot reacted so strongly to the imputation of debt.[44]

The exchange of opinion was potentially another form of literary interaction, but Eliot was generally unwilling either to solicit or to accept advice. Whereas Gaskell cheerfully invited opinions from Anna Jameson, Charlotte Brontë, and the Winkworth sisters, Eliot, like Brontë, regarded her fiction 'once committed to paper, [as] like the laws of the Medes and Persians that alter not' (*EL* I. 27). Similarly Eliot was scarcely more willing to offer guidance. Her fervent respect for her craft and her preoccupation with excellence made her unlikely to enter into the struggles of mediocre authoresses, as an anecdote from Cross's biography of an incident in which any feeling in Eliot of fellowship for co-workers was quickly subsumed into critical sternness, indicates:

. . . when I was urging her to write her autobiography, she said, half sighing, half smiling, 'The only thing I should care to dwell on would be the absolute despair I suffered from of ever being able to achieve anything. No one could ever have felt greater despair, and a knowledge of this might be a help to some other struggler'—adding with a smile, 'but on the other hand, it might only lead to an increase of bad writing.'[45]

Eliot wrote of her unwillingness to offer advice in a letter to Elizabeth Phelps, an American author who had sent Eliot a copy of her novel *The Story of Avis* in 1877: 'do not expect "criticism" from me. . . . In general—perhaps I may have told you—it is my rule not to read

---

[44] Gaskell's influence might also have been suggested in *Felix Holt*, in which the courtroom scene provides marked parallels to the trial scene in *Mary Barton*. In each case the intervention of the heroine on behalf of the unjustly accused hero is instrumental, with the physical appearance of both women having a dramatic effect on the onlookers. Both women are bewildered by the proceedings, but determined to bear public witness to their previously undeclared love, and after the strain of the moment Mary collapses, while Esther feels 'so tremulous' and 'exhausted of her energy' that she is forced to grasp Mrs. Transome lest she 'lose her self-command' (Elizabeth Gaskell, *Mary Barton*, p. 376; George Eliot, *Felix Holt*, Clarendon edn., 1866; rpt. Oxford: Oxford University Press, 1980, pp. 376–7).

[45] Cross, *George Eliot's Life*, I. 43.

contemporary fiction, and I have had to say so in many cases to country-women of yours' (*EL* VI. 418). At another point Eliot instructed her stepson Charles Lewes to write in discouragement of an aspiring authoress:

At the same time indicate that there is little hope for her sister of a remuner-ation which would dispense with her continuing other forms of work. . . . (I should hope, poor thing, that the authoress has conquered the use of the auxiliary verbs better than the letter writer). (*EL* VII. 178)

Eliot's letter provides an interesting contrast in its forbidding tone with the gentler, more approachable manner of Gaskell, who when responding to much the same situation, wrote a lengthy letter of advice and comfort, and concluded: 'If this letter has been of *any* use to you, do not scruple to write to me again, if I can help you.'[46]

VI

In contrast with Gaskell and Brontë, Eliot was not so urgently af-fected by the problems of the 'superabundant' woman because of the educational opportunities and the modest financial independence provided by her middle-class background, and, later, the protective partnership with Lewes. However, in one sense Eliot's literary reputation marked her out as a focus for the women's movement and consequently she was frequently approached with appeals for support on a range of women-related issues. And although Eliot's circle of female friends was small, the relative number of those women who provided her with contact with the wider women's movement was large. As a result Eliot was familiar with controversies surrounding the Woman Question, and her opinions on the subject are more substantially documented than those of either Gaskell or Brontë.

As we have seen, Eliot's two friends Barbara Bodichon and Bessie Parkes were activists for the women's cause, and they introduced Eliot to other similarly dedicated women such as Bodichon's aunt Julia Smith, an outspoken advocate of women's rights and the founder of Bedford College (which Eliot attended for a geometry course in 1851), Emily Davies, the founder of Girton College, Isa Craig, the poet and co-worker at the *English Woman's Journal* and Dr Elizabeth Blackwell, the pioneer of medical education for women. In addition, the feminist activist Clementia [Mrs Peter] Taylor was a

[46] See Chapter 2 above, p. 29.

long standing friend and correspondent, who consistently discussed women's issues with Eliot, urging her at one point, for example, to speak publicly for women's suffrage (*EL* VII. 44). Eliot was also acquainted with Barbara Bodichon's cousin Florence Nightingale, with Octavia Hill, the housing reformer and campaigner for women's education, whose sister Gertrude married Lewes's son Charles, and with Caroline Cornwallis, the feminist writer and co-contributor to the *Westminster Review*. Prompted by these women, Eliot did associate herself practically with the cause in some ways, signing the Married Women's Property Bill petition and soliciting further signatures from friends (*EL* II. 225), contributing money to Girton and encouraging 'rich friends' to do likewise, donating £200 in 1874 to a fund to enable Octavia Hill to devote herself to her philanthropic works, and maintaining a solicitous interest in the publishing venture of Parkes and her co-workers.[47]

The basis of Eliot's sympathy, such as it was, with the women's movement was her 'mildly Radical conviction' that women should have opened to them 'the same store of acquired truth or beliefs as men have' (*EL* IV. 468).[48] Accordingly she wrote to Barbara Bodichon: 'the better Education of Women is one of the subjects about which I have no doubt' (*EL* IV. 399). Yet even her enthusiasm on this one point of whole-hearted agreement with women's reforms was tempered by other more conservative considerations. Cross indicates that Eliot was worried that women's participation in a collegiate system, as at Girton, could possibly weaken 'the bonds of family affection and family duties', and she wrote to Emily Davies urging that the 'primary difference' between the sexes should not be lost sight of:

And there lies just that kernel of truth in the vulgar alarm of men lest women should be 'unsexed.' We can no longer afford to part with that exquisite type of gentleness, tenderness and possible maternity suffusing a woman's being

---

[47] It is ironic that at the same time as Eliot concerned herself with the efforts of the founders of the *English Woman's Journal* she subscribed to its arch-enemy, the *Saturday Review*, which she recommended as the 'best weekly paper in point of talent' (*EL* IV. 311). The irony is compounded by the fact that the notoriously anti-feminist weekly reviewed *The Mill on the Floss* in decidedly sexist terms. Describing the novel as 'too good for a woman's story' and written by a lady 'who with the usual pretty affectation of her sex, likes to look on paper as much like a man as possible', the reviewer went on to declare that 'the whole delineation of passionate love, as painted by female novelists, is open to very serious criticism' (*Saturday Review*, IX (1860), 470).

[48] Thomas Pinney, Introduction, *Essays of George Eliot* (London: Routledge & Kegan Paul, 1963), p. 8.

with affectionateness, which makes what we mean by the female character. (*EL* IV. 468)[49]

Whereas Eliot's support for women's education may have been 'mildly Radical', her vision of its effects was not. Emily Davies reported that Eliot was anxious to discourage political ambitiousness: 'She hoped my friend would teach the girls not to think too much of political measures for improving society—as leading away from individual efforts to be good, I understand her to mean' (*EL* VI. 287). Similarly she wrote to Barbara Bodichon that no good could come to women 'while each aims at doing the highest kind of work'. Cheerful resignation rather than disquieted ambition was the result she hoped for from higher education for women: 'recognition of the great amount of social unproductive labour which needs to be done by women' (*EL* IV. 425).

Furthermore, Eliot's enthusiasm for women's education stemmed as much from her disapproval of women as from any sympathy for women's lot. Her low estimation of the contemporary state of women emerges clearly, for example, from her essay 'Margaret Fuller and Mary Wollstonecraft': 'But we want freedom and culture for woman, because subjection and ignorance have debased her, and with her, Man; for—"If she be small, slight-natured, miserable / How shall men grow?"'[50] It is also reflected in her serious reservations about women's suffrage, which she considered 'an extemely doubtful good' (*EL* IV. 390). She was pleased, therefore, that the efforts to secure the franchise for women made only 'creeping progress', for 'woman does not yet deserve a much better lot than man gives her' (*EL* II. 86).

Temperamentally Eliot was not a political being, for she was ill disposed toward activism—at once 'utterly unfit' for, and 'aloof from', practical matters (*EL* IV. 500; VI. 47)—and she wished to avoid 'fruitless agitation'.[51] That general predisposition against activism extended in the case of the women's movement to the activists themselves, with many of whom Eliot felt 'too imperfect a sympathy . . . to give any practical adhesion to them' (*EL* V. 58). Fundamentally disapproving of the one-sidedness of polemic, Eliot believed that no cause justified distortion and the merest suggestion of propaganda was anathema. She admired Margaret Fuller, for example, precisely

---

[49] Cross, *George Eliot's Life*, p. 283.

[50] George Eliot, 'Margaret Fuller and Mary Wollstonecraft', *The Leader*, 13 Oct. 1855, p. 989.

[51] Edith Simcox, 'George Eliot', *Nineteenth Century*, IX (1881), 797.

because she avoided 'exaggeration of woman's moral excellence or intellectual capabilities'.[52]

Even if Eliot's sympathies had been more unequivocally engaged with the women's movement, her principles as an artist would have prohibited any kind of special pleading. Thus, in a review of Geraldine Jewsbury's *Constance Herbert* in the *Westminster Review* of July 1855, Eliot felt compelled to remonstrate with Jewsbury,

> . . . chiefly because we value her influence, and should like to see it always in what seems to us the right scale. With the exception of Mr. Harrap, who is simply a cipher awaiting a wife to give him any value, there is not a man in her book who is not either weak, perfidious, or rascally, while almost all the women are models of magnanimity and devotedness. The lions, i.e., the ladies have got the brush in their hands with a vengeance now, and are retaliating for the calumnies of men from Adam downwards. Perhaps it is but fair to allow them a little exaggeration. Still we must meekly suggest that we cannot accept an *ex parte* statement, even from that paragon Aunt Margaret, as altogether decisive. . . . Seriously we care too much for the attainment of a better understanding as to woman's true position not to be sorry when a writer like Miss Jewsbury only adds her voice to swell the confusion on this subject.[53]

As an artist Eliot felt it her duty to refrain from public utterance: 'My function is that of the *aesthetic* not doctrinal teacher—the rousing of the nobler emotions, which make mankind desire the social right, not the prescribing of social measures, concerning which the artistic mind, however strongly moved by social sympathy, is often not the best judge' (*EL* VII. 44). Thus, while Eliot respected the enterprise of novels such as *Ruth* and *Uncle Tom's Cabin*, she shared with Brontë a disinclination to write books concerning the 'topics of the day'.

VII

As a woman writer Eliot knew the dangers of critical double standards applied on the basis of sex. In October 1855, for example, she wrote to Charles Bray about her essay in the *Westminster Review*, 'Evangelical Teaching: Dr. Cumming': 'The article appears to have produced a strong impression, and that impression would be a little counteracted if the author were known to be a *woman*' (*EL* II. 218). Similarly, in adopting a male pseudonym Eliot sought to avoid such a double standard, as Lewes made explicit to Barbara Bodichon, when the

---

[52] Eliot, 'Margaret Fuller', p. 988.
[53] George Eliot, 'Belles Lettres', *Westminster Review*, July 1855, p. 295.

controversy raged over *Adam Bede*'s authorship: 'the object of anonymity was to get the book judged on its own merits, and not prejudged as the work of a woman, or of a particular woman' (*EL* III. 106).

In a memoir of Eliot, Edith Simcox claimed that Eliot held 'the same [intellectual] standard for both sexes', and certainly in Eliot's essay on Margaret Fuller, for example, she rejected the use of ideas of 'femininity' as a measure of value and singled out for praise Fuller's remarks on the 'folly of absolute definitions of woman's nature and absolute demarcations of woman's mission'.[54] However, although such thinking suggests similarities with Charlotte Brontë's views on the subject, Eliot operated with a far stricter sense of the demarcations of gender than the Fuller essay might indicate. She extolled an 'exquisite type' of femininity—'of gentleness, tenderness, possible maternity' (*EL* IV. 468)—and longed for 'some woman's duty, some possibility of devoting [her]self' (*EL* II. 322), and, as we shall see, this directly affected her conception of women's relationships. While Eliot recognized the possibility of aspects of the feminine existing in the masculine—'an element of almost maternal tenderness in man's protecting love'—she reacted instinctively against the prospect of the reverse: 'particularly dislik[ing] everything generally associated with the idea of the "masculine woman." '[55]

Furthermore, Eliot upheld her sense of 'primary difference' in literature and declared it, 'an immense mistake to maintain that there is no sex in literature'.[56] Whereas Brontë as an artist refused to be preoccupied with 'femininity', Eliot feared lest it be forgotten. Eliot consistently appealed to characteristics of gender as a criteria for judgement:

Mrs. Browning is, perhaps, the first woman who has produced a work which exhibits all the peculiar powers without the negations of her sex; which superadds to masculine vigour, breadth, and culture, feminine subtlety of perception, feminine quickness of sensibility, and feminine tenderness. It is difficult to point to a woman of genius who is not either too little feminine, or

[54] Simcox, 'George Eliot', p. 797; Eliot, 'Margaret Fuller', p. 989.

[55] Simcox, 'George Eliot', p. 783; Cross, *George Eliot's Life*, IV. 282. Ironically, more than any other woman writing in her period Eliot was admired for the weight and scope of her 'masculine intellect' (Mathilde Blind, *George Eliot*, London: W. H. Allen & Co., 1883, p. 5), or for what Dinah Mulock characterized as ' "the brain of a man and the heart of a woman," united with what we may call a sexless intelligence' ('To Novelists and a Novelist', *Macmillan's Magazine*, Apr. 1861, p. 446).

[56] Eliot, 'Woman in France', p. 499.

too excessively so. But in this, her longest and greatest poem, Mrs. Browning has shown herself all the greater poet because she is intensely a poetess.[57]

The very form of a woman's novel was distinctive according to Eliot, having a 'precious speciality, lying quite apart from masculine aptitudes and experience'.[58] Indeed, so confident was Eliot of the validity of the distinction that only three months after writing to Charles Bray of the necessity of anonymity to prevent the possibility of being judged by a double standard, she wrote in a review of Holme Lee's novel *Gilbert Massenger*: 'we venture to use the feminine pronoun, because though the name is *epicene*, the style of Holme Lee is unmistakably feminine.'[59]

In the face of Eliot's ambivalence toward the women's movement and her tendency to dissociate herself from the common lot of women, apologists frequently focus not so much on Eliot's attitudes as on her achievements. Typically the contention goes: 'George Eliot herself, as an artist, was one of the best arguments for the feminist cause', or '*Middlemarch* itself is a testament to the possibility of "far-resonant action", and "long-recognizable deed". No feminist need feel disappointed.'[60] Such argument should not be discounted, for as Margaret Fuller testified in *Woman in the Nineteenth Century*,

Another sign of the times is furnished by the triumphs of female authorship. These have been great and constantly increasing. Women have taken possession of so many provinces for which men have pronounced them unfit, that though these still declare there are some inaccessible to them, it is difficult to say just *where* they must stop.

The shining names of famous women have cast light upon the path of the sex, and many obstructions have been removed.[61]

However, given the daunting magnitude of Eliot's reputation, it is well to remember that as well as inspire other women writers, Eliot could equally oppress them. The obverse of Fuller's argument is in fact provided earlier in her own book, when she recognizes the double-edged quality of the celebration of an exceptional individual:

[57] George Eliot, 'Belles Lettres', *Westminster Review*, Jan. 1857, p. 306.

[58] Eliot, 'Silly Novels', p. 324.

[59] George Eliot, 'Belles Lettres', *Westminster Review*, Jan. 1856, p. 300.

[60] Catherine McMahon, 'George Eliot and the Feminist Movement in Nineteenth Century England', Diss. Stanford, 1961, p. 322; Kathleen Blake, '*Middlemarch* and the Woman Question', *Nineteenth Century Fiction*, Vol. 21, No. 3, p. 312.

[61] Margaret Fuller, *Woman in the Nineteenth Century* (London: H. G. Clark, 1845), p. 87.

Wherever she has herself arisen in national or private history, and nobly shone forth in any form of excellence, men have received her, not only willingly, but with triumph. Their encomiums indeed, are always, in some sense mortifying; they show too much surprise. Can this be you? he cries to the transfigured Cinderella: well, I should never have thought it, but I am very glad. We will tell everyone that you have 'surpassed your sex.'[62]

Nevertheless, as we have argued throughout this study, it was the literature of the major women writers as much—or indeed more—than their lives that contributed to the controversy over women's friendships and communities. In the discussion of Eliot's fiction in the following chapter we shall consider whether the depiction of women's relationships in her novels confirms or contradicts the stern, frequently unsympathetic detachment from women in her life.

[62] Ibid., p. 36.

7

George Eliot's Fiction

Patient in Our Prison House

I

George Eliot's treatment of women's relationships resembles Charlotte Brontë's in its tendencies to define female characters in relation to men rather than to each other and to create male mentors as the crucial figures in the heroines' lives. However, unlike Brontë, Eliot values acquiescence more highly than assertion in her women and her ideal heterosexual relationships are not the struggles for equality one finds in Brontë.

All three major authors considered in this study portray their women characters as under threat, but whereas Gaskell and Brontë locate that threat primarily in the external world, for Eliot's female characters the enemy is within. In Eliot's view the threat stems from a peculiarly feminine instability, and the solution to it lies in the stability of an external, masculine world. Consequently women are dependent on men in a most fundamental way, and Eliot's conception of what women might offer each other in friendship is more severely circumscribed than either Gaskell's or Brontë's.

Eliot's view of the nature of women's relations is deeply ambivalent, recognizing at once the positive, sustaining role and the divisive, destructive element in women's various and inevitable interactions— as community members, participants in the same rites of womanhood, sexual rivals, spinsters and wives, mothers and daughters.

Like Gaskell and Brontë, for example, Eliot perceives the relationships between servants and their mistresses as like a 'family bond', 'all "sisters" together'. So Nanny supports and protects Milly Barton in 'Amos Barton', and Denner provides unswerving loyalty and affection for Mrs. Transome in *Felix Holt*, just as Tantripp does for Dorothea in *Middlemarch*. Like Gaskell, too, Eliot presents characters such as Dolly Winthrop, Mrs. Pettifer, and Janet Dempster who are bonded together through mutual attendance as nurses. However, Eliot distinguishes sharply between healing and nursing, depicting medical treatment as largely a male prerogative and folk medicine, as practised by Mrs. Holt or the Wise Woman at Tarley in *Silas Marner*, as mere quackery.

Indeed, Eliot seems to regard nursing as a part of that 'great amount of social unproductive labour which needs to be done by women' (*EL* IV. 425). Unlike Gaskell's Ruth, who embraces and justifies nursing as a profession, Mrs. Pettifer remains proudly unpaid, Dolly Winthrop remedies the failure of the hired monthly nurse, and Janet Dempster introduces a finer element into the sickroom previously occupied by Mr. Pilgrim's professional nurses.

Although both Eliot and Brontë accord a primary importance to male figures in their fiction, Eliot is more inclined to imagine her central relationships within the context of a wider community in which women play an important and creative role. Repeatedly galleries of secondary female characters are represented not merely as part of a backdrop to the community, but as the initiators and creators of communality. So, for example, in 'Amos Barton' when Milly falls ill, the Shepperton women set aside their disapproval of the Countess Czerlaski's presence at the vicarage to visit the sick-room, send food, and take care of the children. Similarly the softening of feeling towards Silas Marner after he has been robbed is 'accompanied with a more active sympathy, especially amongst the women'.[1] In all, it is this 'salt of goodness' in communities which is cohesive—'which keeps the world together.'[2]

Like the women in Gaskell's *Mary Barton*, whose memories and shared domestic tasks bind the community and give it continuity with the past, Eliot's female characters are also frequently the custodians of group history. Characters are linked through a domestic network of kitchen and hearth in which news is received, exchanged, and assessed. For example, the Hackit's housemaid hears the news of Milly Barton's illness from the shepherd and relays it to her mistress, who hurries out to question the shepherd (recalling a similar sequence in *Cranford* when the news of Captain Brown's death passes from the carter through the maid to Miss Jenkyns, who, like Mrs. Hackit, promptly intervenes to offer assistance). Mrs. Patten, the hostess of the fireside gathering to which the narrator directs the reader for information in 'Amos Barton', is recognized in 'Mr. Gilfil's Love-Story'

---

[1] George Eliot, *Silas Marner* (Edinburgh: William Blackwood & Sons, 1861), p. 242. All further references to this work appear in the text, abbreviated as *SM*.

[2] George Eliot, *Scenes of Clerical Life* (Edinburgh: William Blackwood & Sons, 1858), II. 77. All further references to this work appear in the text, abbreviated as *Scenes.*

as 'a great source of oral tradition in Shepperton' (*Scenes*, I. 178). Similarly, Mrs. Cadwallader functions as 'the diplomatist of Tipton and Freshitt' in *Middlemarch*, carrying news and advice in her round of domestic visits.[3]

At the same time this importance of women in the oral tradition of communities is inseparable from Eliot's more negative sense of women instigating scandal and gossip. Even though the men of St. Oggs in *The Mill on the Floss*, for example, are not exempt from a fondness of scandal, Eliot sees this preoccupation as essentially feminine. Gossip gives the men's conversation an 'effeminate character', and the males remain bemused by the 'mutual hatred of the women', just as Mr. Phipps in 'Janet's Repentance' wonders 'how it was women were so fond of running each other down' (*Scenes*, II. 228).[4] When Eliot depicts the good-natured Mrs. Hacket as also having a tongue 'as sharp as [a] lancet' and taking the 'utmost enjoyment [in] spoiling a friend's self-satisfaction' (*Scenes*, I. 13), she anticipates her acid satire against the wives of Middlemarch whose 'ardent charity' works at 'setting the virtuous mind to make a neighbour unhappy for her good' (*M*. IV. 196).

This conception of the positive and negative aspects of women in communities is balanced in Eliot's vision in *Middlemarch* with the kind of even-handedness that she urged on writers like Jewsbury for the sake of a 'better understanding as to women's true position'.[5] Thus, although Eliot is fully aware of the reductive 'hampering thread-like pressure' of a community, she also recognizes that the interdependence and mutual responsibility within a community like Middlemarch are sources of strength and goodness. They give effectiveness to the best, as well as the worst, impulses in human nature, enabling Dorothea, for example, to exert 'the saving influence of a noble nature' (*M* IV. 309) and to hold up 'an ideal for others in her believing conception of them' (*M* IV. 252). Significantly, Dorothea is drawn to community living, ill at ease with the isolation of Lowick, where she lives like country gentry 'in a rarified social air: dotted apart' (*M* II. 185), and she dreams of taking a great deal of land and making 'a little colony, where everybody should work, and all the work should be

---

[3] George Eliot, *Middlemarch* (Edinburgh: William Blackwood & Sons, 1871–2), I. 100. All further references to this work appear in the text, abbreviated as *M*.

[4] George Eliot, *The Mill on the Floss*, Clarendon edn. (1860; rpt. Oxford: Oxford University Press, 1980), p. 445. All further references to this work appear in the text, abbreviated as *MF*.

[5] Eliot, 'Belles Lettres', *Westminster Review*, July 1855, p. 295.

done well. [She] should know every one of the people, and be their friend' (*M* III. 224).

Female characters in Eliot share a particular understanding which stems from their common experience as women. It is evident in the 'watchful eyes' of Mrs. Hackit, who perceives accurately, and despite Milly's apparent improved health, that Milly '"won't stan' havin' many more children"' (*Scenes*, I. 89)—something Milly's husband fails to recognize. More characteristically, it takes the form of the recognition by women of the rules that govern their own behaviour in the dynamics of their relationships with men. For example, Mrs. Bede detects Dinah's love for Adam before it occurs to her son: '"I know she's fond on him, as I know th' wind's comin' in at the door, an' that's anoof"', and Mrs. Poyser has 'her own rules of propriety' on the matter:

> . . . she considered that a young girl was not to be treated sharply in the presence of a respectable man who was courting her. That would not be fair-play: every woman was young in her turn, and had her chances of matrimony, which it was a point of honour for other women not to spoil—just as one market-woman who has sold her own eggs must not try to balk another of a customer.[6]

Sharing an understanding of those rules, women are much less likely to be deceived by each other. Thus, Amos Barton remains blinded to the selfishness of the Countess long after Milly has faced the truth: 'for women never betray themselves to men as they do to each other' (*Scenes*, I. 127), and in *Adam Bede* Mrs. Poyser is never duped by Hetty's appearance in the way her husband is: 'It is generally a feminine eye that first detects the moral deficiences hidden under the "dear deceit" of beauty' (*AB* I. 289).

Such shared understanding could potentially either unite women as fellow-travellers with the solidarity of 'fair-play' or divide them as their own most informed, and therefore most threatening, rivals. We have seen, for example, that Gaskell's conception of women's relationships challenges a view such as Eliza Lynn Linton's that no 'woman's friendship ever existed free from jealousy'.[7] While Gaskell does not deny a capacity for jealousy amongst women, she sees it as less disruptive and divisive than male jealousy. Her view is partly

---

[6] George Eliot, *Adam Bede* (Edinburgh: William Blackwood & Sons, 1859), III. 248; *Adam Bede*, II. 97. All further references to this work appear in the text, abbreviated as *AB*.

[7] See Chapter 3 above, p. 66.

due to a conventional sense that women are devoid of libidinous feeling and therefore incapable of the obsessive, desperate jealousy of some of her male characters. However, it also derives from a belief that a shared object of affection can be a source of union rather than division, as she suggests in the recurring image of Ruth and Naomi. In contrast, sexual rivalry almost inevitably plays a more prominent part in women's relations for Brontë and Eliot, given the central role assumed by the male in the lives of their female characters. For example, it is precisely this understanding shared by women that makes Lucy Snowe such a dangerous protégée for Madame Beck, for once Lucy sees through Madame Beck's 'habitual disguise' she is able to triumph over her. Eliot, likewise, has no expectations of female solidarity, and when she writes in *Middlemarch* of 'that dissatisfaction which in women's minds is continually turning into trivial jealousy, referring to no real claims, springing from no deeper passion than the vague exactingness of egoism, and yet capable of impelling action as well as speech' (*M* III. 317), her position seems not far removed from Lynn Linton's.[8] In 'Mr. Gilfil's Love-Story' Caterina's life is transformed by her obsessive jealousy toward Capt. Wybrow's fiancée, Beatrice, and the female rivalry extends beyond the two lovers to encompass the mothers, Lady Cheverel and Lady Assher. Eliot stresses the satisfaction that a woman like Lady Cheverel derives from such competitiveness. She is 'serenely radiant' in the assurance a single glance had given her of Lady Assher's inferiority (*Scenes*, I. 254), and 'having quite her share of the critical acumen which characterizes the mutual estimates of the fair sex' (*Scenes*, I. 305), she holds a similar reassuring, low opinion of Lady Assher's daughter Beatrice.

Not all Eliot's female characters are given to sexual rivalry and jealousy, but the absence of such feeling toward other women is seen as a particular virtue, the 'rarest quality' in a character such as Lucy in *The Mill on the Floss*: 'a woman who was loving and thoughtful for other women, not giving them Judas-kisses with eyes askance on their welcome defects, but with real care and vision for their half-hidden pains and mortifications, with long ruminating enjoyment of little pleasures prepared for them' (*MF* 325). And far from seeing sexual jealousy as less disruptive in women's lives than in men's, in 'Mr. Gilfil's Love-Story' Eliot contrasts Maynard's self-control as he is

---

8 Lynn Linton's views first appeared in serial publication in the *Saturday Review*, Eliot's favourite weekly.

forced to witness Caterina's infatuation with Capt. Wybrow against the passionate, almost insane rage that takes possession of Caterina as she watches Wybrow with Beatrice Assher. In *Daniel Deronda*, when Mirah comes to feel ' "the love that makes jealousy" ', it is at the cost of all her former serenity, producing 'a jarring shock through her frame' (*DD* IV).[9]

The comparison between Hetty and Dinah in 'The Two Bed-Chambers', Chapter XV of *Adam Bede*, which revealingly typifies the tendency in Eliot to present relationships between women through dramatic moments of confrontation and contrast in which the support offered is essentially one-way and the relationship unequal—Maggie and Lucy, Romola and Tessa, Dorothea and Rosamond, Gwendolen and Mirah—also reaffirms the serenity that springs from unconcern for sexual rivalry. So while Dinah adjourns to her room to look out onto a natural world beyond herself and contemplate 'all the dear people whom she had learned to care about amongst these peaceful fields' (*AB* I. 292), Hetty in the adjacent chamber is absorbed with her reflection in the mirror. The openness of Dinah's room is contrasted with the secrecy of Hetty's room, its door bolted against intrusion upon her ritual of self-adornment. Hetty understands only the logic of sexual attraction and regards other women as nuisances at best, and rivals at worst. Thus she rebuffs Dinah's 'anxious affection . . . push[ing] her away impatiently' (*AB* I. 300), just as she later repels Molly who offers her smelling salts in church (*AB* II. 45).

Gwendolen's similarly exclusive preoccupation with men is equally divisive in *Daniel Deronda*, where Eliot describes her heroine's isolation from her sex:

In the ladies' dining-room it was evident that Gwendolen was not a general favourite with her own sex; there were no beginnings of intimacy between her and other girls, and in conversation they rather noticed what she said than spoke to her in free exchange. Perhaps it was that she was not much interested in them, and when left alone in their company had a sense of empty benches. Mrs. Vulcany once remarked that Miss Harleth was too fond of the gentlemen; but we know that she was not in the least fond of them—she was only fond of their homage—and women did not give her homage. (*DD* I. 205)

Gwendolen measures her relationships with women in terms of the threat they present in the competition for male approval. Recogniz-

[9] George Eliot, *Daniel Deronda* (Edinburgh: William Blackwood & Sons, 1876), IV. 219 and IV. 79. All further references to this work appear in the text, abbreviated as *DD*.

ing in her cousin Anna's 'timid appearance and miniature figure'
that she and Anna 'could hardly be rivals', she deigns to kiss her cousin
'with real cordiality' (*DD* I. 50). Gwendolen is more disconcerted
by Catherine Arrowpoint. Catherine possesses 'a certain mental
superiority which could not be explained away' (*DD* I. 87), and
Gwendolen suspects condescension in Catherine's 'kindly solicitude'
(*DD* I. 86). When Gwendolen applies to Klesmer for advice in
launching a stage career, his discouraging response is galling in itself,
but the 'suggestion of Miss Arrowpoint as a patroness was . . .
another detail to its repulsiveness' (*DD* II. 109).

Lydia Glasher is the one woman with whom Gwendolen might
conceivably feel some solidarity as a fellow victim of Grandcourt's exquisite cruelty, and yet the passionate pride and divisive jealousy of
the two women make them the bitterest of enemies. In this relationship the special understanding women have of each other affords only
a sureness of 'exactly where to wound'.[10] Gwendolen betrays her sex
in her dealings with Lydia and is brought bitterly to recognize the
nature of her action: 'That unhappy-faced women and her children
. . . kept repeating themselves in her imagination like the clinging
memory of a disgrace' (*DD* II. 197). For her part, Lydia Glasher
channels the hatred and anger which might more appropriately be
directed against Grandcourt, her tormentor, against her fellow
victim.

II

As her letters indicate, Eliot was scarcely an apologist for unmarried
women, and she recognized 'complete union' and 'perfection' only in
the 'mutual subjection of the soul between a man and woman' (*EL*
IV. 468). Likewise in her fiction exclusively female groupings and
unmarried women are distinguished by a sense of lack and never
realize their full, feminine potential.

Whereas Brontë at least offers some challenge through her heroine
Caroline Helstone to the stereotyped generalities applied to spinsters,
Eliot actually employs them repeatedly in her fiction. Miss Winifred
Farebrother in *Middlemarch*, for example, is 'nipped and subdued as
single women are apt to be who spend their lives in uninterrupted
subjection to their elders' (*M* I. 302), and the kindly Mr. Irwin in
Adam Bede is burdened by 'two hopelessly-maiden sisters'—one

---

10 Ellis, *The Women of England*, p. 225.

'sickly', the other 'spoken of without adjective'—who are 'old maids for the prosaic reason, that they never received an eligible offer' (*AB* I. 120).

In 'Amos Barton' the emotional sterility of the Cross Farm's female household, which Mrs. Patten shares with her fifty-year-old maiden neice Janet Gibbs, is deliberately contrasted to the warmth and fulsomeness of their natural surroundings. Mrs. Patten is a 'childless old lady' (*Scenes*, I. 10), who 'used to adore her husband, and now she adores her money, cherishing a quiet blood-relations hatred for her niece, Janet Gibbs, who, she knows, expects a large legacy, and whom she is determined to disappoint' (*Scenes*, I. 14). Janet's life is equally sterile in its way, exemplifying waste and frustration. She has 'refused the most ineligible offers out of devotion to her aged aunt' (*Scenes*, I. 11), who in turn taunts Janet with being inexperienced—' "it's fine talking . . . old maids' husbands are al'ys well-managed" ' (*Scenes*, I. 22).

Eliot does create a lively and capable spinster in *Silas Marner* in the figure of Priscilla Lammeter, who manages the family farm and controls her father with equal aplomb. Priscilla is not touched by the emotional sterility of most of Eliot's old maids, and behind a certain bluster she betrays 'a good-natured, self-forgetful cheeriness' (*SM* 190), especially in the supportive role she fulfils toward her sister Nancy. Nevertheless much of Priscilla's vigour comes from her self-parody, and derives its sharpness from her own sense of conformity to a spinsterly stereotype:

'For I *am* ugly—there's no denying that . . . . The pretty uns do for fly-catchers—they keep the men off us. I've no opinion o' the men, Miss Gunn—I don't know what *you* have. And as for fretting and stewing about what *they*'ll think of you . . . it's a folly no woman need be guilty of, if she's got a good father and a good home . . . if you've got a man by the chimney-corner, it doesn't matter if he's childish—the business needn't be broke up.' (*SM* 186)

Furthermore, such female self-sufficiency is hardly endorsed by Eliot, for the portrait of Priscilla managing the farm remains little more than a caricature of competence and self-fulfilment in comparison with the depiction of her married counterparts, Mrs. Poyser and Mrs. Garth. The strength and independence of both these women do not rely, like Priscilla's, on a waspish repudiation of men. Mrs. Poyser, who 'has the spirit of three men' (*AB* II. 343), works in partnership none the less with her husband, 'mak[ing] one quarter o' the rent, and sav[ing] th' other quarter' (*AB* II. 337), and she contentedly takes her place on winter's evenings, 'when the whole family, in patriarchal fashion . . . assembled in that glorious kitchen' (*AB* I. 179). Mrs. Garth is even more insistently identified with a male world. She is 'disproportionately indulgent toward the failings of men', and her loyalty is consistently toward males: '[she] had never poured any pathetic confidences into the ears of her feminine neighbours concerning Mr. Garth's want of prudence' (*M* II. 29). Her role in the family as a decision-maker on 'ninety-nine points' is strictly balanced by a 'womanly . . . principle of subordination' (*M* III. 226) on the hundredth.

Although few authors have more brilliantly anatomized failed marriages, Eliot nevertheless defines the married state as the most fulfilling. In *Felix Holt*, although she concedes that 'since Adam's marriage, it has been good for some men to be alone, and for some women also', it is precisely because Esther is 'intensely of the feminine type' that she is 'not one of these [presumably unfeminine] women'.[11] Rather, the feminine Esther is ' "a fair divided excellence, whose fulness of perfection" must be in marriage' (*FH* 360). More revealingly still, Eliot describes the effect that Gwendolen's albeit disastrous marriage has had on her character in terms of almost mystical transfiguration:

Mrs. Grandcourt was handsomer than Gwendolen Harleth: her grace and expression were informed by a greater variety of inward experience, giving new play to the facial muscles, new attitudes in movement and repose; her whole person and air had the nameless something which often makes a woman more interesting after marriage than before, less confident that all things are according to her opinion, and yet with less of deer-like shyness—more fully a human being. (*DD* IV. 118)

Groups of women without men have no more satisfactory a lot than single women in Eliot's fiction. In *Daniel Deronda*, for example, Gwendolen reigns as a 'princess in exile' (*DD* I. 36) in the Harleth household, 'waited on by mother, sisters, governess, and maids' (*DD* I. 36), but it is at best an uneasy dominion within which the roles of the participants are ill defined. Gwendolen's haughty dominance dissolves at times into child-like dependence and fear, and the lack of

[11] George Eliot, *Felix Holt*, Clarendon edn. (1866; rpt. Oxford: Oxford University Press, 1980), p. 360. All further references to this work appear in the text, abbreviated as *FH*.

a focus of authority within the domestic group leaves her looking beyond it. With the move to Offendene, Gwendolen regards 'as a matter of extreme interest to her that she was to have the near countenance of a dignified male relative, and that the family would cease to be entirely, insipidly feminine' (*DD* I. 49), and she carefully cultivates 'the shelter of [Mr. Gascoigne's] fatherly indulgence' (*DD* I. 171). More generally, in moments of crisis Gwendolen consistently looks to male figures outside her home—Mr. Gascoigne, Klesmer, Grandcourt, and Deronda.

In the same novel the Meyrick family group presents an apparent contrast to the Harleth women. When Deronda takes Mirah to the Meyrick house for refuge, he entrusts her, like the Maenads to the Delphic women, to a female domain: 'a motherly figure of quakerish neatness, and three girls who hardly knew any evil closer to them than what lay in history books' (*DD* I. 354). The group becomes literally exclusive in its femaleness when Hans is banished in the interests of propriety to allow the Meyrick women to take Mirah in, and yet Eliot continues to represent it in positive, indeed idyllic, terms: 'But mother and daughters were all united by a triple bond—family love; admiration for the finest work, the best action; and habitual industry' (*DD* I. 358). Significantly, the Meyrick household escapes sterility or the sense of lack precisely because of its receptiveness to, rather than exclusion of, males. The sororal act of giving refuge to Mirah is at the same time an act of service to Deronda, whom they revere. Also, although Hans is ostensibly banished, he remains the favoured child of Mrs. Meyrick, and his presence enlivens the group in a way reminiscent of Rochester's advent in *Jane Eyre*'s female world at Thornfield: '"We hardly thought that Mirah could laugh till Hans came"' (*DD* III. 120).

The ending of *Romola* offers points of comparison with the kind of sisterly solidarity Gaskell explores in 'The Grey Woman'. Romola, aware of her husband's illicit relationship with the peasant girl, Tessa, wishes 'above all things to find that young woman and her children, and to take care of them'.[12] She succeeds in her search, and with the assistance of her cousin Monna Brigida sets up a home for them all in the Borgo degli Albizzi. However, Romola is in some

---

[12] George Eliot, *Romola* (London: Smith, Elder & Co., 1863), III. 261. All further references to this work will appear in the text, abbreviated as *R*. In this, Eliot's heroine is also comparable to Aurora Leigh, the heroine of Elizabeth Barrett Browning's epic poem published six years earlier.

ways a reluctant sister to Tessa. Not only does she feel an inevitable 'woman's sense of indignity' (*R* III. 72) at her position in relation to her husband's mistress, but throughout the novel Romola consistently reacts against the all-female world of convents with 'dread lest she should be drawn at last into fellowship with some wretched superstition—into the company of the howling fanatics and weeping nuns who had been her contempt from childhood till now' (*R* II. 204).

Indeed the predominant feeling that distinguishes this novel's ending from that of Gaskell's tale is resignation. Monna Brigida's home is not so much a genuine and fulfilling alternative as a last resort. Romola has been betrayed by the male world in which she has sought so variously and so hard to believe, and her retreat in the end to Borgo degli Albizzi is conditioned, even forced, by that unworthy world: 'She never for a moment told herself that it was heroism or exalted charity in her to seek these beings; she needed something that she was bound specially to care for; she yearned to clasp the children and to make them love her' (*R* III. 263). Even so, Romola's final impulse is, significantly, a desire to believe in the male world she has forsaken: 'her soul cried out for some explanation of his lapses which would make it still possible for her to believe that the main striving of his life had been pure and grand' (*R* III. 273). A comparable feeling of resignation in the face of disappointment imbues both Gwendolen's return to the female world of Offendene at the end of *Daniel Deronda* and Armgart's retreat into retirement to Walpurga's birthplace at the conclusion of *Armgart.*

III

In *Jane Eyre*, as we have seen, the heroine's conscious choice of a sexual, rather than a maternal, bond is underscored by her unconscious rejection of motherhood and equally by the imagery of the novel which at times startlingly violates conventional maternal images. In Eliot, however, the imagined maternal violence of Brontë's novel becomes real, and motherhood, rather than invariably uniting women as it does in Gaskell, often operates as a divisive and destructive force.

Eliot does present maternal ideals in her fiction, but she is frequently at her least impressive in doing so. The portrait of Milly Barton, for example, is remarkably for its sentimentality and conventionality, with Milly depicted as a 'gentle Madonna' (*Scenes*, I. 28), the essence of patience, thrift, and motherly love. A similar sentimentality marks Eliot's description of Mirah's feelings for her lost mother in *Daniel Deronda*. In her first confidential exchange with Mrs. Meyrick, for example, Mirah opens the conversation with the unlikely declaration: ' "I think my life began with waking up and loving my mother's face" ' (*DD* II. 13), and later, in a moment worthy of the dialogue Eliot satirizes in 'Silly Novels by Lady Novelists', Mirah interrupts Deronda and the Meyrick sisters to announce: ' "I think I can say what I mean, now . . . . When the best thing comes into our thoughts, it is like what my mother has been to me" ' (*DD* III. 124).

Eliot's imaginative power is more impressively engaged, however, when she explores the failure of motherhood. For a number of her female characters the experience of motherhood is not the fulfilling solution to life's ills that Eliot's own eulogy suggests it might be:

Mighty is the force of motherhood . . . . It transforms all things by its vital heat: it turns timidity into fierce courage, and dreadless defiance into tremulous submission; it turns thoughtlessness into foresight, and yet stills all anxiety into calm content; it makes selfishness become self-denial, and gives even to hard vanity the glance of admiring love. Yes; if Janet had been a mother, she might have been saved from much sin, and therefore from much sorrow. (*Scenes*, II. 224)

It is ironic that such celebration is found in 'Janet's Repentance', for in the same tale Eliot presents in the characters of Janet's mother and mother-in-law two women whose sorrow and disappointment arise out of their maternity. The portrait of Janet's mother, Mrs Raynor, hanging in the room where Janet is beaten by her husband, inspires the narrator to exclaim: 'Poor grey-haired woman! Was it for this you suffered a mother's pangs in your lone widowhood five-and-thirty years ago?', while the mother herself 'lies sleepless and praying in her lonely house weeping the hard tears of age' (*Scenes*, II. 124). With corresponding disappointment, Dempster's mother lives in her son's home bearing mute witness to his violence:

O it is piteous—that sorrow of aged women! In early youth, perhaps, they said to themselves, 'I shall be happy when I have a husband to love me best of all;' then when the husband was too careless, 'My child will comfort me;' then through the mother's watching and toil, 'My child will repay me all when it grows up.' And at last, after the long journey of years has been wearily travelled through, the mother's heart is weighed down by a heavier burthen and no hope remains but the grave. (*Scenes*, II. 148)

Similarly in *Felix Holt*, when Harold's return crushes Mrs. Transome's hopes and she finds herself afraid of a son 'who was utterly unmanageable' (*FH* 99), Mrs. Transome is left bitterly wondering who would be a mother 'if she could foresee what a slight thing she will be to her son when she is old' (*FH* 36). Mrs. Transome's delusion in imagining that 'a beautiful man-child' will bring her abundant happiness is, Eliot insists, a 'common dream', and the recognition of 'a fact perhaps kept a little too much in the background, that mothers have a self larger than their maternity' (*FH* 98) seems far removed from such earlier sentimental portraits as that of Milly Barton.

Whereas Gaskell tends to portray mothers united in a 'sisterhood of shared pain' transcending other antipathies, Eliot more readily envisages the intensities of maternal emotion directed against other women. For example, the shared disappointment of Mrs. Raynor and Mrs. Dempster only serves to exacerbate hostilities between them with Mrs. Dempster reproaching Mrs. Raynor 'for encouraging her daughter's faults by a too exclusive sympathy' (*Scenes*, II. 147). And in *Daniel Deronda* Lydia Glasher's hatred of Gwendolen is deepened by her love for her children: 'The equivocal position which she had not minded about for herself was now telling upon her through her children, whom she loved with the added passion of atonement' (*DD* II. 250).

Even within families in Eliot's fiction the bonds of womanhood are frequently betrayed. So mothers acquiesce to a conspiracy of silence as they give their daughters up to be married. Janet's demand of her mother, '"How could I help it? How could I know what would come? Why didn't you tell me, mother?—why did you let me marry? You knew what brutes men could be; and there's no help for me—no hope,"' (*Scenes*, II. 234), could just as well be made by Gwendolen to Mrs. Davilow when she is left in naïve ignorance after asking '"Mamma, have men generally children before they are married?"' (*DD* II. 237).

Equally divisive is the partiality Eliot's mothers often demonstrate toward their male children. For example, as Mrs. Tulliver channels all her love to Tom, the family becomes torn by fluctuating jealousies and resentments. Similarly in *Adam Bede* Mr. Irvine's mother demonstrates a 'hardness towards her daughters, which was the more striking from its contrast with her doting fondness towards [her son]' (*AB* I. 121), and even Mrs. Bede's 'idolatrous love of Adam' (*AB* I. 74) has something of that unfair allegiance to a male world, discriminating as it does against the 'gentle' Seth, who 'had learned to make himself, as Adam said, "very handy in the housework," that he might save his mother from too great weariness' (*AB* III. 238).

Gaskell and Brontë also depict failed mothers, although neither perhaps with the same frequency as Eliot. However, Eliot extends the possibilities and implications of that failure to challenge conceptions of motherly love and tenderness in much more disturbing ways than do either of her predecessors. In characters such as Hetty and Mrs. Transome the most negative aspects of their personalities actually find focus in their maternal, or more accurately anti-maternal, feelings. Whereas Jane Eyre may dream of accidently causing the death of the child that 'clung round her neck in terror' (*JE* 357), Hetty actually murders her infant which—recalling the image from Brontë's novel —'was like a heavy weight hanging around [her] neck' and which she 'seemed to hate' (*AB* III. 166). While the birth of Ruth's illegitimate child is instrumental in her salvation, the same event in Hetty's life seals her damnation. Admittedly, Hetty's infanticide results more from her consuming selfishness than considered hostility toward the child, but even after the event Hetty remains essentially unrepentant, and the fundamental instinct that Gaskell trusts as a positive force is simply lacking in Hetty: 'Hetty's counsel . . . tried, without result, to elicit evidence that the prisoner had shown some movements of maternal affection towards the child' (*AB* III. 128).

Similarly in *Daniel Deronda* the Princess Halm-Eberstein is devoid of maternal feelings, abandoning her child in the act of rejecting the role of 'mere daughter and mother' (*DD* IV. 93), and neither expecting nor offering affection in the reunion with her son: ' "I have not the foolish notion that you can love me merely because I am your mother" ' (*DD* IV. 19). As evidence of Eliot's greater imaginative engagement with the negative aspects of motherhood, the bitter, concentrated force of the Princess's declarations balance, and indeed almost obscure, the more conventional example offered by Mrs. Meyrick in the same novel.

Maternal instincts are not so much absent as perverted in the character of Mrs. Transome in *Felix Holt*. Her character is in many ways more disturbing than Hetty's, for although she is not guilty of any overt crime, she actively nurtures the idea of infanticide: 'The mother's early raptures had lasted but a short time, and even while they lasted there had grown up in the midst of them a hungry desire, like a black poisonous plant feeding in the sunlight,—the desire that her first, rickety, ugly, imbecile child should die, and leave room for her darling, of whom she could be proud' (*FH* 22). Likewise she later wishes her second son 'should never have been born' (*FH* 317). She is incapable

of the 'suppression of self' that Eliot sees as necessary if the early exclusive absorption of motherly love is to 'continue to be a joy . . . [like]
other long-lived love' (*FH* 22). Mrs. Transome regards her child as a
possession, and her disappointment at Harold's return stems from the
reversal of power relations: 'she had been accustomed to dictate, and
. . . as he had left her when he was a boy, she had perhaps indulged the
dream that he would come back a boy' (*FH* 321). Even in the pitiful
descriptions toward the end of the novel of Mrs. Transome's loneliness,
in which she longs for the affection she has alienated and wishes that
Esther were her daughter, Eliot is uncompromising in her recognition
that Mrs. Transome cannot relinquish the framework of power that has
defined all her relationships. Thus the solace that Esther provides
comes from 'the charm of [her] sweet young deference' (*FH* 310).

IV

While it should be acknowledged that Eliot's view of women is deeply
ambivalent, it is also necessary to recognize more broadly that those
relationships between women remain fundamentally secondary to their
relationships with men. Nevertheless this centrality of the male in
Eliot's fiction is not in itself a repudiation of all things feminine,
because she invests her heroes with positive female qualities, explicitly
blending characteristics which she still insists on categorizing in terms
of gender with the same strictness she applied in her criticism. For example, Daniel Deronda possesses a 'mental balance . . . moved by an
affectionateness such as we are apt to call feminine, disposing him to
yield in ordinary details, while he had a certain inflexibility of judgment, an independence of opinion, held to be rightfully masculine'
(*DD* II. 215). The description of his 'ardent clinging nature' (*DD* I.
307) recalls the terms Eliot uses for the portrait of Dorothea, and like
Dorothea—and, indeed, Romola—Deronda performs the function of
Milton's daughter, reading for his friend Hans whose eyes have failed,
just as Dorothea reads for Casaubon and Romola for her father. Also,
like many female heroines, Deronda is haunted by thoughts of his
mother 'about whose character and lot he continually wondered, and
never dared to ask' (*DD* I. 339). Will Ladislaw too is preoccupied
with thoughts of his lost mother, and in both heroes their foreignness
and the uncertainty of their backgrounds make them seem dispossessed, as the heroines of the novels are both literally and figuratively,
in a male world of wills, codicils and entails.

Male characters in Eliot's fiction also frequently demonstrate the 'maternal tenderness in a man's protective love'.[13] Mordecai, for example, shows a 'maternal' caring in his relationship with Jacob Cohen (*DD* III. 145), and Caterina's natural father in 'Mr. Gilfil's Love-Story' 'seemed to exist for nothing but the child: he tended it, he dandled it, he chatted to it' (*Scenes*, I. 216), in marked contrast to Lady Cheverel's 'uncaressing authoritative goodwill' (*Scenes*, II. 29). Similarly in *Adam Bede* Mr. Irwine adopts a maternal tenderness toward his sisters, compensating for his mother's hardness; Will Ladislaw demonstrates 'a fondness, half artistic, half affectionate, for little children' (*M* III. 503); and in *Felix Holt* it is Felix, and not his mother, who undertakes the upbringing of the orphan Job.

The positiveness of Eliot's response to this feminization of her male characters, though, depends very much on a confidence in the masculinity of those figures—on her sense that it is ' "the strong, skilful men [who] are often the gentlest to the women and children" ' (*AB* I. 264). Eliot distinguishes sharply, however, between that strength and the weakness and inadequacy which can also feminize males, and she responds to the latter with distaste. Silas Marner, for example, is almost entirely associated with a feminine world, willingly embracing a maternal role toward the abandoned Eppie under the attentive supervision of Dolly Winthrop. His occupation as a weaver makes him ' "partly as handy as a woman, for weaving comes next to spinning" ' (*SM* 263), and correspondingly he succeeds the Wise Woman at Tarley in the practice of folk medicine, having 'inherited from his mother some acquaintance with medicinal herbs and their preparation' (*SM* 12). However, it is Silas's weakness and his status as an outcast, rather than any positive mixture of strength and gentleness, that contributes to the feminization of his world. Nearly blind and epileptic, he is more pitiful than impressive, and Eliot frequently represents him through images that suggest a reduction, rather than a wholeness, of humanity, as he weaves 'like a spider' (*SM* 26) and with 'the unquestioning activity of a spinning insect' (*SM* 27).

Similarly, in *The Mill on the Floss* Philip Wakem is consistently defined in feminine terms. His pale face is 'full of pleading, timid love —like a woman's (*MF* 296) and he is 'by nature half feminine in sensitiveness' (*MF* 291). Philip's response to his feelings of jealousy toward Stephen—'his irritable, susceptible nerves . . . pressed upon almost to frenzy' (*MF* 405)—is more reminiscent of Caterina's 'fierce

<hr />

[13] Simcox, 'George Eliot', p. 783.

palpitations' than the 'manly' response typified by Maynard Gilfil's restraint or even Adam Bede's violence toward Arthur Donnithorne. In his deformity and weakness Philip is seen as something of a failed male, and if Tom Tulliver 'never thoroughly over[comes] his repulsion to Philip's deformity' (*MF* 145), it is not clear that Eliot does either. Most tellingly, he cannot answer all Maggie's needs, and his 'appeal was more strongly to her pity and womanly devotedness than to her vanity or other egotistic excitability' (*MF* 361).

Eliot's treatment of Seth Bede provides a rather less obvious example of essentially the same negative response to perceived weakness. In some respects Seth's womanly ways provide an attractive counterbalance to Adam's gruffness. In the workshop fight at the beginning of the novel Seth is conciliatory while Adam is pugnacious, and where 'idle tramps always felt sure they could get a copper from Seth; they scarcely ever spoke to Adam' (*AB* I. 4). Seth is more attentive to his mother, humouring her 'little unjust plaints' of which Adam 'never took notice' (*AB* II. 53). However, in another sense the repeated comparisons with Adam work against Seth. When Adam cries, Eliot notes that he 'had never sobbed before' (*AB* III. 63), whereas Seth's tears are the mark of a man 'who was easily touched' (*AB* II. 49). And while Seth can subjugate his passion: 'it was better to be Dinah's friend and brother than any other woman's husband' (*AB* III. 62), Adam explodes with 'instinctive fierceness' (*AB* II. 247) in his fight with Arthur. Throughout the novel the difference is stressed: 'there was something in the dark penetrating glance of this strong man so different from the mildness and timidity of his brother Seth' (*AB* I. 216), and such comparisons anticipate the ending of the novel, where Adam's manliness is, in effect, rewarded with the love of Dinah. Mrs. Bede rather bluntly articulates her sense of Seth's inadequacy as a husband for Dinah. ' "Thee couldstna put up wi' Seth . . . he's as handy as can be at doin' things for me when I'm bad; an' he's as fond o' th' Bible an' chappellin' as thee a't thysen. But happen, thee'dst like a husband better as isna just the cut o' thysen: the runnin' brook isna athirst for th' rain" ' (*AB* III. 246). And whatever Eliot's ironic detachment from Lisbeth Bede, masculine inadequacy tinged with saintliness is almost the only explanation for the rather absurd reconciliation of Seth to the loss of Dinah: 'But Seth? Would the lad be hurt? Hardly; for he had seemed quite contented of late, and there was no selfish jealously in him' (*AB* III. 262); and 'to walk by Dinah's

side, and be tyrannized over by Dinah and Adam's children, was uncle
Seth's earthly happiness' (*AB* III. 328).

V

This endowing of the male with feminine characteristics is similar in
some respects to Brontë's challenge to dichotomized sex roles in
Shirley. In that novel, as we have seen, Louis Moore and William Farrer
demonstrate a maternal tenderness toward their charges, and Robert
Moore's development from his early arrogance and disregard to
a more compassionate and identifiably feminine understanding and
acquiescence to feelings of love for Caroline, provides parallels with
the gradual emergence of the softer aspects of character in Felix Holt,
Adam Bede, and even to some extent Harold Transome, and their
forsaking of the scorn with which they have regarded romantic love
and marriage.

However, the real similarities in this attraction to a 'hero as mentor',
endowed with both strength and gentleness, can disguise important
differences between the two authors.[14] Brontë's ideal is essentially
androgynous, for she seeks an integrated wholeness in male and female
relations. So her attraction to the gentler characteristics of Louis
Moore is matched by admiration of the 'masculine' strengths of
Shirley. The same kind of duality and equality is evident in the
resolution of *Jane Eyre*, where Jane finds at Ferndean a totality of relationship hitherto lacking, which combines the intensity of a love
relationship with a mutuality of dependence, where Rochester's
mastery is balanced by his reliance on Jane due to his blindness. In
Villette too the business partnership of Lucy and Paul is indicative of
a more comprehensive equality. Appropriately, Brontë's heroines are
attracted to teachers—William Crimsworth, Louis Moore, and Paul
Emmanuel by profession, and even Rochester in the sense that in taking up a governess as his protégée, he educates Jane in the ways and
the confidence of a more elevated role—for the very nature of these
relationships holds at least the possibility of a developing equality as the
teacher shares knowledge and the discrepancy between dispossessed
and possessed is lessened. The relationships are, as Ellen Moers suggests, 'the result of pride rather than humility'.[15]

---

[14] Barbara Hardy, *The Novels of George Eliot: a Study in Form* (London: Athlone Press,
1963), p. 57.
[15] Moers, *Literary Women*, p. 157.

Significantly, Eliot disapproved of the blinding of Rochester, as she makes clear in a review of *Aurora Leigh* in the *Westminster Review*:

The *story* of 'Aurora Leigh' . . . has nothing either fresh or felicitous in structure or incident; and we are especially sorry that Mrs. Browning has added one more to the imitations of the catastrophe in 'Jane Eyre' by smiting her hero with blindness before he is made happy in the love of Aurora. Life has sadness and bitterness enough for a disappointed philanthropist like Romney Leigh, short of maiming or blindness; and the outflow of love and compassion towards physical ills is less rare in woman than complete sympathy with mental sorrows. Hence we think the lavish mutilation of heroes' bodies, which has become the habit of novelists, while it happily does not represent probabilities in the present state of things, weakens instead of strengthening tragic effect; and, as we said, we regret that Mrs. Browning has given this habit her strong sanction.[16]

The function that Rochester's blinding serves in the equalizing of his relationship with Jane is overlooked by Eliot, but were it not, Eliot would probably still be unsympathetic, for though like Brontë she views male and female relationships as essentially complementary, she does not see them as fundamentally equal. Eliot's attraction to certain feminine characteristics in her male characters is not matched by an admiration for masculine strengths in her fictional women. Her particular dislike of 'everything generally associated with the idea of the "masculine woman"' is evident in her fiction in, for example, the caricature of Priscilla Lammeter and, more chillingly, in the sterility of the world over which Mrs. Transome presides as 'master' (*FH* 10) and 'chief bailiff' (*FH* 20) with its dead leaves on the path, 'tarnished gilding and dinginess of the walls and furniture' (*FH* 14), and her decrepit, senile husband attending his collection of dried insects.[17] Similarly, whereas Brontë's perfect union involves the emergence and fulfilment of the self, Eliot's depends on self-suppression: 'that subjection to her husband's mind which is felt by every wife who loves her husband with passionate devotedness and full reliance' (*R* II. 69). Indeed, as Elaine Showalter observes: 'The legends attached to Brontë and Eliot in their lives were reversed in the heroines of their novels. Brontë's Jane Eyre is the heroine of fulfillment, Eliot's Maggie Tulliver is the heroine of renunciation.'[18]

Eliot regards the capacity to love as a fundamental virtue, which is in many ways especially feminine. In contrast to her friend Barbara

[16] Eliot, 'Belles Lettres', *Westminster Review*, Jan. 1857, p. 306.
[17] Cross, *George Eliot's Life*, IV. 282.
[18] Showalter, *A Literature of Their Own*, p. 112.

Bodichon's protest that love should never become the vocation of women, Eliot represents the act of loving as an end in itself for her female characters.[19] Despite its ironic detachment from Casaubon, Eliot's fiction endorses his observation that 'the great charm' of womanhood is 'its capability of an ardent self-sacrificing affection' (*M* I. 80), and in 'Mr. Gilfil's Love-Story', for example, Eliot suggests that with the 'one exception' of her ability to sing, Caterina's 'only talent lay in loving' (*Scenes*, I. 237). Furthermore, Eliot's perception of the nature of womanly love implies an intrinsic inequality in heterosexual relationships. In *Felix Holt*, for example, Eliot argues that 'the best part of a woman's love is worship' (*FH* 302), and consequently Esther's feeling that she is weak—'"my husband must be greater and nobler"' (*FH* 397)—is seen as appropriate. Esther's 'best feeling' is 'her most precious dependence', and her 'clinging of the heart' is a 'great and mysterious gift' (*FH* 359). Similarly, in *Adam Bede* Hetty is shaken by her 'first passion' and experiences 'for the first time that sense of helpless dependence on another's feeling which awakens the clinging deprecating womanhood even in the shallowest girl' (*AB* II. 89).

The consequence of such a conception of womanly love is that women are seen as living through male figures and finding fulfilment in them. In *Adam Bede* the death of old Mr. Donnithorne threatens the very rationale of his daughter Lydia's life: 'after the manner of women, she mourned for the father who had made her life important' (*AB* III. 146). And in *Silas Marner* Nancy Lammeter's acceptance of her childlessness in contrast to her husband's discontent depends on her sense that '"a woman could always be satisfied with devoting herself to her husband, but a man wanted something that would make him look forward more"' (*SM* 310). Similarly, in 'Amos Barton' Eliot describes Milly's devotion in images that strikingly encapsulate the difference between her conception of her heroines' relation to men and that of Brontë: 'A loving woman's world lies within the four walls of her own home; and it is only through her husband that she is in any electric communication with the world beyond' (*Scenes*, I. 119). Against this 'suppression of self' in enclosure, the impulse in Brontë's fiction is repeatedly to escape from constriction—the Red Room at Gateshead, Thornfield, Mr. Helstone's vicarage on the night of the riot, Miss Marchmont's over-heated rooms, the attic to which M.

[19] Barbara Bodichon, *Women and Work* (1857; rpt. New York: C. S. Francis & Co., 1859), p. 27.

Paul has consigned Lucy, and the drugged imprisonment of Lucy by Madame Beck on the night of the festival.

It is important to recognize, however, that the absence of such figurative protest against confinement in Eliot, and the value she places on acquiescence and containment are not simply the result of a difference in the perception of woman's lot or a failure to perceive the kinds of constriction that Brontë finds so threatening in women's lives. Dorothea, for example, marries Casaubon under the mistaken impression that she will be liberated from 'the shallows' of her previous learning and experience by the 'wide embrace' of 'the un-gauged reservoir of Mr. Casaubon's mind' (*M* I. 31). Instead, she becomes 'fettered' with 'the ideal, and not the real yoke of marriage' (*M* III. 98). At Lowick she experiences the 'stifling oppression of [the] gentlewoman's world' (*M* II. 89), where she feels both an emotional and 'moral imprisonment' (*M* II. 90). It is within such a world that 'the mere chance of seeing Will occasionally [is] like a lunette opened in the wall of her prison' (*M* II. 252), and she declares in exasperation to Celia: '"I only want not to have my feelings checked at every turn"' (*M* IV. 185).

Dorothea is in many ways typical of Eliot's heroines, who with noble natures are forced to struggle 'in the bands of narrow teaching, hemmed in by a social life which seemed nothing but a labyrinth of petty courses, a walled-in maze of small paths that led no whither' (*M* I. 40). In fifteenth-century Florence Romola, for example, is ostensibly a privileged woman in her time, given access to the wider learning and knowledge that Dorothea craves, but she is, in fact, treated with comparably slight regard within a misogynistic environment where her father considers 'the unbeaten paths of knowledge' closed to 'the wandering, vagrant propensity of the feminine mind' (*R* I. 85). Like Dorothea, Romola's life is absorbed in the dubious scholarship of another, and her entrapment continues after the death of the male, as she struggles with 'something like guilt' (*R* II. 66) to fulfil the project her father has bequeathed to her. The parallel can be extended further, for the release that Romola, like Dorothea, imagines in marriage proves a 'dream' and she, too, is trapped both literally and figuratively by her husband: 'He had locked in his wife's anger and scorn, but he had been obliged to lock himself in with it' (*R* II. 136).

Maggie Tulliver is also consistently undermined and undervalued in a world in which '"an over-'cute woman's no better nor a long-tailed sheep"' (*MF* 11), and like many of Eliot's and Brontë's heroines, Maggie seeks to escape from the constrictions of such a world, in her case by running away to join the gypsies, where she might gain respect for her intelligence and power as their queen. In the stark reality of adulthood, however, the wider world offers Maggie only a 'dreary schoolroom' in which to teach and a new kind of imprisonment: ' "It is with me as I used to think it would be with the poor uneasy white bear I saw at the show. I thought he must have got so stupid with the habit of turning backwards and forwards in that narrow space, that he would keep doing it if they set him free" ' (*MF* 327).

Beyond a general sense of constraint Maggie Tulliver provides specific echoes of Brontë's Lucy Snowe. Like Lucy, Maggie fantasizes that she will starve herself, and she enjoys the 'luxury of vengeance' by beating nails into the head of her fetish like 'Jael destroying Sisera' (*MF* 25) just as Lucy Snowe quells her longing 'after the manner of Jael to Sisera' (*V* I. 212). Similarly Maggie undertakes the obliteration of her ego in the systematic self-denial and resignation suggested by Thomas à Kempis just as Lucy narrows 'all within her' to the tameness and stillness of Miss Marchmont's two rooms (*V* I. 67).

In addition to her perception of the constriction felt by her heroines, Eliot also recognizes that women's capacity for loving makes them particularly vulnerable: 'We women are always in danger of living too exclusively in the affections . . . though our affections are perhaps the best gifts we have' (*EL* V. 107). Most simply, a world defined through devotion to another is liable to disintegrate as Lydia Donnithorne's does with the death of her father, and more generally women find themselves trapped by their dependence solely on emotional fulfilment. Thus Maggie Tulliver laments: ' "I have always had so much pain mingled with [loving]. I wish I could make myself a world outside it, as men do" ' (*MF* 363). Similarly Janet Dempster is threatened by 'the blank that lay for her outside her married home' (*Scenes*, II. 226). Indeed Janet is doubly vulnerable because her 'talent' for loving means that she is 'subdued in a moment by a word or a look that recalled the old days of fondness' (*Scenes*, II. 225), and her devotion convinces her that she 'must go back' (*Scenes*, II. 289) to the 'difficult duties' (*Scenes*, II. 300) of life with a brutal husband, who feels no such womanly compunction. In *Felix Holt* Mrs. Transome acknowledges the vulnerability for women of such inequity in bitterly ironic terms in her final confrontation with Jermyn: ' "I might almost have let myself starve, rather than have scenes of quarrel with the man I had loved, in which I must accuse him of turning my love into a good bargain. . . . I suppose if a lover picked one's pocket, there's no woman would like to own it"' (*FH* 337). Most dramatically, Maggie Tulliver undertakes the ultimate self-sacrifice in her unequal love for her brother Tom. Maggie's distinctly feminine wish even as a child to 'keep Tom's house, and . . . always live together' (*MF* 27) is contrasted against Tom's harsher conception of the same plan: 'Still he was very fond of his sister, and meant always to take care of her, make her his housekeeper, and punish her when she did wrong' (*MF* 35). Like Janet, Maggie is loyal to a shared past, with her first memory being of '"standing with Tom by the side of the Floss, while he held my hand"' (*MF* 270) and her 'perpetual yearning' for harmony with Tom 'that had its root deeper than all change' (*MF* 399). In contrast, Tom feels no such loyalty to a continuing bond of love: 'There had arisen in Tom a repulsion towards Maggie that derived its very intensity from their early childish love in the time when they clasped tiny fingers together' (*MF* 439). What does remain constant is Tom's enjoyment of punishing Maggie (*MF* 306), and as a woman made vulnerable by loving more than she is loved, Maggie, like Janet Dempster, lives 'with that fear which springs in us when we love one who is inexorable, unbending, unmodifiable—with a mind that we can never mould ourselves upon, and yet that we cannot endure to alienate from us' (*MF* 425).

VI

Eliot does recognize the vulnerability in women's 'talent' for loving, then, and like Brontë demonstrates the frustration and injustice of women's confinement and restraint. None the less she consistently values the self-sacrificing, passive acquiescent qualities of her female characters and reacts against the self-assertive, combative, and rebellious impulses upholding Fedalma's claim in *The Spanish Gypsy*: '"We must be patient in our prison-house, / And find our space in loving."'[20] Significantly, just as Eliot has used spatial imagery to suggest confinement, she employs precisely the same imagery to convey her sense of the paradox of self-fulfilment through self-abnegation and the liberation achieved through selfless love. For example, in 'Amos Barton' the difficulties of Milly Barton's lot are not seen as regrettable: 'for her sublime capacity of loving will have all the more

[20] George Eliot, *The Spanish Gypsy* (Edinburgh: Blackwood & Sons, 1868), p. 107.

scope; and I venture to say, Mrs. Barton's nature would never have grown half so angelic if she had married the man you would perhaps have had in your eye for her—a man with sufficient income and abundant personal éclat' (*Scenes*, I. 31). Similarly, in *The Mill on the Floss* Tom's masculine temperament suffers more keenly from the family's ruin: 'for Maggie, with all her keen susceptibility, yet felt as if the sorrow made larger room for her love to flow in, and gave breathing-space to her passionate nature. No true boy feels that' (*MF* 226).

It is a difficult position to maintain, and yet one which Eliot endorses with a sense of its dangers. So, for example, the potential for self-abnegation to become self-destruction is evident in the fate of those heroines who become victims of their nobility of nature. Milly Barton, malnourished and exhausted, dies, as Mrs. Hackit predicts she will, bearing her sixth child, and Dorothea is only saved from the living death of her devotion to Casaubon by his timely demise. Maggie Tulliver sacrifices her life in the attempt to save her brother's, offering a sharp and revealing contrast to the fate of Gaskell's 'prototype' Maggie Browne in 'The Moorland Cottage'. In Gaskell's story the heroine demonstrates her sisterly self-sacrifice in her determination to forsake her lover and accompany her brother to America. She, however, is saved from drowning in the shipwreck that claims her brother's life, and the ultimate reconciliation is not with her difficult brother but with her mother.

Furthermore, while Eliot suggests that passivity gives women a certain negative power, she also recognizes its vulnerability. So, on the one hand the apparent limitation for women 'whose power lies solely in their influence' (*FH* 279) assumes more significant dimensions in the 'saving influence of a noble nature' such as Dorothea's (*M* IV. 308). Her capacity to hold up an ideal for others 'in her believing capacity of them' is seen by Eliot as 'one of the great powers of her womanhood' (*M* IV. 252). Likewise, behind the acknowledgement in *Felix Holt* that a woman's lot 'is made for her by the love she accepts' (*FH* 342) lies a paradoxical sense of the power of refusing, which Esther demonstrates in rebuffing Harold Transome.

On the other hand, while Esther's power to reject Harold is in one sense absolute, Esther is nevertheless dependent on men to offer her scope for the worthy channelling of affections and energy. So she characterizes the dilemma of all Eliot's heroines when she complains to Felix: '"A woman must choose meaner things, because only meaner things are offered to her"' (*FH* 342). Recalling Gaskell's sense of women's vulnerability in sexual politics, Esther is forced to wait for love 'like a woman, as she was . . . never able to ask for it' (*FH* 262), and in Eliot's fiction such passivity makes women even more vulnerable because the conjugal relationship for which they wait is endowed with such overwhelming importance: 'A supreme love, a motive that gives a sublime rhythm to a woman's life, and exalts habit into partnership with the soul's highest needs, is not to be had where and how she wills' (*FH* 389). Thus Esther's power to refuse, like Dorothea's power to influence, is essentially a secondary power to react, not to initiate.

Eliot's perception of women's capacity to repress their emotions is also characterized by an ambivalence which raises doubts about her doctrine of self-abnegation. She seems consistently to admire self-control. Mrs. Transome, for example, has nothing of 'the feminine tendency to seek influence through pathos' (*FH* 17), and her bitterness is carefully suppressed 'because she could not endure that the degradation she inwardly felt should ever become visible or audible' (*FH* 101). In part, such control is seen as politic, given her son's hatred of all those 'who defeated their own projects by the indulgence of momentary impulses' (*FH* 38), but beyond that the character acquires a certain dignity through her restraint, and the narrative voice betrays an attitude not far removed from that expressed by Harold Transome: 'half the sorrows of women would be averted if they could repress the speech they know to be useless; nay, the speech they have resolved not to utter' (*FH* 36). Indeed, when Mrs. Transome abandons her control and gives vent to her repressed feelings, Eliot represents the gesture as self-defeating and regrettably characteristic of feminine folly:

She did not dare to ask questions, and yet she had not resisted the temptation to say something bitter about Harold's failure to get returned as a Radical, helping, with feminine self-defeat, to exclude herself more completely from any consultation by him. In this way poor women, whose power lies solely in their influence, make themselves like music out of tune, and only move men to run away. (*FH* 279)

Mrs. Garth, in contrast, proves herself an 'exemplary' wife in sparing her husband the admonitory anger she feels over Fred's use of Mr. Farebrother to intercede for him with Mary. At the same time, Eliot recognizes the necessity for the release of such anger, which 'had fermented the more actively because of its total repression towards her husband' (*M* III. 266), and Fred Vincy, deservedly, becomes her 'scape-goat'. So too Mrs. Poyser finds welcome release from her habitual self-control with her diatribe directed against the Squire: '"There's no pleasure i' living, if you're to be corked up for iver, and only dribble your mind out by the sly, like a leaky barrel"' (*AB* II. 339). Like the circumspect Mrs. Garth, Mrs. Poyser chooses her time and her victim well.

Not all such negative impulses can be resolved, however, and this remains a problem for any doctrine of acquiescence and renunciation. When Tito locks Romola's crucifix in the cabinet and claims to '"have locked all sadness away"', Romola accurately senses the futility of the gesture: '"But it is still there—it is only hidden," said Romola, in a low tone, hardly conscious that she spoke' (*R* I. 336). Equally, for all Gwendolen's efforts to ensure that the haunting portrait stays safely locked behind the door to which she holds the key, she is unable to anticipate her sister's interference and is reduced to hysterical fear during the performance of the charade. Concealment offers no guarantee of control for Gwendolen. As the images that embody Gwendolen's dread indicate—the 'adder' in the jewel box sent by Lydia Glasher or the 'dangerous serpent ornamentally coiled in her cabin' (*DD* IV. 106)—fear lives with her, threatening always to burst forth, and is only exacerbated by the uncertainty of its being hidden. When she locks the dagger in a drawer of her cabinet, Gwendolen exposes the problematic nature of many attempts at self-control. Although her action indicates a determination to repress her desire to kill Grandcourt, the gesture lacks finality because the impulse it symbolically quashes has not been satisfied or resolved. And whereas Eliot apparently endorses such restraint as much as Deronda does, she also recognizes the danger of anger 'fermented' or 'corked', which has the ability, as Stephen warns Maggie, suddenly to '"assault you with a savage appetite"' (*MF* 289).

VII

Given the reservations, not merely possible in theory, but actually recognized by Eliot in her endorsement of womanly acquiescence and renunciation—the masochistic aspect of self-abnegation, the fundamentally secondary nature of women's power of influence and choice, the danger of the unresolved in self-suppression—one might reasonably wonder what leads Eliot to such different conclusions from those of Brontë, or even those of Gaskell, after a certain agreement in initial perceptions. The answer, quite simply, is that despite her reservations Eliot perceives more danger to women in rebellion than in acquiescence.

Careerism in women is one area of self-assertion which Eliot deplores in such characters as Deronda's mother, the Princess Halm-Eberstein, and Armgart. For the sake of her 'genius' Deronda's mother asserts her 'right to be an artist', established by natural 'charter' (*DD* IV. 93), just as Armgart claims to be 'an artist by my birth— / By the same warrant that I am a woman.'[21] But each character demonstrates Eliot's sense of the sterility of such assertion, violating conceptions of womanhood in the rejection of conventional roles. So in the Princess's refusal to be 'a mere daughter and mother' (*DD* IV. 93) or in Armgart's insistence that she will be 'more than wife' and not accept:

> The oft-taught Gospel: 'Woman, thy desire
> Shall be that all superlatives on earth
> Belong to men, save the one highest kind—
> To be a mother.' (*Jubal*, 101)

each character is 'unwomaned'. Ambition has led both women to manipulate those around them and to betray equally valid 'charters' of affection—the Princess's to her son and Armgart's to her devoted friend, Walpurga. Both women, significantly, are stricken with the loss of their voices, the essence of their talent, as though punished by their divine, and more temporal, creators.[22]

Eliot's judgement against the Princess in *Daniel Deronda* is under-scored by the contrast offered by the character of Mirah. Although the two women are initially linked in Deronda's mind, with his first sight of Mirah accompanied by the thought '"perhaps my mother was like this one"' (*DD* I. 347), the similarities between them prove to be those of a mirror image—the Princess defies her manipulative

---

[21] George Eliot, *Jubal and other Poems* (Edinburgh: William Blackwood & Sons, 1874), p. 104. All further references to this work appear in the text, abbreviated as *Jubal*.

[22] This seems ironic because it comes not only from the century's greatest woman writer, but from the woman who wrote so approvingly of Margaret Fuller's *Woman in the Nineteenth Century*, in which Fuller declares that women artists 'rich in genius . . . ought not to find themselves, by birth, in a place so narrow, that, in breaking bounds, they become outlaws' (London: H. G. Clark, 1845, p. 67). Christina Rossetti under-takes a similar act of self-renunciation in her tale *Maude*, where Magdalen, having shown some poetic talent, forsakes it and enters a convent, while Maude becomes ab-sorbed with her writing genius to the cost of her religion and health. When Maude dies, the 'locked book' of her writings 'with all its words of folly, sin, vanity' is placed in her coffin (London: James Bowden, 1897), p. 78.

father, while Mirah is humbly submissive; the Princess forsakes all to satisfy a desire to perform, while Mirah is forced on the stage; the Princess repudiates her faith, whereas Mirah clings to Judaism. Even Mirah's talent, while remarkable, is suitably demure with her voice more suited to parlours than concert halls (just as Catherine Arrowpoint's musical talent is modest enough to present no challenge or obstacle to her love for Klesmer).

Mirah's willingness to forsake her career for her love of Deronda is also reminiscent of a similarly approved choice by Dinah at the end of *Adam Bede*. Despite Eliot's sympathetic attempts early in the novel to suggest a real validity in Dinah's vocation, she comes in the end to suggest that Dinah's self is not fully realized as ' "one o' those women that feels no drawing towards having a husband and children o' their own" ' (*AB* III. 236) and to feel with Adam the pity that ' "she shouldna be a mother herself" ' (*AB* III. 265). The issue of Dinah's final renunciation of her vocation as a preacher is evaded by an appeal to an external circumstance, so that the Methodist conference forbids women from preaching and Dinah decides, with Adam's hearty approval, ' "to set the example o' submitting" ' (*AB* III. 332). Seth's opposition to Dinah's decision—' "If Dinah had seen as I did, we'd ha' left the Wesleyans and joined a body that 'ud put no bonds on Christian liberty" ' (*AB* III. 331)—raises another possibility for action and corresponds exactly to the response of Eliot's aunt Elizabeth Evans, the figure who 'suggested Dinah' and '*left the society when women were no longer allowed to preach*, and joined the New Wesleyans' (*EL* III. 175).

Eliot also sees female assertiveness in the dynamics of heterosexual relationships as an area where women's energy is not only misplaced, but destructive. We have seen that the 'crisis' of Jane Eyre's sexual contest with Rochester is 'perilous' for Brontë's heroine, but 'not without its charm', and that the continuing struggle for mastery between the two is essentially a playing out of sexual attraction and energy. In some respects the courtship between Gwendolen and Grandcourt takes on a similar aspect, but, in marked contrast, such a contest is portrayed far more negatively by Eliot. The notion that Gwendolen and Grandcourt will 'match' each other, which might be a promise of the health of the relationship in Brontë, is a guarantee of its doom in Eliot. The combative excitement of the courtship, suggested by the repeated use of hunting imagery, comes to fruition in the emotional violence of the marriage, in which Grandcourt calculates his comments, 'conscious of using pincers on that white creature' (*DD* III. 345), and Gwendolen's truthfulness and sense of justice have been 'throttled into silence, collared and dragged behind [Grandcourt] to witness what he would, without remonstrance' (*DD* IV. 101). For Gwendolen the assertiveness of sexual contest has been 'perilous' indeed. Significantly, the 'peaceful melancholy' that Gwendolen achieves by the end of the novel is a product of 'the renunciation of demands for self' (*DD* IV. 337) and brings her closer to Deronda's choice of wife, Mirah, whose nature knows 'only to submit' (*DD* II. 39).

An equally destructive contest poisons the relationship between Rosamond and Lydgate, in which Rosamond's inflexible selfishness keeps Lydgate held 'as with pincers' (*M* IV. 56). And in marked contrast to the benevolent influence exercised by Eliot's selfless female characters, Rosamond's impervious egoism inspires Lydgate to 'violent movements of . . . anger' (*M* IV. 56) and Will to a desire 'to stay and shatter Rosamond with his anger' (*M* IV. 262).

Not only are Eliot's passionate women destructive in their relationships, but their passion is also self-destroying. For example, Lydia Glasher's external withering—'the blooming curves which had once been where now was sunken pallor' (*DD* II. 256)—reflects the inner wasting and taint of 'gathering venom' (*DD* II. 251) and recalls the 'black poisonous plant' in Mrs. Transome's mind. Those women in Eliot's fiction who lack womanly passivity and want 'everything' are 'secure of nothing' (*FH* 316). They create for themselves their own kind of vulnerability, for 'a passionate woman's love is always overshadowed by fear' (*Scenes*, I. 241).

Perhaps the most revealing example in this aspect of Eliot's thinking on women is the portrait of Romola. Although she shares many of the characteristics of those passionate, assertive women already discussed, Romola's triumph is one of control and her strength is proved 'in submission' (*R* II. 253). Like Gwendolen, for example, Romola 'love[s] homage' (*R* I. 227) and has a 'disposition to rebel against command' (*R* I, 262), but checking her natural inclinations, she also has a strong sense of appropriate womanly behaviour. She quiets 'half awakened' doubts by 'that subjection to her husband's mind which is felt by every wife who loves her husband with passionate devotedness and full reliance' (*R* II. 69) and labours 'as every loving woman must, to subdue her nature to her husband's' (*R* II. 70). Eliot is keenly aware both of the unjust, corrupt nature of the world around Romola and of the threat that Tito's determination to master her poses for Romola. Nevertheless she contemplates the prospect of escape for her heroine only to reject it, because she recognizes too that the cost to Romola's nature of rebellion is desperately high: 'In the act of rebelling she was bruising her own reverence' (R III. 135). Far from the fulfilment that Jane Eyre seeks, and eventually finds, in her exodus from Thornfield, Romola's 'new rebellion' gives birth to 'new despair' (R III. 156), and she turns back on her escape from Florence on two occasions—the first under the direction of Savonarola and the second of her own volition. As a woman who channels her passionate nature, throwing 'all the energy of her will into renunciation' (R II. 269), she becomes one of Eliot's most potent heroines of submission.

Underlying Eliot's mistrust of passionate, assertive women and her sense of the danger of their rebelliousness is a more fundamental mistrust of the stability of the female temperament, perhaps reflecting her own 'horror of mental breakdown' (EL V. 56). In the 'madness' of her jealousy, and her 'ungovernable impulses of resentment and vindictiveness' (Scenes, I. 315) Caterina is 'frightened at her own sensations' (Scenes, I. 336). She, like Mrs. Transome and Gwendolen, can contemplate murder, while Hetty and Madame Laure actually prove capable of its execution. When Caterina runs away from Cheverel Manor, Maynard's fear alternates between the understandable thought that she might be dead and the more revealing dread that he might find her 'with madness in her eyes, looking and looking, and yet not seeing him' (Scenes, II. 7). Accordingly, when Caterina cries on seeing him, the tears are precious to Maynard, 'who day after day had been shuddering at the continually recurring image of Tina with the dry scorching stare of insanity' (Scenes, II. 21). In the same way Deronda's 'dominant' anxiety arising from his first impression of Mirah is 'that her mind might be disordered' (DD I. 350), and later Mirah confesses that she is haunted by ' "a picture of a madhouse, that she could never forget" ' (DD II. 30). Maggie Tulliver's girlhood in which she 'rushed to her deeds with passionate impulse' (MF 57), bewildering others with her irrationality, gives way to a womanhood in which she is continually liable to be overwhelmed—assaulted by 'savage appetite' (MF 289), made vulnerable by her 'passionate sensibility' to 'the supreme excitement of music' (MF 352), and finally running off with Stephen as though 'taken hold of and shaken by the invisible influence . . . borne along by a wave too strong for her' (MF 367). Romola's 'touch of fanaticism', which makes Tito joke that she shall soon be 'seeing visions' (*R* II. 77), links her with the seer Camilla, 'whose faculties seemed all wrought up into fantasies, leaving nothing for emotion and thought' (*R* III. 61), even though Camilla's 'shallow excitability' disgusts Romola. Janet Dempster suffers from 'vague indefinable states of susceptibility . . . states of excitement or depression, half mental, half physical—that determine many a tragedy in women's lives' (*Scenes*, II. 343). And in this she anticipates Gwendolen Harleth's 'fits of spiritual dread' (*DD* I. 109), which seem to her 'like a brief remembered madness' (*DD* I. 108). Gwendolen is perhaps the most vulnerable of all Eliot's women, haunted by memories of moments of lost control such as the strangling of her sister's canary and her hysteria during the charades and, even more, by internal forces that threaten to overwhelm her. She lives in 'perilously-poised terror' (*DD* III. 24), fearing 'subjection to a possible self, a self not to be absolutely predicted about' (*DD* I. 245). Finally, even the remarkably down-to-earth Mrs. Cadwallader contemplates the danger of madness for Dorothea in her isolation at Lowick after Casaubon's death: ' "You will certainly go mad in that house alone, my dear. You will see visions. We have all got to assert ourselves a little to keep sane, and call things by the same names as other people call them by" ' (*M* III. 199).

VIII

In the face of such instability, feminine dependence becomes not only virtuous but wise, and submission is not merely seemly but necessary. This perception clearly conditions Eliot's sense of female communities and friendships, for logically extended it suggests that women's relationships by their very nature are partial—women without men are fundamentally vulnerable, self-sufficiency such as Lucy Snowe attains is not possible, and complementary heterosexual relationships are crucial to feminine salvation.[23]

Accordingly, Eliot's imagery repeatedly stresses a religious, saving role for her male figures, with the 'male as mentor' fulfilling a role as redeemer in women's lives. Such redemptive power is made quite explicit in the early work 'Janet's Repentance', and the central male figure Mr. Tryan appears as a religious minister. Throughout the tale

[23] The contemporary debate on Protestant sisterhoods, discussed in Chapter 1, provides interesting parallels to Eliot's view, for it demonstrated similar elements of mistrust and most often located its solutions in the requirement of 'submission to priestly office' or some equivalent external male authority.

the play of images of day and night, light and darkness, further empha-
size an aspect of revelation. So Janet feels 'no gladness' in the 'morning light', but finds 'every coming night more impossible to brave'
(*Scenes*, II. 222) and dreads 'the oncoming of the utter dark' (*Scenes*,
II. 223). It is only after she confesses to Tryan, submitting to his
direction and love, that she can face her solitary night walk—' "There
is no real reason why I should not go alone" '—which is seen overtly
in terms of absolution: 'That walk in the dewy starlight remained for
ever in Janet's memory as one of those baptismal epochs' (*Scenes*, II.
352).

In *Adam Bede* Dinah's religion is displaced in a real sense by Adam,
not only in so far as she relinquishes her preaching when she marries
him, but also in the way that Adam can become her ' "idol in the
temple" ' (*AB* III. 279). Maggie Tulliver turns to Dr. Kenn in order
to 'tell . . . everything' (*MF* 434), and, like Mr. Tryan, Kenn intervenes on her behalf with the townswomen (*MF* 444–5). Romola too
finds a religious mentor Savonarola, and in her case the 'sacrament
. . . of yearning passivity on which she had newly entered' (*R* II. 265)
is apparently consecrated by the language Romola uses—' "Father,
I will be guided" '—and by the religious garb she is wearing as disguise. Furthermore, it seems almost emblematic that Romola's initial
quest is for a female guide, having determined 'to go to the most
learned woman in the world, Cassandra Fedele, at Venice, and ask
her how an instructed woman could support herself in a lonely life
there' (*R* II. 196), but Savonarola intervenes and she is turned back
to Florence with a new male mentor and a new determination to fulfil
her role as a wife.

Even the more overtly secular heroes are sanctified by Eliot's descriptions and are endowed with redemptive powers. For example, Esther
feels that if Felix would love her, 'her life would be exalted into something quite new—into a sort of difficult blessedness' (*FH* 197), and as
his wife she could be 'a good woman', although she has 'no trust that
she could ever be good without him' (*FH* 262). Her love for Felix is
seen as the 'first religious experience of her life' (*FH* 227) and appropriately so since her life is transformed by her desire 'to be worthy of
what she reverenced' (*FH* 262). In fact, it is difficult to credit that the
evil from which Esther is saved is quite so grave as her speech suggests. Beyond a diminution of self-indulgence and frivolity there
seems little obvious substance to the 'inward revolution' Esther has
undergone since meeting Felix.

Similarly Daniel Deronda's role as a saviour is enhanced by his enigmatic appearances at times of crisis—to Gwendolen in the gaming room, to Mirah by the river, and with almost beatific splendour to Mordecai on the bridge. Gwendolen's feelings toward Deronda have 'turned this man, only a few years older than herself, into a priest' (*DD* III. 56). He assumes a 'restraining power' in her life, and echoing Esther, Gwendolen declares: '"If you had not been good, I should have been more wicked"' (*DD* IV. 162). Like Esther, too, part of Gwendolen's growth comes from her recognition of unworthiness: 'the year's experience . . . had turned the brilliant, self-confident Gwendolen Harleth of the Archery Meeting into the crushed penitent impelled to confess her unworthiness where it would have been her happiness to be held worthy' (*DD* IV. 166). Ultimately Deronda becomes her 'outer conscience', serving 'in the stead of God' (*DD* IV. 276). Indeed, there is an element of the self-styled saviour in Deronda's character: 'Persons attracted him, as Hans Meyrick had done, in proportion to the possibility of his defending them, rescuing them, telling upon their lives with some sort of redeeming influence' (*DD* II. 220), and it is difficult not to feel something of Gwendolen's unease with his 'halo of superiority' (*DD* IV. 149). However, it is unlikely that any irony is intended in the contrast between Gwendolen's readiness to kneel before Deronda (*DD* IV. 149) and her forced assumption of that posture with Grandcourt (*DD* II. 212), or between Grandcourt's sadism and Deronda's exalted pleasure at Gwendolen's overwhelming remorse: 'Deronda could not utter one word to diminish that sacred aversion to her worst self—that thorn-pressure which must come with the crowning of the sorrowful Better, suffering because of the Worse' (*DD* IV. 153).

The religious aura surrounding Eliot's heroes is in keeping with her general conception of the sacred nature of 'supreme love', which is 'hardly distinguishable from religious feeling' (*AB* I. 62). Such a view removes the love relationships of her heroines from the realm of passionate, libidinous love, which, as we have seen, Eliot generally portrays negatively in terms of its threatening, destructive power for women. For example, Esther is oblivious to Felix's handsomeness until the courtroom scene, long after other kinds of attraction have been established, and Gwendolen's consideration of Deronda, in marked contrast to her sexually charged interaction with Grandcourt, is likewise free from such profane thoughts:

Her imagination had not been turned to a future union with Deronda by any other than the spiritual tie which had been continually strengthening; but also it had not been turned towards a future separation from him. Love-making and marriage—how could they now be the imagery in which poor Gwendolen's deepest attachment could spontaneously clothe itself? Mighty love had laid its hand upon her; but what had he demanded of her? Acceptance of rebuke—the hard task of self-change—confession—endurance. (*DD* IV. 292)

Further, the recurring imagery of adult–child relationships not only deepens the sense of 'precious dependence' but diffuses and dispels the issue of sexuality from these central relationships. With Tryan's guidance Janet feels 'like a child whose hand is firmly grasped by its father' (*Scenes*, II. 351), and Dinah waits on Adam's words and looks 'almost as a little child waits on the help and tenderness of the strong on whom it depends' (*AB* III. 279). Esther, Romola, and Eppie all remain with their fathers after marriage, creating a 'triple life' (*R* II. 62) in which the conjugal is absorbed into the familial. Esther is drawn to Felix like 'a frightened child towards its protector' (*FH* 365), Romola is 'as simple and unreserved as a child in her love for Tito' (*R* I. 294), and in *Middlemarch* Will and Dorothea, who perhaps represent Eliot's closest, if somewhat unlikely, approach to a positive passionate relationship, their happiness conveniently consigned to the brief finale, still regard each other 'like two fond children' (*M* II. 309). Even reversed, when Mary Garth feels for Fred Vincy 'something like what a mother feels at the imagined sobs or cries of her naughty truant child' (*M* II. 53), the relation retains that sense of non-sexual bonding.

Gwendolen's relationship to Deronda is described in terms of 'a half-soothed child' (*DD* IV. 357), who cries 'to be taken by the hand' (*DD* IV. 293), and there is, too, a strangely innocent quality in her desire to please by reading a wildly random selection of authors: 'hoping that by dipping into them all in succession, with her rapid understanding she might get to a point of view nearer his level' (*DD* III. 271). Significantly, what she receives for the first time from Deronda is 'a sign of tenderness' which she has 'never before had from any man' (*DD* IV. 141). In so far as sexual considerations enter the relationship between Deronda and Gwendolen, they do so as vexations in the form of Grandcourt's jealousy and Sir Hugo's warning to Deronda that he should avoid entanglements with married women. Unlike most men, Deronda is neither mesmerized nor even attracted to Gwendolen's physical beauty, but rather regards it with almost clinical disgust: 'Strange and piteous to think what a centre of wretchedness a delicate piece of human flesh like that might be, wrapped round with fine raiment, her ears pierced for gems, her head held loftily, her mouth all smiling pretence, the poor soul within her sitting in sick distaste of all things' (*DD* III. 23). Accordingly, Deronda's relationship toward Mirah is suitably non-sexual. Not only is Mirah described as 'like a tired child' (*DD* I. 354), whose natural inclination is 'to submit' (*DD* II. 39), but her figure is represented as so demure and ennervated that sexual vigour seems entirely beyond the realm of their wedded bliss in Zion.

IX

Given women's temperamental instability and the redemptive role of male figures, then, the feminine 'talent' for loving becomes a means not only of self-definition, but of self-survival. Just as Caterina 'must have something to cling to' (*Scenes*, II. 35), 'the need of being loved' is the strongest desire in Maggie Tulliver's nature. And the crucial nature of that love, expressed in the image of a flower's dependence on 'the sunshine or the cloud' (*MF* 344), is extended through images of hunger and nourishment in which, contrary to Jane Eyre's nourishment by maternal figures, it is the male figure who provides sustenance. So when Maggie retreats to the attic determined to 'starve' (*MF* 32) and feeling a 'hunger of heart—as peremptory as that other hunger by which Nature forces us to submit to the yoke' (*MF* 34), Tom arrives to feed her, and she takes that nourishment in a revealingly passive fashion, 'put[ting] out her mouth for the cake' (*MF* 34). In later life she remembers that moment when she and Tom 'bit their cake together as a sacrament of conciliation' (*MF* 346). Similarly, in submission to Savonarola Romola finds 'an immediate satisfaction for moral needs which all the previous culture and experience of her life had left hungering' (*R* II. 303).

Without that 'nourishment' of love the prospect for Eliot's women is a kind of disintegration as fatal for the psyche as starvation is for the body. Romola declares to Tito that her whole life has been 'a preparation to love' (*R* I. 299), and her purpose in living is located in a succession of dedications—to her father, to Tito, to Savonarola, to her godfather, and finally to her husband's grim legacy, Tessa and her children. The prospect of 'ceasing to love' is for Romola 'like the hideous nightmare in which the world seemed to break away all round her, and leave her feet overhanging the darkness' (*R* II. 71), and similarly a crisis of faith in 'the beings to whom she could cling' provides 'an illumination that made all life look ghastly' (*R* III. 65). In such crises Romola feels the helplessness of one overwhelmed: 'alone in the presence of the earth and sky, with no human presence interposing and making a law for her' (*R* II. 250) and 'orphaned in those wide spaces of sea and sky' (*R* III. 163).

As we have seen, this threat of instability is pervasive in Eliot's studies of women, and the solution lies in the counterbalancing stability and fixity of a peculiarly masculine world of laws and codes. The contrast between the two worlds is clear in the study of the Tulliver children. Tom, for example, lives in a world of maxims: '. . . he was particularly clear and positive on one point—namely, that he would punish everybody who deserved it' (*MF* 34). He never regrets his actions, 'whereas Maggie was always wishing she had done something different' (*MF* 46). Tom shapes his actions in terms of his 'duty [as] a son and a brother' (*MF* 302), and he readily swears to his father's inflexible pact of vengeance. In the simplicity of his world with 'no impulses . . . that led him to expect what did not present itself to him as a right to be demanded' (*MF* 197), Tom is never vulnerable to the impulsiveness of his sister. Maggie's tragedy is that she cannot embrace the narrow rigidity of Tom's world, but finds no alternative scheme or system that will suffice. The endeavour is there in her devotion to Thomas à Kempis, for example, but in the end she remains vulnerable to being 'borne along by a wave too strong for her' (*MF* 367).

The recourse of Eliot's women to the stability of a male world is evident, for example, in the way Romola's terror of 'her feet overhanging the darkness' (*R* II. 71) is directly remedied by her 'trust in Savonarola [which] was something like a rope suspended securely by her path' (*R* II. 304). For a period Savonarola offers Romola the security of that 'interposing' human presence 'making a law for her' (*R* II. 309), the absence of which has been so threatening. Romola's 'new presentiment of the strength there might be in submission' when she meets Savonarola, is dependent upon his having 'some valid law to show her' (*R* II. 254). She is not disappointed, for Savonarola immediately and authoritatively defines roles for Romola, and the difficulties of choice are removed by the striking rigidity of his categories: '"You have no vocation. . . . You are a wife"' (*R* II. 260). Even if Tito were a malefactor, he contends, Romola's place '"would be in the prison beside him"' (*R* II. 262).

Against the vacancy and metaphysical vagueness of Romola's feminine world, Savonarola's is a world of clarity, of contrasts and obligations: '"you were warned before marriage, when you might still have lawfully chosen to be free from the marriage-bond. But you chose the bond; and in wilfully breaking it—I speak to you as a pagan, if the holy mystery of matrimony is not sacred to you—you are breaking a pledge"' (R II. 254). Under Savonarola's direction Romola assumes a new philanthropic role for which she has 'no innate taste' (R II. 301), but in her submissive execution of that role she finds herself 'recovering a firm footing in her works of womanly sympathy' (R II. 301). And even after the masculine world has betrayed Romola's trust, she retains the lesson she has learned of its laws and duties in her dedication to Tessa and her children: 'she needed something that she was bound specially to care for' (R III. 263).

In a comparable way Gwendolen Harleth is fascinated with the judgement of males, who provide a standard of measurement external to herself. For example, the idea that Deronda is 'looking down on her as an inferior' in the gaming room at Leubronn endows him with a 'different quality from the human dross around her' and places him 'in a region outside and above her' (DD I. 9). And later her helplessness in her marriage to Grandcourt gives 'fresh force to the hold Deronda had from the first taken on her mind, as one who had an unknown standard by which he judged her' (DD III. 55). Similarly, although Gwendolen dreads Klesmer as 'part of that unmanageable world which was independent of her wishes' (DD II. 91), she seeks his judgement none the less on her plans to take up acting, requesting his advice, as she later desires that Deronda tell her '"what to think and what to do"' (DD III. 85). Like Savonarola for Romola, Deronda becomes an externalized source of authority, 'an outer conscience' (DD IV. 275), for Gwendolen, and she looks forward to a future in which 'she would be continually assimilating herself to some type that he would hold before her' (DD IV. 338). Echoing the fear and insecurity of Romola's conception of a world without a guide, Gwendolen cries 'as the child cries whose little feet have fallen backward—cried to be taken by the hand, lest she should lose herself' (DD IV. 293). The same fear of vastness and vacancy torments Gwendolen: 'Solitude in any wide scene impressed her with an undefined feeling of immeasurable existence aloof from her, in the midst of which she was helplessly incapable of asserting herself. The little astronomy taught her at school used sometimes to set her imagination at work, in a way that made her tremble' (*DD* I. 110), and she finally finds a stability in her reliance on Deronda, 'which had become to her imagination like the firmness of the earth, the only condition of her walking' (*DD* IV. 339).

Dorothea Brooke is another victim of the 'indefiniteness with which the Supreme Power has fashioned the natures of women' (*M* I. vii). Without a 'coherent social faith and order', she too is threatened by 'inconsistency and formlessness' (*M* I. vi). Her attraction to Casaubon with his ultimate system, the *Key to all Mythologies*, may be misguided, but it represents a characteristic effort to 'shape' the world through a male figure. In the end Dorothea succeeds in defining her role through Will 'as a wife and mother' (*M* IV. 366). Eliot recognizes the limitations of such a lot for 'so substantive and rare a creature' (*M* IV. 366), but she recognizes as well that the obverse of confinement and restraint is not simply liberation. Given her sense of women's capacities and temperament, neither woman alone nor women apart from men can exist satisfactorily. Where Gaskell's heroines can turn at some point to a maternal figure, and Brontë's to sexual partners or the power of an 'empire over self', Eliot's women must have a spiritual guide to protect them from the threat without and within—otherwise escapees from the 'prison-house' are likely to become lost souls.

Conclusion: Telling their Own Story

We have seen that Elizabeth Gaskell, Charlotte Brontë, and George Eliot shared new opportunities for literary communality and that each woman was touched in differing degrees by a wider female literary subculture. Between all three writers, in fact, there was a significant overlap of friends and acquaintances. In addition, as writers about women they wrote in a particularly controversial climate, at a time when the Woman Question occupied a great deal of public attention in a variety of forms. Woman's character, place in society, rights, employment, and education were all hotly debated, and in their individual ways Gaskell, Brontë, and Eliot addressed those issues.

Many of the problems confronting women in the mid-nineteenth century were facts of daily life for Gaskell and Brontë. As the mother of four daughters, Gaskell was faced with the uncertainty of the future for her children if they remained single women, and she sought to provide for their later life from her literary earnings. Also, as the most philanthropically active of the three authors, Gaskell concerned herself with issues of female employment, emigration, and the rehabilitation of prostitutes. Similarly, Charlotte Brontë lived out a struggle for employment and education, making substantial sacrifices to gain teaching qualifications and earn a living. George Eliot, while not so directly involved, became the focus for many appeals from female activists and she took an interest in female education, the women's press, and related issues of the Woman Question. None of these three women, then, wrote in splendid isolation, oblivious to their times, and a good deal of common experience as women writers was shared between them. Hence we may well be inclined to look for a certain uniformity of vision, the 'woman's view' that George Lewes anticipated, on such issues as communality and women's relationships.[1]

However, as we have also seen in this study, against a common social background, Gaskell, Brontë, and Eliot demonstrated widely diverging attitudes to that shared experience. Gaskell was more socially active and gregarious within the literary community, at ease with her more amateur self-image as a writer, and more directly con-

---

[1] Lewes, 'The Lady Novelists', p. 131.

cerned and involved with the social problems confronting women in the period. Charlotte Brontë, in contrast, was much more socially and temperamentally isolated than her friend Gaskell, and felt deeply ambivalent in her attitudes to the literary community, torn between an ambitious desire to participate on the one hand and a painful sense of social inadequacy and strain on the other. And while in personal terms Brontë was passionately aware of the problems and injustices faced by women, she was oddly quietistic about any broader political action on women's behalf. George Eliot's personal disposition combined with her social circumstances and her awesome professional stature ensured that she was relatively detached from her sister authors, maintaining very little contact with other women writers. She was no less theoretically aware than either Gaskell or Brontë of the problems facing women, but her sympathies with the activists were reserved and her engagement with the cause was distinctly limited.

Those differences of attitude and experience in the individual lives were in the end more telling for the fiction these women created than was the shared experience of their historical background, and consequently they represented the possibilities for and realities of female friendships and communities in significantly different ways. For example, the spirit of camaraderie evident in Gaskell's dealings with her sister authors and in her relationships with female friends is reflected in her fiction in a primary allegiance between women, in which Gaskell consistently depicts women united together by choice or by circumstance. Accordingly, in her community of women at Cranford she explores the possibility, which was stressed in the wider contemporary debate considered in Chapter 1, that friendships between women might provide a substitute for heterosexual relationships, and in her tale 'The Grey Woman' she extends that exploration to encompass the possibility of all-female relationships providing not simply a substitute but a chosen alternative. For Gaskell, the bonding between women is both natural and political—the former based primarily on shared maternal feelings and experiences of motherhood, the latter on women's common lot as victims of social and sexual passivity.

In her life, as in her fiction, Charlotte Brontë was much more divided in her attitude to women's relationships, and was considerably less at ease with any exclusiveness in female friendships or communities. So although her heroines are haunted by that 'mother-want' which testifies to the importance of the female bond, and the friendship between Shirley and Caroline in *Shirley* is represented as having a value unique to its female qualities, at decisive moments Brontë's fiction tends to validate conjugal relationships ahead of maternal or sororal bonds. Ultimately Brontë's impulse to repudiate relationships finds expression in *Villette* in a movement away from mutuality toward an insulating self-containment and self-preservation, with the solitary and unsociable Lucy Snowe establishing her own domain at Faubourg Clotilde.

In shunning social interaction as too stressful, George Eliot was temperamentally more akin to Charlotte Brontë, and indeed each of them lived in relative isolation. Eliot's social world was more diverse, none the less, and included, like Gaskell's, acquaintance with many female reformers. However, her relationship to that world was both problematic and constrained, and in the most decisive areas, Eliot's life was more markedly male-centred than either Gaskell's or Brontë's, not merely in the moral and social taboo on women entering Eliot's circle but in her dependence on a succession of male figures throughout her career. In her fiction Eliot, like Brontë, demonstrates a tendency to define female characters in relation to men. However, whereas Brontë creates heroines who are assertive and combative, Eliot distrusts the aggressive and passionate capacity in her female characters. So while Brontë celebrates the assertion of the self, Eliot extols subjection; where Brontë channels aggression, Eliot diffuses it. Brontë's conception of the male as a sexual partner is transformed by Eliot into a sense of the male as a saviour. The prospects of Cranford and Faubourg Clotilde—women together or alone—are equally unsatisfactory for Eliot, since in her fictional world the insecurity of the female temperament craves the stability of a male-centred world.

Bibliography

I   Primary material: works of Charlotte Brontë, Elizabeth Gaskell, and George Eliot

(i) Charlotte Brontë

Emma: a Fragment, introduced by W. M. Thackeray, *Cornhill Magazine*, Jan. 1860, pp. 485–98.

Five Novelettes, ed. Winifred Gérin (London: Folio Press, 1971).

Jane Eyre, Clarendon edn., eds. Jane Jack and Margaret Smith (1847; rpt. Oxford: Oxford Univ. Press, 1969).

The Brontës: Their Lives, Friendships and Correspondence, eds. T. J. Wise and J. A. Symington, 4 vols. (Oxford: Shakespeare Head, 1932).

The Miscellanies and Unpublished Writings of Charlotte and Patrick Brontë, eds. T. J. Wise and J. A. Symington, 2 vols. (Oxford: Shakespeare Head, 1934).

Poems, by Acton, Ellis, and Currer Bell (London: Aylott & Jones, 1846).

The Professor, 2 vols. (London: Smith, Elder & Co., 1857).

Shirley, Clarendon edn., eds. Herbert Rosengarten and Margaret Smith (1849; rpt. Oxford: Oxford Univ. Press, 1979).

Tales from Angria, ed. Phyllis Bentley (London: Collins, 1954).

Villette, 3 vols. (London: Smith, Elder & Co., 1853).

(ii) George Eliot

Adam Bede, 3 vols. (Edinburgh: William Blackwood & Sons, 1859).

'Art and Belles Lettres', *Westminster Review*, Apr. 1856, pp. 625–50.

'Belles Lettres', *Westminster Review*, July 1855, pp. 288–307; Oct. 1855, pp. 596–615; Jan. 1856, pp. 290–312; Oct. 1856, pp. 325–34; Jan. 1857, pp. 306–26.

Daniel Deronda, 4 vols. (Edinburgh: William Blackwood & Sons, 1876).

Essays and Leaves from a Note-book, Vol. XXI of *The Works of George Eliot* (London: Virtue & Co., n.d.).

Essays of George Eliot, ed. Thomas Pinney (London: Routledge & Kegan Paul, 1963).

'Evangelical Teaching: Dr. Cumming', *Westminster Review*, Oct. 1855, pp. 436–62.

Felix Holt the Radical, Clarendon edn., ed. Frederick Thomson (1866; rpt. Oxford: Oxford Univ. Press, 1980).

'German Wit: Heinrich Heine', *Westminster Review*, Jan. 1856, pp. 1–33.

'History, Biography, Voyages and Travels', *Westminster Review*, Jan. 1857, pp. 288–306.

Impressions of Theophrastus Such (Edinburgh: William Blackwood & Sons, 1879).

George Eliot's Journal, MS Journals, Yale.

The Legend of Jubal and Other Poems (Edinburgh: William Blackwood & Sons, 1874).

The George Eliot Letters, ed. Gordon S. Haight, 9 vols. (London: Oxford Univ. Press, 1954–78).

George Eliot's Life as Related in Her Letters and Journals, ed. J. W. Cross, 4 vols. (Leipzig: Tauchnitz, 1885).

'Life and Opinions of Milton', *Leader*, Aug. 1855, pp. 750–2.

'Margaret Fuller and Mary Wollstonecraft', *Leader*, Oct. 1855, pp. 988–9.

'Memoirs of the Court of Austria', *Westminster Review*, Apr. 1855, pp. 303–35.

Middlemarch, a Study of Provincial Life, 4 vols. (Edinburgh: William Blackwood & Sons, 1871–2).

The Mill on the Floss, Clarendon edn., ed. Gordon S. Haight (1860; rpt. Oxford: Oxford Univ. Press, 1980).

'The Natural History of German Life: Riehl', *Works of George Eliot*, XXI. 188–236.

Romola, 3 vols. (London: Smith, Elder & Co., 1863).

Scenes of Clerical Life, 2 vols. (Edinburgh: William Blackwood & Sons, 1858).

'Servant's Logic', *Pall Mall Gazette*, Mar. 1865, pp. 310–11.

Silas Marner, the Weaver of Raveloe (Edinburgh: William Blackwood & Sons, 1861).

'Silly Novels by Lady Novelists', *Westminster Review*, Oct. 1856, pp. 442–61.

The Spanish Gypsy (Edinburgh: William Blackwood & Sons, 1868).

'Woman in France: Madame de Sablé', *Westminster Review*, Oct. 1854, pp. 448–73.

'Worldliness and Other Worldliness: the Poet Young', *Westminster Review*, Jan. 1857, pp. 1–42.

(iii) Elizabeth Gaskell

The Letters of Mrs. Gaskell, eds. J. A. Chapple and Arthur Pollard (Manchester: Manchester Univ. Press, 1966).

'Some Unpublished Gaskell Letters', *Notes and Queries*, Dec. 1980, pp. 507–14.

The Life of Charlotte Brontë, 2 vols. (London: Smith, Elder & Co., 1857).

My Diary: the early years of my daughter Marianne (London: privately printed by Clement Shorter, 1923).

'Sketches among the Poor', by Elizabeth and William Gaskell. *Blackwood's Magazine*, Jan. 1837, pp. 48–51.

The Works of Mrs. Gaskell, ed. A. W. Ward, 8 vols. (London: Smith, Elder & Co., 1906).

Vol. I   *Mary Barton and Other Tales*
Vol. II   *Cranford and Other Tales*
Vol. III   *Ruth and Other Tales, Etc.*
Vol. IV   *North and South*
Vol. V   *My Lady Ludlow and Other Tales*
Vol. VI   *Sylvia's Lovers, Etc.*
Vol. VII   *Cousin Phillis and Other Tales*
Vol. VIII   *Wives and Daughters*

II   Secondary material: contemporary background

ABERDEEN, The Countess of (Ishbel Gordon), 'The International Council of Women in Congress', *Nineteenth Century Review*, July 1899, pp. 18–25.

AUSTEN, JANE, *Persuasion* (1818; rpt. Oxford: Oxford Univ. Press, 1980).

BLACKWELL, ELIZABETH and EMILY, 'Medicine as a Profession for Women', *English Woman's Journal*, May 1860, pp. 145–60.

BLIND, MATHILDE, *George Eliot* (London: W. H. Allen, 1883).

BODICHON, BARBARA (Leigh Smith), *Women and Work* (1857; rpt. New York: C. S. Francis & Co., 1859).

BOUCHERETT, JESSIE, 'Provision for Superfluous Women', *Woman's Work and Woman's Culture: a Series of Essays*, ed. Josephine Butler (London: Macmillan, 1869).

BROWNING, ELIZABETH BARRETT, *Letters of Elizabeth Barrett Browning*, ed. F. G. Kenyon, 2 vols. (London: Smith, Elder & Co., 1897).

——, *The Poetical Works of Elizabeth Barrett Browning* (London: Henry Frowde, 1904).

BURNS, JOHN, 'The Unemployed', *Nineteenth Century Review*, Dec. 1892, pp. 845–63.

BUTLER, JOSEPHINE, 'The Lovers of the Lost', *Contemporary Review*, Jan. 1870, pp. 16–40.

——, ed. *Woman's Work and Woman's Culture* (London: Macmillan & Co., 1869).

The Census of Great Britain in 1851 (London: Longman, Brown, Green, & Longmans, 1854).

COBBE, FRANCES POWER, 'Celibacy v. Marriage. Old Maids, their Sorrows and Pleasures', *Fraser's Magazine*, Feb. 1862, pp. 228–35.

—— 'Female Charity—Lay and Monastic', *Fraser's Magazine*, Dec. 1862, pp. 774–88.

—— *Life of Frances Power Cobbe as Told by Herself* (London: Swan, Sonnenschein & Co., 1904).

—— 'What Shall We Do with Our Old Maids?', *Fraser's Magazine*, Nov. 1862, pp. 594–610.

CORNWALLIS, CAROLINE, 'The Capabilities and Disabilities of Women', *Westminster Review*, Jan. 1857, pp. 42–72.

CROSS, J. W., ed., *George Eliot's Life as Related in Her Letters and Journals*, 4 vols. (Leipzig: Tauchnitz, 1885).

DAVENANT, FRANCES, 'Old Maids', *Belgravia: a Magazine of Fashion and Amusement*, Jan. 1867, pp. 442–8.

DILKE, LADY EMILIA, 'Benefit Societies and Trade Unions for Women', *Fortnightly Review*, June 1889, pp. 852–6.

ELLIS, SARAH, *The Women of England: Their Social Duties and Domestic Habits* (London: Fisher & Son, 1839).

English Woman's Journal, Vols. I–XIII (1858–64).

Englishwoman's Review: a Journal of Women's Work, Nos. 1–12 (1866–8).

'THE EXCLUSIVENESS OF WOMEN', *Saturday Review*, 19 Feb. 1870, pp. 242–3.

FAITHFULL, EMILY, 'Open Council', *English Woman's Journal*, Sept. 1862, p. 70.

—— 'Women Compositors', *English Woman's Journal*, Sept. 1861, pp. 37–40.

FAWCETT, MILLICENT GARRETT, *Some Eminent Women of Our Times* (London: Macmillan & Co., 1889).

'FRIENDSHIP', *Saturday Review*, 15 Jan. 1870, pp. 77–8.

'FRIENDSHIP', *Victoria Magazine*, Oct. 1871, pp. 544–8.

FULLER, MARGARET, *Woman in the Nineteenth Century* (London: H. G. Clark, 1845).

'GEORGE SAND and GEORGE ELIOT', *Saturday Review*, 4 Nov. 1876, pp. 561–62.

GOODMAN, MARGARET, *Experiences of an English Sister of Mercy* (London: Smith, Elder & Co., 1862).

—— *Sisterhoods of the Church of England* (1862; rpt. London: Smith, Elder & Co., 1864).

GREENWELL, DORA, *Essays* (London: Alexander Strahan, 1866).

GREGORY, SAMUEL, 'Female Physicians', *English Woman's Journal*, Mar. 1862, pp. 1–11.

—— 'Letter to Ladies in Favor of Female Physicians for their own Sex', *English Woman's Journal*, Nov. 1860, p. 278.

'A GROUP OF FEMALE PHILANTHROPISTS', *London Quarterly Review*, Oct. 1881, pp. 49–81.

HALDANE, ELIZABETH, 'Registered Friendly Societies for Women', *National Review*, Dec. 1896, pp. 559–66.

HAMILTON, LADY MAUD, 'Mission Women', *Nineteenth Century Review*, 1884, pp. 984–90.

HARTLEY, MAY, 'Convent Boarding-Schools for Young Ladies', *Fraser's Magazine*, June 1874, pp. 778–86.

HOLLAND, PENELOPE, 'A Few More Words on Convents and on English Girls', *Macmillan's Magazine*, Apr. 1869, pp. 534–9.

HOLYOAKE, EMILY, 'The Capacity of Women for Industrial Union', *Westminster Review*, Feb. 1893, pp. 164–68.

HOWITT, MARY, *Mary Howitt: an Autobiography*, ed. Margaret Howitt. 2 vols. (London: Isbiter, 1889).

HUBBARD, LOUISA M., 'Englishwomen and their Work in Queen Victoria's

Reign', *The Englishwoman's Year-Book*, Vol. VIII (London: Hatchards, 1888), pp. 1–79.

INGPEN, ADA, ed., *Women as Letter-Writers: a Collection of Letters* (London: Hutchinson and Co., 1909).

IRELAND, ANNIE, 'George Eliot and Jane Welsh Carlyle', *Gentleman's Magazine*, Vol. 264 (1888), pp. 229–38.

—— 'A Monograph on Miss Jewsbury', *Selections from the Letters of Geraldine Endsor Jewsbury to Jane Welsh Carlyle* (London: Longmans, Green, & Co., 1892).

JAMESON, ANNA, *Anna Jameson: Letters and Friendships (1812–1860)*, ed. Mrs. Steuart Erskine (London: T. Fisher Unwin Ltd., 1915).

—— *The Communion of Labour: Social Employments of Women* (London: L.B.G.L. & Roberts, 1856).

—— *Sisters of Charity: Catholic and Protestant* (London: Longman, Brown, Green & Longmans, 1855).

JEWSBURY, GERALDINE, Review of *Adam Bede*, *Athenaeum*, 26 Feb. 1859, p. 284.

—— Review of *The Afternoon of Unmarried Life*, *Athenaeum*, 27 Nov. 1858, p. 676.

—— Review of *The Mill on the Floss*, *Athenaeum*, 7 Apr. 1860, pp. 467–8.

—— Review of *Silas Marner*, *Athenaeum*, 6 Apr. 1861, pp. 464–5.

—— *Selection from the Letters of Geraldine Endsor Jewsbury to Jane Welsh Carlyle*, ed. Annie E. Ireland (London: Longmans, Green & Company, 1892).

JEX-BLAKE, SOPHIA, 'Medical Women in Fiction', *Nineteenth Century Review*, Feb. 1893, pp. 261–72.

—— *Medical Women: Two Essays* (Edinburgh: William Oliphant, 1872).

KAVANAGH, JULIA, *English Women of Letters* (London: Hurst & Blackett, 1863).

LAW REPORTS, *The Times*, 15 Jan. 1869–4 Feb. 1869.

LEE, ELIZABETH, 'A Literary Friendship', *Cornhill Magazine*, Jan. 1898, pp. 58–71.

LEWES, GEORGE, 'The Lady Novelists', *Westminster Review*, July 1852, pp. 129–41.

LIBRI, MELANIE, 'Nuns of Port Royal', *Quarterly Review*, Sept. 1856, pp. 491–521.

LINTON, ELIZA LYNN, *The Girl of the Period and other Social Essays*, 2 vols. (London: Richard Bentley, 1883).

—— *My Literary Life* (London: Hodder & Stoughton, 1899).

—— *Ourselves. A Series of Essays on Women* (London: G. Routledge & Son, 1870).

—— 'The Partisans of Wild Women', *Nineteenth Century Review*, Mar. 1892, pp. 455–64.

—— 'The Wild Women as Politicians', *Nineteenth Century Review*, July 1891, pp. 79–88; and Oct. 1891, pp. 596–605.

—— *Witch Stories* (London: Chapman Hall, 1861).

MCILQUHAM, HARRIET, 'Lady Mary Wortley Montagu and Mary Astell', *Westminster Review*, Mar. 1899, pp. 289–99.

MARCH-PHILLIPS, EVELYN, 'Women's Newspapers', *Fortnightly Review*, Nov. 1894, pp. 661–70.

MARTINEAU, HARRIET, *Deerbrook*. 3 vols. (London: Edward Moxon, 1839).

—— *Harriet Martineau's Autobiography, with Memorials*, ed. Maria Weston Chapman, 3 vols. (London: Smith, Elder & Co., 1877).

—— 'Nurses Wanted', *Cornhill Magazine*, Apr. 1865, pp. 409–25.

—— Review of *Notes on Nursing* by Florence Nightingale, *Quarterly Review*, Apr. 1860, pp. 392–422.

'MATRON'S AID SOCIETY', *Englishwoman's Review*, May 1881, pp. 196–203.

MILL, JOHN STUART, *The Letters of John Stuart Mill*, ed. Hugh Elliot, 2 vols. (London: Longmans, Green & Co., 1910).

'MISS PARKES' ESSAYS ON WOMEN'S WORK', *Victoria Magazine*, June 1865, pp. 173–8.

MITFORD, MARY R., *Notes on a Literary Life: or Books, Places and People*, 3 vols. (London: Richard Bentley, 1857).

MOZLEY, ANNE, 'Clever Women', *Blackwood's Magazine*, Oct. 1868, pp. 410–27.

—— 'Convent Life', *Blackwood's Magazine*, May 1869, pp. 607–21.

—— 'Some Aspects of Friendship', *Blackwood's Magazine*, Mar. 1876, pp. 297–313.

—— 'Vapours, Fears and Tremors', *Blackwood's Magazine*, Feb. 1869, pp. 228–37.

'MRS. LYNN LINTON ON WOMEN', *Victoria Magazine*, July 1876, pp. 244–8.

MULOCK, DINAH, *About Money and Other Things* (London: Macmillan & Co., 1886).

—— *Concerning Men and Other Papers* (London: Macmillan & Co., 1888).

—— 'To Novelists—and a Novelist', *Macmillan's Magazine*, Apr. 1861, pp. 441–8.

—— *A Woman's Thoughts about Women* (London: Hurst & Blackett, 1858).

NIGHTINGALE, FLORENCE, *Florence Nightingale to her Nurses* (London: Macmillan & Co., 1914).

—— *Notes on Hospitals* (London: John Parker & Son, 1859).

—— *Notes on Nursing: What it is, and What it is Not* (London: Harrison, 1860).

—— *Suggestions for Thought to Searchers after Religious Truth*. 3 vols. (Privately printed. London: Eyre & Spottiswoode, 1860).

OLIPHANT, MARGARET, *Autobiography and Letters of Mrs. Oliphant*, ed. Mrs. Harry Coghill (Edinburgh: Blackwood & Sons, 1899).

—— 'The Condition of Women', *Blackwood's Magazine*, Feb. 1858, pp. 139–54.

—— 'The Grievances of Women', *Fraser's Magazine*, May 1880, pp. 698–710.

—— 'The Laws Concerning Women', *Blackwood's Magazine*, Apr. 1856, pp. 379–87.

—— 'Harriet Martineau', *Blackwood's Magazine*, Apr. 1877, pp. 472–96.

—— 'Mary Russell Mitford', *Blackwood's Magazine*, June 1854, pp. 658–70.

—— 'Men and Women', *Blackwood's Magazine*, Apr. 1895, pp. 620–50.

—— 'Miss Austen and Miss Mitford', *Blackwood's Magazine*, Mar. 1870, pp. 290–313.

—— 'Modern Novelists—Great and Small', *Blackwood's Magazine*, May 1855, pp. 554–68.

—— *et. al., Women Novelists of Queen Victoria's Reign: a Book of Appreciations* (London: Hurst & Blackett, 1897).

'OUTLINE FOR A PLAN FOR THE FORMATION OF INDUSTRIAL ASSOCIATIONS AMONGST WORKWOMEN', *English Woman's Journal*, Oct. 1860, pp. 73–6.

PARKES, BESSIE, 'Address to a Meeting of the National Association for the Promotion of Social Science in Dublin in August, 1861', *English Woman's Journal*, Sept. 1861, pp. 52–61.

—— 'Dorothea Casaubon and George Eliot', *Contemporary Review*, Feb. 1894, pp. 207–16.

—— *Essays on Woman's Work* (London: Alexander Strahan, 1865).

—— *Historic Nuns* (London: Duckworth, 1898).

—— 'A Review of the Last Six Years', *English Woman's Journal*, Feb. 1864, pp. 361–8.

—— 'The Use of a Special Periodical', *Alexandra Magazine and Englishwoman's Journal*, Dec. 1864, pp. 257–63.

'PAROCHIAL MISSION WOMEN'S FIRST REPORT', *English Woman's Journal*, June 1861, p. 281.

PROCTOR, ADELAIDE, ed., *Victoria Regia: a Volume of Original Contributions in Poetry and Prose* (London: Victoria Press, 1861).

'PROPERTY OF MARRIED WOMEN', *English Woman's Journal*, Mar. 1858, pp. 58–9.

REVIEW OF *Daniel Deronda, Saturday Review*, 23 Sept. 1876, pp. 390–2.

REVIEW OF *English Women and the Age* by Mrs. Horace Roscoe St. John, *English Woman's Journal*, July 1860, p. 351.

REVIEW OF *A Life for a Life* by Dinah Mulock, *English Woman's Journal*, Sept. 1859, p. 60.

REVIEW OF *The Mill on the Floss, Saturday Review*, 14 Apr. 1860, pp. 470–1.

REVIEW OF *On Sisterhoods* by F. D. Maurice, *Victoria Magazine*, Aug. 1863, p. 290.

RITCHIE, LADY ANNE, 'In Friendship', *Cornhill Magazine*, June 1873, pp. 666–70.

ROSSETTI, CHRISTINA, *Maude: a Story for Girls* (London: James Bowden, 1897).

—— *The Poetical Works of Christina Georgina Rossetti* (London: Macmillan & Co., 1904).

SIMCOX, EDITH, 'Autobiography of a Shirt-maker'. MS, Bodleian Library, Oxford.

—— 'The Capacity of Women', *Nineteenth Century Review*, Sept. 1887, pp. 391–402.

—— 'Eight Years of Co-operative Shirtmaking', *Nineteenth Century Review*, June 1884, pp. 1037–54.

—— 'George Eliot', *Nineteenth Century Review*, Sept. 1881, pp. 778–801.

—— Review of *Middlemarch, Academy*, Jan. 1873, pp. 1–4.

STANLEY, MISS, *Hospitals and Sisterhoods* (London: John Murray, 1854).

STOWE, HARRIET BEECHER, 'The True Story of Lady Byron's Life', *Macmillan's Magazine*, Sept. 1869, pp. 377–96.

SWINBURNE, ALGERNON, *A Note on Charlotte Brontë* (London: Chatto & Windus, 1877).

TAYLOR, FRANCES, 'Works of Charity', *Dublin Review*, Mar. 1857, pp. 123–42.

TAYLOR, HARRIET, 'The Enfranchisement of Women', *Westminster Review*, July 1851, pp. 149–61.

TAYLOR, MARY, *The First Duty of Women: a Series of Articles Reprinted from the Victoria Magazine 1865 to 1870* (London: Emily Faithfull, 1870).

—— *Miss Miles or a Tale of Yorkshire Life 60 Years Ago* (London: Remington & Co., 1890).

THOMAS, ANNIE, *New Grooves* (London: Charlton Tucker, 1871).

THOMSON, MRS., *Celebrated Friendships*, 2 vols. (London: James Hogg & Son, 1861).

Transactions of the National Association for the Promotion of Social Science, 1860 (London: Parker & Bourne, 1861).

TRENCH, MARIA, 'English Sisterhoods', *Nineteenth Century Review*, Aug. 1884, pp. 339–52.

TROLLOPE, T. ADOLPHUS, *The Girlhood of Catherine de' Medici* (London: Chapman & Hall, 1856).

Victoria Magazine, Vols. 1–9, 11, 13–32 (1863–78).

WALLER, R. D., ed., *Letters Addressed to Mrs. Gaskell by Celebrated Contemporaries* (Manchester: Manchester Univ. Press, 1935).

WILLIAMS, JANE, *The Literary Women of England* (London: Saunders, Otley & Co., 1861).

WINKWORTH, SUSANNA AND CATHERINE, *Memorials of Two Sisters: Susanna and Catherine Winkworth*, ed. M. J. Shaen (London: Longmans, Green & Co., 1908).

WOLLSTONECRAFT, MARY, *Mary, and The Wrongs of Woman*, ed. G. Kelly (London: Oxford Univ. Press, 1976).

'THE WOMEN OF THE DAY', *Victoria Magazine*, Oct. 1868, pp. 551–64.

YONGE, CHARLOTTE, 'George Eliot and Her Critics', *Monthly Packet*, Sept. 1885, pp. 471–94.

—— *Womankind* (Leipzig: Bernhard Tauchnitz, 1878).

Index

Austen, Jane 1, 6, 56, 154

Bedford College 160
Belloc, Mme Louis *see* Bessie Rayner
    Parkes
Blackwell, Elizabeth 25, 160
Blackwell, Emily 25
Bodichon, Barbara (Leigh-Smith) 9, 19,
    34, 35, 36, 143, 144, 148, 149–51,
    153, 160, 161, 162, 163, 186
Boucherett, Jessie 9
Brontë, Anne 33, 84
Brontë, Branwell 32
Brontë, Charlotte 2, 3, 5, 15, 27, 28,
    29, 30, 38, 44, 80, 83–140 *passim*,
    141, 143, 154, 155, 167, 192,
    204–7; on androgyny 117–18, 119,
    123–4, 184; antagonism between
    sexes 109, 112–17; critical double
    standards 32, 87, 164; confinement
    186–8; female bonding 104–8, 135;
    female communities 100, 103, 125,
    126–7, 140; female friendships 100,
    104, 112, 115–16, 118–21, 125;
    female jealousy 171; female maso-
    chism 134–5; female medical prac-
    tice 102; female powerlessness
    127–32, 135–6; female violence
    108–9; letters 96–7, 137–9; loneli-
    ness 84, 86–7; motherhood 107–8,
    109–11, 116–17, 123–4, 177, 180;
    primacy of male 111–12, 168, 176;
    servants 102; single women 93, 99,
    112, 117, 121–2, 173; sisterhoods
    100, 102–3; threat of violation
    132–4, 139; the Woman Question
    99–100, 160; women's employment
    99–100, 101
  relationships: and Elizabeth Barrett
    Browning 33; family ties 83–4,
    112; Elizabeth Gaskell 28, 30, 31–3,
    34, 37, 88, 89, 91–2, 98, 100, 101;
    Julia Kavanagh 87–8; the literary
    community 84–7, 92, 146, 159;
    Harriet Martineau 86, 88–91, 101,
    152; Ellen Nussey 87, 89, 93–4,
    98, 148; George Smith 87, 89, 92;
    Harriet Beecher Stowe 91, 101;

Mary Taylor 34, 93, 94–8, 112,
    149; W. S. Williams 84, 85, 87,
    100; Margaret Wooler 85, 89, 99
  works: *Jane Eyre* 5, 32, 47, 84, 88,
    91, 92, 93, 97, 98, 101, 102, 104–
    12, 113, 123, 124, 135, 139, 180,
    184, 185, 194, 196, 201; *The Profes-
    sor* 102, 124, 125–33, 139, 184;
    Shirley 84, 85, 88, 91, 93, 94, 97,
    101, 102, 104, 112–24, 139, 173,
    184, 207; *Villette* 31, 84, 86, 87,
    88, 89–90, 97, 101, 103, 104,
    124–40, 171, 184, 188, 197, 207
Brontë, Emily 33, 84, 87, 94, 112
Brontë, Patrick 32, 98
Browning, Elizabeth Barrett 9, 24, 25,
    30, 33, 44, 73, 78, 154, 164–5,
    176, 185
Brunton, Mary 1
Burney, Fanny 1

Carlyle, Jane 9, 79
Carpenter, Mary 79
Carter, Elizabeth 1
Chapman, John 141, 147, 151
Cobbe, Frances Power 4, 7, 8, 13, 15,
    19, 21, 23–4, 25, 36, 39, 79, 99
Committee for the Ladies' Address to
    their American Sisters on Slavery 10
Cornwallis, Caroline 23, 161
Craig, Isa 9, 148, 160
Craigie, Pearl 147
Craik, Mrs *see* Dinah Mulock
critical double standards 15, 32, 87,
    163–5
Cross, John 147, 159, 161

Davies, Emily 160, 161–2
demographic imbalance 2, 3, 7
Dickens, Charles 3, 23, 154
Disraeli, Benjamin 3

Edgeworth, Maria 1
Eliot, George 2, 3, 5, 9, 14, 27, 28, 29,
    30, 38, 44, 80, 141–207 *passim*; on
    Jane Austen 154; Mary Braddon
    157; Charlotte Brontë 154, 155,
    185; Elizabeth Barrett Browning